Toward a Better Future

EDUCATION AND TRAINING FOR ECONOMIC DEVELOPMENT IN SINGAPORE SINCE 1965

Edited by LEE Sing Kong, GOH Chor Boon, Birger FREDRIKSEN, and TAN Jee Peng

NIE
NATIONAL INSTITUTE OF EDUCATION
SINGAPORE

THE WORLD BANK
Washington, D.C.

1818 H Street NW
Washington DC 20433
Telephone: 202-473-1000
Internet: www.worldbank.org
E-mail: feedback@worldbank.org

1 2 3 4 5 11 10 09 08

A copublication of The World Bank and the National Institute of Education (NIE) at Nanyang Technological University in Singapore.

National Institute of Education
Nanyang Technological University
1 Nanyang Walk
Singapore 637616

ISBN: 978-0-8213-7375-0
eISBN: 978-0-8213-7376-7
DOI: 10.1596/978-0-8213-7375-0

Library of Congress Cataloging-in-Publication Information

Toward a better future : education and training for economic development in Singapore since 1965 / edited by Sing Kong Lee, Chor Boon Goh, Birger Fredriksen, and Jee-Peng Tan.
p. cm.
ISBN 978-0-8213-7375-0
1. Education—Singapore—Aims and objectives. 2. Education—Economic aspects—Singapore. 3. Vocational education—Singapore. 4. Singapore—Economic conditions. I. Lee, Sing-Kong. II. Goh, Chor Boon, III. Fredriksen, Birger. IV. Tan, Jee-Peng.
LA1239.5.T69 2008
370.95957'09045—dc22

Cover design: Critical Stages.

Toward a Better Future

EDUCATION AND TRAINING FOR ECONOMIC DEVELOPMENT IN SINGAPORE SINCE 1965

Contents

FIGURES

TABLES

Foreword

Education is at the core of a nation's development. Over the past four decades, Singapore has transformed its education system so as to develop a cohesive society and prepare generations of young people to make the most of a globalized future.

Development of education in Singapore has evolved with changing national and global circumstances. In the early years of nationhood, schools were built rapidly, teachers were recruited on a large scale, the ethnically diverse educational streams the country inherited were merged into a single national system, and bilingual education for all students was introduced. By the early 1980s, Singapore had moved from a one-size-fits-all education approach to one that enabled pupils of different abilities and aptitudes to develop at their own pace. A differentiated approach reduced school attrition and allowed less academically inclined students to gain basic literacy and numeracy skills before moving on to acquire technical skills in demand in the workplace.

Since 1997, when Singapore launched its vision of "Thinking Schools, Learning Nation," the country has geared its education system toward nurturing an innovative society attuned to the demands and opportunities of the 21st century. Time and space has been freed to allow schools and teachers to develop engaging approaches to helping students learn and think for themselves. Diverse paths are being provided for students with different talents to take them as far as they can go, and more opportunities are being developed for all-around education—not just academic knowledge, but also the character development, resilience, and the social skills that young people need to embrace change and do well in life.

At the heart of development of education in Singapore has been the way the country recruits and trains teachers, develops outstanding school leaders, and deploys these people across the system. They are the source of quality in education, and the reason why every school is considered a good school in Singapore. It is a key strategy that requires continuous work, both in equipping beginning teachers with the skills they need and in giving existing teachers the opportunity to refresh and update themselves throughout their careers, expand their horizons, and get a sense of innovations outside the school.

A unique feature of Singapore's education system is its robust and broad-based technical and vocational education segment. Polytechnics and the Institute of Technical Education educate some two-thirds of students, equipping them with skills for employment or entrepreneurship in a high-value economy and for further education. Singapore's state-funded, autonomous universities have taken bold steps forward in building excellence in teaching and research.

At each stage of development of its education system, Singapore has learned to do important things first. Investment in basic education to build a broad base was followed by the injection of modern management methods to strengthen quality, along with continuous development of teachers and school leaders. Diverse pathways in schools and the increasing flexibility and free play needed to develop distinct talents, is being built on a system with solid, common foundations. And a tertiary system that was initially aimed at providing the manpower for an industrializing economy is now focused on developing continuous learning that can sustain a high-value economy in a globalizing world.

Academics, education policy makers, and practitioners may find some useful pointers from Singapore's experience, just as Singapore has constantly found relevance in ideas and lessons elsewhere in the world. Though it is a challenge to distill a journey of four decades into a single volume, this book is an admirable effort.

Tharman Shanmugaratnam
Minister for Finance and Minister for Education

Acknowledgments

A book that captures 40 years of education change and development is never the work of a few individuals. Publication of this work would not have been possible without the help and support of many dedicated individuals and organizations. We would like to name and thank those who were involved in different phases of this collective effort.

The project that led to this book was the June 2006 Asia Education Study Tour for African Policy Makers, sponsored by the World Bank and, for the Singapore segment of the study program, coordinated by Singapore's National Institute of Education with support from International Enterprise Singapore and the Singapore Ministry of Foreign Affairs. The purpose of the tour was to offer African education officials and their World Bank counterparts an opportunity to study education development and reform processes undertaken by several East Asian countries. Following the presentation of three papers on aspects of the Singapore education system, it was later decided that the publication of a Singapore volume providing a comprehensive analysis of the evolution of education change would be a useful follow-up. In this respect, we would like to thank the World Bank for its management support of the project and the study tour participants for their active engagement during the visit. The exchange and policy dialogue among African practitioners and their counterparts in Singapore provided a particularly rich backdrop for this book.

In the course of preparing this book, all chapter contributors have been generous in putting time and effort despite their busy schedules and professional responsibilities. They have also been accommodating and patient with us during the process of editing, research, and verification of facts. The chapter authors are Lee Sing Kong, Leo Tan Wee Hin, S. Gopinathan, Ang Wai Hoong, Law Song Seng, David Ng Foo Seong, Koh Thiam Seng, Lee Sai Choo, Chan Lee Mun, and Goh Chor Boon.

We also place on record our gratitude to our colleagues at the Ministry of Education who made this book possible. In particular, we want to mention the thoughtful comments and suggestions made by Mrs. Tan Ching Yee, Permanent Secretary of the Ministry of Education, as well as others who provided significant help to the editorial team in verifying information and helping make sense of the sequence of historical and contemporary developments. We are especially grateful to Chee Hong Tat, Bernard Ong, and Lim Wan Yong for their meticulous reading of the draft manuscript. Finally, we would like to thank Cherie Lek Yian Ping for her administrative efficiency and coordination efforts.

About the Authors

ANG Wai Hoong teaches part-time at the National Institute of Education (NIE) at Nanyang Technological University in Singapore and is a consultant for private education projects in China, Indonesia, and Vietnam.

CHAN Lee Mun is the principal and CEO (designate) of Nanyang Polytechnic in Singapore.

GOH Chor Boon is an associate professor and associate dean in the External Programs Office at the NIE.

S. GOPINATHAN is a professor at the NIE and vice dean (policy) at the Centre for Research in Pedagogy and Practice in the NIE.

KOH Thiam Seng is the director of educational technology at the Ministry of Education, Singapore, and deputy director at the NIE.

LAW Song Seng is chairman and CEO of ITE Education Services Pte Ltd, a fully owned subsidiary of the Institute of Technical Education (ITE).

LEE Sai Choo is assistant director, professional development and consultancy at the Educational Technology Division, Ministry of Education, Singapore.

LEE Sing Kong is director of the NIE.

David NG Foo Seong is associate dean for leadership programs at the NIE.

Leo TAN Wee Hin is a professor at the Natural Sciences and Science Education Academic Group in the NIE.

Abbreviations

AEB	Adult Education Board
CDIS	Curriculum Development System of Singapore
CET	continuing education and training
CPDD	Curriculum Planning and Development Department
CPE	College of Physical Education
DET	Division of Educational Technology
DMR	digital media repository
EDB	Economic Development Board
EFL	education for living
EOI	export-oriented industrialization
EPB	Education Publication Bureau
ETD	Educational Technology Division (of the Ministry of Education)
GCE	General Certificate in Education
GDP	gross domestic product
ICT	information and communication technology
iDA	Infocomm Development Authority of Singapore
IE	Institute of Education
ISI	import substitution industrialization
ITB	Industrial Training Board
ITE	Institute of Technical Education
KBE	knowledge-based education
MNC	multinational corporation
MOE	Ministry of Education
MOM	Ministry of Manpower
MTI	Ministry of Trade and Industry
NCB	National Computer Board
NES	New Education System

NIE	National Institute of Education
Nitec	National ITE Certificate
NMC	National Manpower Council
NTC	National Trade Certificate
NTU	Nanyang Technological University
NUS	National University of Singapore
NYP	Nanyang Polytechnic
OECD	Organisation for Economic Co-operation and Development
PAP	People's Action Party
PD	personal development
PDCM	Professional Development Curriculum Model
PET	preemployment training
PPP	Primary Pilot Project
PSLE	Primary School Leaving Examination
PSP	Primary Science Project
R&D	research and development
SDF	Skills Development Fund
SMU	Singapore Management University
SVI	Singapore Vocational Institute
TED	Technical Education Department
TIMSS	Trends in International Mathematics and Science Study
TSLN	Thinking Schools, Learning Nation
TTC	Teachers Training College
VITB	Vocational and Industrial Training Board
VTE	vocational technical education

Introduction

The story of Singapore's economic success has been related many times over and documented in countless articles and books. At one point, academics, economists, and international observers began referring to the city-state's economic achievements, especially during the 1970s and 1980s, as a "miracle," putting it among the highly successful East Asian economies of Japan, South Korea, Taiwan (China), and Hong Kong (China). The Singapore economy has undergone significant stages of development since the 1960s. It has grown from its traditional role as a regional port and distribution center in the 1960s to an international manufacturing and service center in the 1970s and 1980s, and now into a center of science-based manufacturing and knowledge-intensive technical services. Much has been written to explain this success. Emphasis has been placed on the early adoption of an export-oriented strategy for industrialization, high savings and investment rates, a stable macroeconomic environment, and even sociocultural traits that support successful industrialization. This volume documents a less-explored aspect of Singapore's economic development: it examines the transformation of the education and training system since the country's independence in 1965 and how the process contributed to skills formation and, hence, economic change.

Led by the country's first prime minister, Lee Kuan Yew, Singapore's rapid economic progress since 1965 centers largely on the role of the state and the state-led economic policies that were so effectively implemented by the nation's key financial and economic institutions. The foundation for sustainable growth was laid on a few basic principles: fiscal discipline; the use of price incentives in public service delivery; equitable sharing of the opportunities for economic progress; strong basic institutions to foster political stability, good governance, and the rule of law; and a well-functioning social contract. These elements of Singapore's version of the East Asian development model were identified by development economists and politicians alike as the key to unlocking the complexities of underdevelopment. Singapore's economic transformation, commonly divided into three main stages, was all the more spectacular when judged against the backdrop of the unpromising conditions at the time the country gained independence.

The initial stage of Singapore's economic development was closely influenced by the political situation in the region at the time. In 1965, with its separation from Malaysia, the Singapore government, under the People's Action Party (PAP), inherited a narrow economic structure that depended mainly on the entrepot trade. The government could not follow an import-substitution strategy because of the lack of a large domestic market. In the 1960s and 1970s, multinational corporations (MNCs) from the developed nations, especially those in the electronics and textile industries, were facing rising production costs and market saturation. They were pressured to transfer part or all of their production and technological resources to low-cost locations in Southeast Asia. This interest was eagerly reciprocated; the countries in the region, especially Singapore, were eager to attract the MNCs. In 1966, foreign direct investment in the Singapore manufacturing sector amounted to S$239 million. As a result of proactive promotion on the part of the government through a range of tax and investment incentives, the figure multiplied by more than six times to reach S$1,575 million in 1971, and quadrupled to S$6,349 million in 1979 (Department of Statistics, various years). Singapore had made a swift change toward export-oriented industrialization (EOI) with the primary objective of providing jobs for the people. The MNCs were seen as critical channels through which Singapore could acquire the latest in managerial and technological knowledge. Foreign technology became an effective means to overcome domestic limitations, such as the lack of an indigenous technological base.

The success of Singapore's EOI strategy in the late 1960s and 1970s was dependent to a large extent on adopting modern science and technology to catch up with the more advanced countries. But the task of closing the technological gap was more easily said than done. British colonial rule had not produced the necessary development in technical and vocational education. Furthermore, there was a severe shortage of local experts in the field of science and technology who could impart knowledge and skill. The 1961 *Winsemius Report* had highlighted the deficiency in terms of the shortage of skilled workers.[1] At the request of the government, Dr. Albert Winsemius continued to make regular visits to Singapore. In February 1970, he estimated that Singapore would remain short of about 450 to 500 engineers each year over the period 1970 to 1975—despite the government's effort to increase the annual output of engineers from the then—University of Singapore from 80 to 210 by 1974 (Goh 1972, 273). Equally worrisome was the shortage of management personnel, estimated at 200 a year over the next three years, and technicians, estimated at as many as 1,500 to 2,000 each year over the next two years (Goh 1972, 274).

A new ministry, the Ministry of Science and Technology, was established in April 1968 to formulate science policies and coordinate the deployment of the nation's scientific and technological manpower.[2] There was an urgent need to restructure the educational system to provide the requisite technical manpower.

The yawning gap between the enrollment in academic and technical streams was stressed in a ministerial report in 1968. In Japan, the ratio of academic to vocational students was 3:2, while in Singapore the ratio was 7:1, and the ratio of technicians to engineers and scientists was 1:23 (Ministry of Culture 1968, 6–7). To redress the imbalance, the Ministry of Education announced that, from 1969, all secondary school pupils would receive two years of compulsory technical education, after which they would be streamed into technical, commercial, or academic education. Radical changes were introduced in the field of technical education, especially in the face of potential unemployment following the British military withdrawal from Singapore in 1971. These changes would prepare the young people leaving schools to take up the new economic activities that were generated from an expanding manufacturing sector in the 1970s. Several industrial training centers and vocational institutes were built during the 1970s. At the tertiary level, greater emphasis was placed on engineering and technology.

The oil crisis of 1973 led to increased protectionism in the world economy and also exposed Singapore's economic frailties. The government began focusing on economic-upgrading strategies. This skill-upgrading strategy marked the second stage of Singapore's economic development. By upgrading, Singapore could bypass the problem of rising protectionism, which was mostly centered around low-skill production. As countries in Southeast Asia began to compete effectively for foreign investments in low-skilled, labor-intensive industries, Singapore's previous comparative advantage in labor-intensive manufactured products was gradually being eroded. To achieve long-term, sustainable development, the country's economic planners shifted their emphasis to accelerating Singapore's transition from a "third-league" labor-intensive industrializing country to a "second-league" capital-intensive economy.[3] Thus, the Second Industrial Revolution was launched under the Ten-Year Plan, which sought to raise the manufacturing sector's share of gross domestic product from 22 percent in 1979 to 31 percent by 1990.

Singapore, however, entered the 1980s still severely hampered by a shortage of labor at three critical levels: skilled labor, qualified technical and engineering personnel, and management trained in modern techniques. Compared with the newly industrializing countries in East Asia and in Japan, Singapore in the 1970s suffered from low labor productivity growth. Between 1973 and 1978, real productivity growth in Singapore averaged about 3 percent per annum, compared with an average of 7 percent for Hong Kong, Taiwan, and South Korea.[4] Education during this period also failed to keep pace with the rapid expansion of the Singapore economy (Goh 1972, 277). Educational wastage was significant. Moreover, the majority of school leavers and university graduates gravitated toward clerical and administrative occupations, mainly in insurance, banking, trade, and government service. These jobs commanded high prestige and offered the prospects of upward social mobility and job security. The tight labor market for skilled workers and professionals soon led to crimping and countercrimping of such personnel, especially in the fast-expanding shipbuilding and repair industry and the chemicals-petroleum industry (Chia 1971, 219). Unemployment between 1979 and 1984 averaged a low 3.2 percent. In the words of then–Prime Minister Lee Kuan Yew (2000, 82), "By the late 1970s we had left our old problems of unemployment and lack of investments behind us. The new problem was how to improve the quality of the new investments and with it the education and skills levels of our workers." As a short-term solution, the government encouraged the inflow of skilled personnel by liberalizing the conditions under which such people could come to Singapore and acquire permanent residence and eventual citizenship.

The two main strategies of the restructuring program were (a) the continued efforts to attract MNCs to invest in high-technology operations and (b) the promotion of science and technology, including activities in research and development (R&D). The nation's comparative advantage, hitherto based on factor endowments, was gradually becoming a function of manmade conditions fostered by heavy spending on R&D. The technological innovations that MNCs brought when they set up production in Singapore also undermined the long-term viability of the country's labor-intensive EOI model (*Straits Times* Feb. 27, 1986). In the words of then–Prime Minister Goh Chok Tong, "New technology, the microchip revolution, and robotic slaves that do not go on strike for better pay and working conditions have relieved the pressures on American, European and Japanese companies to seek sanctuaries outside their home" (*Straits Times* Feb. 27, 1986). American company Fairchild Semiconductor shifted its integrated circuit assembly operations from Singapore back to Portland, Maine, because automation and robots easily wiped out the cost advantage of cheaper labor in Singapore. Singapore's economic growth would need to be driven by an innovation-led industrial strategy rather than a labor-intensive model. The idea was to provide local firms with windows of opportunity to upgrade, innovate, and commercialize their R&D efforts. For the strategy to work, a sound science and technology policy and a good technology infrastructure were indispensable. Singapore faced an uphill task from the start, mainly because the country lacked a large pool of indigenous research professionals and a workforce with the requisite skills and attitudes. The government responded by embarking on a series of plans spanning several decades to reshape the education system, using it not only as a vehicle for nation building, but also as a tool for building up the skills base to serve the broader goals of economic development.

To match the needs of establishing higher-value-added forms of production, the government had to ensure that the requisite skills were in place. Levels of educational achievement had to be increased and more sophisticated forms of technical education introduced to create the appropriate intermediate-level skills. The government started the task of upgrading education upon the comprehensive and radical recommendations of the *Goh Report* of 1979. In January 1979, a New Education System (NES) was introduced in alignment with the government's strategy for economic restructuring and sustainable growth. Under the NES, the education system was revamped to make it more efficient. The government maintained a bilingual language policy in schools and provided three streams of instruction at both primary and secondary levels. Instructional and curriculum standards were raised through the centralization of writing of instructional materials and textbooks. The Curriculum Development Institute of Singapore (CDIS) was established in June 1980 to produce teaching materials of high quality, including textbooks and multimedia teaching materials. In short, the underlying philosophy of the education system was to let pupils progress at a pace suited to their individual abilities. Its aim was to enable each child to go as far as possible in his or her schooling career, thereby giving everyone the best possible educational foundation for subsequent training and employment. By reducing dropouts, the NES achieved its objective of cutting educational wastage. In tandem with the swift educational reforms, various training schemes were introduced to upgrade the skill formation of the workforce. Singapore's technical and vocational education was reviewed, and concerted efforts were made to elevate the quality and status of skill training programs.

The third stage of Singapore's economic growth trajectory started in the 1990s when increasing regional and international competition motivated Singapore's leaders to initiate The Next Lap—a vision for economic development that would propel the city-state to the league of the industrial economies and to attain the same standard of living as the Swiss by 2020. To achieve this objective, the economic policy continued to be pro-MNCs, but sought to attract only those firms that were able to invest in industrial clusters that were deemed to provide the next wave of economic expansion. Local companies were encouraged to move out into the Asia-Pacific to tap into cheaper production resources and to place Singapore in the center of the region's drive for economic growth. Clearly, the shift was from "Singapore Incorporated" to "Singapore International Incorporated."

To achieve the ambitious nation-building goals of the new millennium, Singapore's education system was comprehensively reviewed and revamped. Ability-driven education—with a focus on innovation, creativity, and entrepreneurship—was introduced at all school levels to implement the Thinking Schools, Learning Nation (TSLN) vision and the various initiatives encapsulated in the information technology master plans to develop 21st-century literacy skills, including computer literacy, in young Singaporeans to prepare them for the future. The period also witnessed the transformation of technical and vocational training, from a generally unpopular postsecondary experience to a much-sought-after route for the more technically inclined youths. At the higher education level, polytechnics and universities were urged not only to achieve excellence in teaching and to offer a wide range of specializations to meet market demands, but also to strive for excellence in R&D programs. The intention was to develop leading-edge tertiary institutions that would help drive R&D and maintain Singapore's role as the leading research hub in the region. Today, many world-class educational institutions are setting up satellite campuses that provide Singaporeans with a wide menu of opportunities to acquire knowledge and skills for the new global economy.

Until recently, Singapore's education system functioned as a centralized, top-down bureaucracy offering standardized services. Though this approach has indeed benefited the country by rapidly expanding educational opportunities and raising the educational profile of Singaporeans, its limits are also beginning to be felt. The challenges posed by globalization are, in fact, raising questions about the relevance of the centralized governance model that has served the country so well for so long, and the need for adaptation to sustain the city-state's continued socio-economic progress in the decades ahead.

Growth theorists, economic historians, and development economists consistently argue that the sustained growth of the East Asian economies stems from several interrelated key factors: substantial investment in infrastructure, an efficient absorption and adaptation of advanced technology, a stable social and political environment, and an impressive commitment to human capital formation. (See, for example, Ogawa, Jones, and Williamson [1993] and Jomo [2006].) One reason for Singapore's economic success is the ability of the state to successfully manage the education system and the demand for skills in tandem with each other. In the words of former Prime Minister Lee Kuan Yew, "Our job was to plan the broad economic objectives and the target periods within which to achieve them. We reviewed these plans regularly and adjusted them as new realities changed the outlook. Infrastructure and the training and education of workers to meet the needs of employers had to be planned years in advance" (Lee 2002, 85). This dynamic synergy continues to be a major source of Singapore's competitive advantage. The key strategy to having a workforce fit for the new economy is to ensure that education stays relevant and keeps pace with economic change. In short, the central thesis of this volume is that Singapore's economic success since independence in 1965 owes much to its leaders' ability to establish, through the education system, a close link between policies for skills formation and the demand for skills at each stage of economic development.

How does one explain Singapore's successful transformation of its education system within the short span of a few decades? In one of its key documentations on the "economic miracles" of the East Asian "Tiger" economies, the World Bank (1995) strongly suggested that substantial investment to achieve universal, high-quality primary education (and also secondary and vocational education) in these countries produced important payoffs for economic efficiency and equity. Excess demand created by primary education for secondary and tertiary education was met by a combination of expansion of public secondary and postsecondary education and a self-financed private system of postsecondary education. In many developing countries, however, the emphasis is on public subsidies for university education, with insufficient attention paid to achieving and reaping the full benefits of universal primary education. Although many developing countries today boast 100 percent primary school enrollment rates and access to secondary education has risen sharply, the improvement in enrollment rates has not always been matched by advances in educational quality.[5] The World Bank's interpretation provides a valid explanation for Singapore's successful development of its labor-intensive industrialization during the 1960s and 1970s, which required mainly unskilled and semiskilled workers with basic education to man its factories—although other factors, such as an influx of foreign workers and external institutional support in manpower training, also played significant roles. However, as the Singapore economy made its transition to capital- and technology-intensive industrialization in the 1980s and beyond, broader theoretical considerations are required to explain Singapore's education change to meet its economic transformation. In today's globalized economy, primary education is necessary but not sufficient for robust and sustained economic development. Improving and expanding secondary and tertiary education remains a national priority even for Singapore, which already has what some might consider an excellent education system and school infrastructure.

This book sets out, within the broader context of Singapore's economic and social change since 1965 and the impact of globalization in recent years, to document the various facets and stages of education reform and how they have contributed to enhancing the nation's economic competitiveness in the global economy. It consists of chapters contributed by educationists who were (and are) intimately linked to the growth and development of education in the city-state. It is written with the primary objective of sharing with developing countries Singapore's experience in synergizing the demands of two key sectors—education and the economy. Our focus is on the institutional mechanisms that deliver system responsiveness and on the sequencing of policies.

We start off with an overview chapter documenting the key features of the development of education in Singapore over the past 40 years, focusing on how Singapore has been able over this period to develop its education system from a level in the early 1960s quite similar to that of many African countries, to reach a level comparable to the best systems in member countries of the Organisation for Economic Co-operation and Development. Education, from preschool to tertiary education (and even adult learning), on the island republic of Singapore in the 21st century is undergoing transformational change. The change is transformational because the education sector prepares the Singapore workforce to meet the challenges of a very competitive, globalized economy. The various components of

Singapore's education sector are elaborated on in the rest of the book. Chapter 2 examines the intimate relationship between Singapore's industrialization strategy and its strategic management of educational reform in primary, secondary, and technical education. The economic and educational successes of Singapore did not happen by accident. Effective planning, a strong political will, and a stable government are key factors in charting the success of Singapore. The chapter discusses in detail the parallel stages of the strategic industrialization and educational reforms in Singapore. In education, the focus of the discussion is on primary, secondary, technical, and tertiary education. It documents the key features of the institutional arrangements, accountability structures, resources allocation, and operational processes that have enabled Singapore's education sector to make an effective contribution to nation building and economic growth.

Many developing countries are looking into best practices relating to textbook publication and the quality of teacher education. In the case of Singapore, improving quality through standardization, such as the centralized production of high-quality curriculum materials, was geared to the requirements of the syllabuses set by the Ministry of Education and national examinations applicable to all schools. Modern methods of instruction in teacher education were implemented from the late 1970s until the late 1990s. Chapters 3 and 4 provide useful illustrations of how Singapore has coped with the need to provide affordable textbooks and to develop teacher education that is responsive and relevant. Education reform, curriculum planning, and the evolution in the design and use of textbooks mirrored the nation's economic, manpower, and technological developments. The transition from using imported textbooks, to copublication of textbooks by the Ministry of Education and local publishers, to commercial publication of textbooks by local publishers (and the impact on the local educational publishing industry) in the late 1990s is explained in chapter 3. The next chapter traces the developments in teacher education especially since the 1990s, when Singapore's education entered into a new era with the TSLN vision. The overall objective was to motivate Singaporeans to continually acquire new knowledge; learn new skills; gain higher levels of technological literacy; and embrace innovation, enterprise, and risk taking—without losing their moral bearings or their commitment to the local community and the nation. In line with these changes, the National Institute of Education (NIE) reviewed its teacher-training curriculum to meet the objectives of TSLN. NIE ensured that its preservice training curriculum and professional development programs stayed relevant and responsive.

Another crucial issue facing developing countries is the development of technical and vocational education and training. Singapore, too, grappled with the difficulty and know-how of propagating and sustaining quality technical and vocational training as a form of postsecondary education. At one stage, technical and vocational education in Singapore was seen as a backwater. Over the decades,

Singapore transformed these educational systems, and chapter 5 explains the processes by which this was achieved. It looks into the evolution of technical and vocational education as an illustration of the successful economic transformation of Singapore since 1965. It argues that the so-called economic miracle was, to a large extent, achieved through the rapid, innovative, and relatively low-cost provision of large-scale technical education.

Chapters 6 and 7 discuss the transformation of polytechnic and university education to meet changing manpower needs. Chapter 6 examines the unique role of polytechnics in Singapore's education system. Absorbing around 40 percent of each primary one cohort, the polytechnics provide a very intense work-related training and education leading to diplomas in specific career-related areas. Students avidly seek polytechnic education because its graduates are in high demand by industry and the universities both in Singapore and abroad. The polytechnics are unique in that they train the critical middle-level workers for business and industry. In many developing economies, polytechnic education is largely neglected, and tertiary education in these countries almost always means degree-level courses. Sadly, the graduates of such courses often lack the mind-set, attitudes, and practical skills to match industry needs. Chapter 7 centers on the important role of university education in a knowledge-based economy, where the emphasis shifts from the mere production of goods and services toward innovation and creativity in economic activity. The faster the Singapore economy changes, the harder it is for the citizens to be confident of their skills and employability. Hence, at the tertiary education level, knowledge generation has been given more attention, together with an emphasis on the linkage between research and its economic impact. This chapter discusses the changing role of Singapore's universities and the strategies taken to integrate them more explicitly into the economic sphere of Singapore.

To support the rapid transformation of education and manpower training, Singapore has always placed great emphasis on enhancing the technological literacy of its people. Indeed, the city-state is consistently ranked as one of the top nations in the world in information and communication technology (ICT) application and development for economic growth. A holistic and well-thought-through policy on the role of ICT provides a strong platform to enhance the economic competitiveness of countries through greater productivity gains. Chapter 8 explains the strategies adopted to develop digital skills in Singapore's education system. It discusses Singapore's strategy in successfully providing an ICT-enabled infrastructure for teaching and learning in schools and the corresponding professional development programs for teachers and school leaders on the use of ICT in education. It argues that one of the main factors accounting for Singapore's present-day entry into the new economy is the alignment of the educational system, manpower needs, and ICT policies with global market forces.

In the final chapter we discuss the question, What lessons emerge from Singapore's experience? For many developing nations, the implication of Singapore's experience is straightforward: It exemplifies a general rule that the development of widespread basic education of good quality is necessary, though not sufficient, for sustainable growth. This implication is consistent with experience elsewhere among fast-growing economies and supports the World Bank's focus on helping all countries accelerate progress in primary education while also supporting efforts to build the skills base for growth. In the concluding chapter, we examine the exportability of Singapore's approach to education and training policy and its lessons for aligning manpower and skills development strategies to the requirements for economic growth.

NOTES

1. In 1961, a United Nations Industry Survey Mission, under the leadership of Dutch economist Dr. Albert Winsemius, was commissioned by the Singapore government. The *Winsemius Report,* as it became known, convinced the Singapore leaders that the traditional dependence on entrepot trade and service industries such as banking would not ensure the economic survival of the small city-state.

2. Despite optimistic expectations at the point of its establishment, the organization was eventually dissolved in 1981. See chapter 1.

3. However, the impact of the industrial policy of expanding the manufacturing base through foreign enterprises to elevate the general skill levels of the workforce was not easily achieved. Local industrial establishments in Singapore during this period were characterized by their small size, low capital input, and use of simple technology. In 1969, 70 percent of manufacturing enterprises employed 10 to 39 workers, while only 10 percent had more than 100 to 300 workers. Though foreign investors were quick to take advantage of Singapore's open-door policy and the many incentives offered by the government, they were also rational in their technological choice and organization of work. The small domestic market and the scarcity of local managerial and technical know-how and expertise imposed a limit on the size of the foreign firm. Therefore, apart from the shipbuilding and repairing industry and the chemical-petroleum industry, industrial firms in Singapore were largely labor-intensive, low-wage, and low-productivity enterprises, requiring the mere repetition of simple operations along the assembly and production line.

4. Speech by the minister of trade and industry, quoted in Lim Joo-Jock (1980, 279).

5. For an assessment of the state of education in the developing world and the impact of globalization on education in these countries, see Bloom (2004).

REFERENCES

Bloom, David E. 2004. "Globalization and Education: An Economic Perspective." In *Globalization: Culture and Education in the New Millennium,* ed. M. Suarez-Orozco and D. B. Qin-Hilliard, 56–77. Berkeley: University of California Press.

Chia, Siow Yue. 1971. "Growth and Pattern of Industrialization." In *The Singapore Economy,* ed. You Poh Seng and Lim Chong Yah. Singapore: Eastern University Press.

Department of Statistics. Various years. *Yearbook of Statistics.* Singapore: Department of Statistics.

Goh Keng Swee. 1972. *The Economics of Modernization.* Singapore: Asia Pacific Press.

Jomo, K. S., ed. 2006. *Manufacturing Competitiveness in Asia: How Internationally Competitive National Firms and Industries Developed in East Asia.* London: Routledge Curzon.

Lee, Kuan Yew. 2002. *From Third World to First: The Singapore Story: 1965–2000.* Singapore: Singapore Press Holdings, Times Editions.

Lim, Joo-Jock. 1980. "Bold Internal Decisions, Emphatic External Outlook." In *Southeast Asian Affairs 1980.* Singapore: Institute of Southeast Asian Studies.

Ministry of Culture. 1968. *The Mirror* (April 22).

Ogawa, Naohira, Gavin W. Jones, and Jeffrey G. Williamson, eds. 1993. *Human Resources in Development along the Asian-Pacific Rim.* Singapore: Oxford University Press.

Straits Times, February 27, 1986.

World Bank. 1995. *The East Asian Miracle: Economic Growth and Public Policy.* New York: Oxford University Press.

CHAPTER 1

The Development of Education in Singapore since 1965

GOH Chor Boon and S. GOPINATHAN

The aftermath of World War II in the Pacific created severe social and economic dislocations for the people of Singapore in 1945. Although the British rulers reclaimed control of the trading port, the people clamored for political freedom and economic opportunities. There were frequent industrial strikes and unrest. The population grew from about 960,000 in 1948 to about 1.6 million in 1954. There was high unemployment and an acute shortage of public housing.

The years 1959 to 1968 represent some of the epochal years in Singapore's modern history.[1] In 1959, the British colony became completely self-governing, and in August 1965 Singapore became a sovereign state after separating from Malaysia. Her political leaders were faced with the unenviable task of ensuring the political and economic survival of the small city-state. Colonialism had produced a lopsided economy strongly dependent on entrepot trade. As science and technology became the vital ingredients that dictated a country's level of competitiveness, the overriding priority of the Singapore government in 1965 was to find the quickest and most effective way to develop an industrialized economy and to develop its own military capability. To compete as a viable economic entity, Singapore was faced with the immediate task of breaking away from the long dependency on entrepot trade and embarking on an export-oriented industrialization strategy.

In the late 1960s and 1970s, individual survival matched well with the state's ideology of survival. Singapore's economic and political fortunes became inseparable. The successful fusion of economic and political survival required the internalization of an entirely new set of social attitudes and beliefs by the people of Singapore. The government called on the people to sacrifice self-interest for the "national interest." In the process of catching up, important policies, especially those in the field of education and manpower development, were speedily implemented.

This chapter highlights key features of the development of education in Singapore over the past 40 years, focusing on how Singapore has been able to develop its education system from a level quite similar to that of many developing countries in the early 1960s to a system comparable to the best in member countries of the Organisation for Economic Co-operation and Development (OECD). The analysis is done in the context of the economic and social transformation of Singapore since 1965.

SURVIVAL ECONOMICS, SURVIVAL-DRIVEN EDUCATION, 1965–78

Since the 1950s, industrialization has been widely acknowledged by the pro-capitalist, independent states of Southeast Asia as the key to survival and economic growth. But the task was not easy because long periods of colonialism had produced imbalanced economic structures that confined the rising indigenous capitalist class to comprador trading activities and limited small-scale manufacturing and processing. The initial response was the adoption of the development strategy strongly recommended by the Argentine economist Raul Prebisch: Import Substitution Industrialization (ISI) aimed at reduced dependence on imported goods (Dixon 1991, 152). Essentially, ISI involves the small-scale production of nondurable consumer goods whose production requirements are compatible with conditions, such as abundant unskilled labor and unsophisticated technology, existing in countries without previous industrial experience. Rapid economic growth was indeed experienced by the countries in Southeast Asia, but by the mid-1960s the limitations and inherent contradictions of the ISI strategy began to be felt. In the case of Singapore, apart from assembling consumer goods, there were few signs of a transition to capital goods production. Manufactured imports were merely replaced by raw materials, capital goods, and components. Pressure for accelerated growth through the development of export markets was emerging from local manufacturing capitalists. The situation was compounded by Singapore's expulsion from Malaysia in 1965; the ISI strategy was seriously undermined by the dramatic reduction in the size of the domestic market. When Singapore was part of Malaysia in 1963–1965, it could hope to take advantage of the wide hinterland market to its north. Following the separation from Malaysia, the development strategy adopted by Singapore leaders gradually shifted toward export-oriented industrialization (EOI), which, by the early 1970s, became the "new orthodoxy" strongly advocated by Bela Balassa of the World Bank for economic growth in the developing countries.

In the late 1950s, Singapore derived 70 percent of its gross domestic product from entrepot activities (Dixon 1991, 158). The country had a small and limited industrial base. The predominant industry was shipbuilding and ship repair, which was largely in the hands of governmental and public bodies, such as the

Singapore Harbor Board and the British Naval Base. The small manufacturing sector consisted mainly of light engineering, assembly of vehicles, marine engineering, printing, and processing (Colony of Singapore 1955). Although employment in the manufacturing sector grew from 22,692 in 1955 to 44,295 in 1961, manufacturing development was slow and stagnated at about 12 percent of gross domestic production in 1960. In the meantime, the postwar baby boom in the early 1950s and the free immigration policy had resulted in an average annual population growth rate of 4.4 percent in 1957. The unemployment rate stood at 5 percent, rising to a high of 9.2 percent in 1966. It was clear to the government that solving the rising unemployment problem was a matter of high priority.

The government became more focused on the need to expand the industrial base, although it still advocated that Singapore must continue to "jealously guard its position as an entrepot" (*Malaya Tribune* 1953). But the task of expanding manufacturing activities for a trading port was not expected to be smooth because of the "dearth of skilled labor in Singapore" (Colony of Singapore 1954). The year 1968 was a watershed in terms of a shift in industrial strategy to more export-oriented manufacturing activities. Because of Singapore's lack of natural resources, the development of the country's human resources was of paramount importance for the government to support its EOI strategy. To achieve this end, an education system that would support the development of a literate and technically trained workforce was introduced.

While under British colonial rule, education was a tool to meet political and ethnic primordial interests. In 1965 and after, an intimate link between education and economic development of the small city-state was strongly emphasized. The government took the conventional path, developing new skills and work attitudes to accommodate new economic strategies. While the economics of education was in focus, the role of education in socialization and the nation-building process, especially in terms of developing a Singapore identity, was not forgotten. National integration through a national education system was seen as the key condition for economic survival. To attain these national objectives, the government rightly recognized the necessity to provide every child with at least six years of education from the age of six—without discrimination on the basis of race, language, sex, wealth, or status.

Bilingualism became a key component in Singapore's education system. In 1960 the learning of a second language was made compulsory in all primary schools, and the policy was extended to all secondary schools in 1966. The decision on bilingualism was not just for the achievement of social cohesion in a largely pluralistic society. The English language was seen as a necessary tool in Singapore's effort to make the world its marketplace. However, with the increasing demand for English, the government was concerned that the young could become less attuned to their own cultures and not use their mother tongues. The bilingual policy would assure parents that their children would not grow up ignorant of their cultures.

Singapore's bilingual policy is perhaps unique in the world. It is an East-West model that allows Singaporeans to attain competency in the use of the English language, the language of the West, and in the use of the Chinese language (or other indigenous languages, such as Tamil and Malay), the language of the East. This approach is particularly useful for Singapore's business internationalization strategy. The Western concept of bilingualism in schools is based more on a Latin model in which pupils will usually learn, for example, German and English or Italian and English.

The years 1959 to 1965 were significant or even epochal in the history of Singapore's educational transformation. In May 1959, Singapore was given self-government status, and a Five-Year Plan (1961–1965) to boost the educational standards of the people was soon implemented. The priority at this point was to provide universal free primary education. It consisted of three main features:

- Equal treatment for the four streams of education: Malay, Chinese, Tamil, and English.
- The establishment of Malay as the national language of the new state.
- Emphasis on the study of mathematics, science, and technical subjects.

The philosophy behind these aims "conserved equal opportunity for all citizens; established the means of maintaining unity in diversity; and instituted a program for training a new generation for the needs of a forward-looking, modern, industrial and technological society" (Ministry of Education 1966).[2] This philosophy, broadly speaking, stays intact even today. Although the government continued to provide for vernacular education, a major consequence of the transformation of the Singapore economy from 1959 onward was the consistently strong tendency for parents to enroll their children in the English language schools. In 1959 only 47 percent of children entering primary one were in the English stream, while 46 percent were in Chinese schools. Twenty years later (in 1979), the English stream enrolled 91 percent of all primary one children, with only 9 percent in the Chinese stream and a negligible number in the Tamil and Malay language streams. This dramatic drift was brought about by the free choice of pragmatic parents in response to the nation's drive toward high-value-added industrialization and to an economy where the language of business is English.

Free primary education was made available to all. In 1962, out of a population of 1.7 million, the student population stood at nearly 400,000. This led to a period of rapid construction of schools. Under British rule, government English schools and missionary English schools had good buildings. However, most of the other vernacular schools, especially in the rural areas, were built and supported by

Table 1.1 Students in Public Educational Institutions

Year	1965	1975	1985	1995	2005
Primary	355,096	328,034	277,875	261,553	290,261
Secondary	104,720	160,556	163,590	180,982	213,063
Pre-university	6,671	13,782	24,699	21,690	28,901
Institute of Technical Education (ITE)	1,193	9,830	18,894	9,476	21,603
Polytechnics	3,208	9,276	21,610	46,841	64,422
National Institute of Education (NIE)	5,603	685	1,125	2,482	3,676
Universities	4,996	8,540	16,958	34,591	59,441

Source: Ministry of Education 2007.

private organizations or individuals and not well resourced. Beginning in 1959, the responsibility for building all new functional schools was passed on to the Ministry of Education.

Total primary and secondary education enrollment in public schools rose from 459,816 in 1965 to 488,590 in 1975. Tables 1.1 and 1.2 show the enrollment figures and gross enrollment ratios in Singapore's public educational institutions, respectively, since 1965. (The early 1970s saw a decline in primary enrollment because of successful family planning strategies implemented by the government.) A total of 83 new school buildings were completed between 1959 and 1965, a rate of about one school a month for seven years. The accelerated building program equaled the demand of the primary-school-going population in 1964. Even with this program, however, it became necessary for school buildings to be used by two sets of children, that is, double sessions, to accommodate the rapid increase in enrollment. In the words of Ong Pang Boon, then the minister for education, "The people of Singapore are becoming so education conscious that we have achieved universal primary education without making it compulsory . . . and once

Table 1.2 Gross Enrollment Ratios (%)

Year	1965	1975	1985	1995	2005[a]
Primary	108	108	110	98	101
Secondary	57	70	90	105	106
Pre-university/ITE	10	20	41	38	69
Polytechnics/NIE/ universities	6	6	14	39	58

Source: Ministry of Education 2007.

a. Figures for 2005 are preliminary and include private educational institutions.

admitted, they [the children] are assured of a 10-year primary and secondary education finishing at the minimum age of 16" (*Straits Times* Sept. 26, 1965, Nov. 25, 1965). Because of the rapid construction of schools, universal lower secondary education was achieved as early as 1970. The overall growth in secondary education, from 104,720 students in 1965 to 160,556 students in 1975, is impressive evidence of the importance parents gave to education (beyond primary education). From a societal point of view, secondary education was the most profitable investment (Pang 1982, 94–95). The rate of return to society is 18.2 percent for a completed secondary education for males and 17.0 percent for females. In terms of types of education, an English-stream education had greater monetary payoffs to society than did other vernacular-stream education.

Although statistics indicated successful outcomes, it was increasingly difficult for the Ministry of Education to meet the intense desire of the people to educate their children. Some obstacles were logistic in nature. There was uneven distribution of population in most urban areas and in certain rural areas. Suitable school sites in the densely populated areas were unavailable. The problem was compounded by the parents' selection and preference for certain schools, such as those with personal affiliation and language stream. Nevertheless, with careful planning and budgeting and ensuring that there were sufficient teachers, universal primary education was attained by the mid-1960s.

In the first year of its independence, the Singapore government allotted 59 percent of the annual education budget to primary education, 27 percent to secondary education, and 14 percent to higher education (as compared with 65 percent, 20 percent, and 15 percent, respectively, in Japan) (*Straits Times* Nov. 25, 1965). Table 1.3 shows the annual expenditure on education from 1959 to 1967.

Table 1.3 Annual Expenditure on Education, 1959–67

Year	Expenditure on Education (S$)	% of Total National Expenditure
1959	60,008,000	23.6
1960	57,100,000	23.5
1961	65,841,000	17.1
1962	82,307,000	23.4
1963	94,644,000	15.8
1964	103,358,000	31.7
1965	112,806,000	28.8
1966	124,076,000	23.4
1967	135,051,000	22.8

Source: Department of Statistics, various years.

Education in Singapore was financed almost entirely from state revenue. The Ministry of Education made its own annual estimates of expenditures, which were presented to the Ministry of Finance for submission to Parliament for approval. Hence, except for a handful of private schools run by private organizations such as clan associations, schools in Singapore were (and are) public or state supported. This is quite different from the case in African countries, where private funding played a significant role in the development of schools, especially secondary schools, and often outstripped the number of state-owned schools.[3] Besides the generous funding from the government, two other strategies were adopted to cater to the rapid expansion of the school population: teacher recruitment and the availability of textbooks.

Corresponding to the increase in pupil enrollment, the number of teachers also increased rapidly, from 10,590 teachers in 1959 to 16,986 in 1965 and 19,216 in 1968. These were trained or qualified teachers. The strategy to achieve the numbers was large-scale recruitment of teachers-in-training (with at least a full ordinary-level, or O-level, Cambridge certificate) at the then–Teachers Training College. During this period, part-time teaching programs were introduced: training in the morning and teaching in the afternoon and vice versa (depending on the type of program). This was a realistic approach during the years of rapid expansion.

In tune with the government policy of equal treatment for all four language streams of education, the government scheme for the loan of free textbooks offered assistance to pupils in all four language streams. This was done in accordance with the "Textbook for All" policy that no needy children from lower-income families should be denied an education merely because of inability to purchase textbooks. The free textbooks scheme was administered by schools, and the books were obtained directly from the Education Publishing Bureau (EPB), which was set up by the government in 1967 to produce common and affordable textbooks for all. The rising cost to the government of this form of aid to needy children can be seen from the annual expenditure on free textbooks, rising from S$79,606 in 1959 to S$259,200 in 1965. The ownership-of-textbook–to–student ratio was close to 1:1, attributable to the low cost of production achieved through a competitive tender system administered by the EPB with private printers. The cost recovery associated with textbook development was not a primary concern because "Singapore has so far been able to finance its own educational expansion program largely because of the resourcefulness of its people" (*Straits Times* Nov. 25, 1965).

The period of survival-driven education also saw the review and upgrade of technical and vocational education. In 1964, the government established secondary vocational schools for the first time, with an enrollment of 4,910 pupils. These were pupils who did not pass the primary-leaving examinations to enter into academic secondary schools. The curriculum, aimed to equip pupils for employment in establishments where basic vocational skills are required, consisted largely of subjects such as woodwork, domestic science, arts and crafts, and technical drawings. By 1968, the Ministry of Finance concluded that the prospective output of technically trained workers produced by the school system would not be sufficient to meet the requirements of new industries. Reaching this conclusion did not require any elaborate process of manpower planning. In 1968, out of the 144,000 students in secondary schools, only some 18,000 were in technical and vocational streams. Accordingly, the government accelerated plans for the expansion of technical education. A Technical Education Department was set up in the Ministry of Education in June 1968, and from 1969 all male lower secondary pupils were required to have two years of training in technical subjects, while girls were given a choice between technical subjects and home economics.

The Technical Education Department made use of all available training facilities (located in four newly built vocational institutes) to turn out skilled workers, such as welders and machinists, to service the shipbuilding, oil refinery, electrochemical, electromechanical, precision engineering, metalworking, and woodworking industries (Clark 1971). From 1970 to 1973, for example, 1,789 trainee welders received formal technical training. While Singapore succeeded in attracting a wide range of foreign-owned new industries, the industrialization effort benefited immensely from technical and financial assistance from a number of foreign governments and from the United Nations Development Programme aimed at producing industrial skills. Foreign governments that donated machinery and expertise included Japan, Britain, and France. Several vocational training centers were set up as a result of this external support.

In an effort to keep pace with the rapid developments in technical and vocational education, extensive teacher training and retraining programs were developed, and the Finance Ministry made funds freely available for such purposes. The number of technical teachers increased from 425 in 1968 to 1,950 in 1972. This was no mean achievement as the labor market was getting increasingly tight. Besides teachers specifically trained in technical subjects, academic subject teachers were also encouraged to be retrained as technical subject teachers. In 1968, some 4,000 teachers received training in metalwork, including fitting and sheet metal, woodwork, printing, motor mechanics, radio and television servicing, and electrical fitting and installation.

The survival-driven system of education continued into the 1970s with the continual propagation of an industrial-oriented education to produce the manpower for industrial development. The Vocational and Industrial Training Board (VITB, the predecessor of the current Institute of Technical Education) was created in 1979 to take in secondary school leavers who were less academically inclined. Vocational training institutes under the VITB offered a wide range of courses, the most popular of which were electrical, electronics, maintenance and repair of motor vehicles, refrigeration, air conditioning, carpentry, masonry, and plumbing.[4] Enrollment at the secondary level continued to grow, rising from about 148,000 in 1969 to 176,000 in 1979. Enrollment in VITB institutes also rose from 2,800 to 14,000 during the same period. By 1976, close to 20 percent of the secondary school population was receiving technical education. At the tertiary level, the total intake at Singapore's two main polytechnics at this time—Singapore Polytechnic and Ngee Ann Polytechnic—rose from about 3,500 in 1966 to about 11,000 in 1980.

While the British laissez faire policy did not produce systemic changes to the educational landscape in colonial Singapore, the Singapore leaders introduced a flurry of "haphazard changes" (*Straits Times* Mar. 24, 1976). Singapore's education planners failed to see early enough that the bilingual requirements of the system were not differentiated in terms of pupil ability. Those who failed to make the grade at the Primary School Leaving Examination (PSLE), which was a selection tool for secondary school, left the system, and only some went on to vocational institutions. As a result the growth in secondary education was slow, with an average of about 70 percent of the leaving-primary cohort entering into secondary schools. As many as seven different ministers were at the helm of educational changes and, at one stage, Singapore had three education ministers within a span of less than 15 months. There was no attempt to hear the views of teachers or parents before new policies were implemented. As pointed out by one member of Parliament, "The point is we were so concerned with objects and objectives that we lost sight of the fact that we were dealing with children and people" (*Straits Times* Mar. 24, 1976). There was a serious communication gap between the Ministry of Education and the schools. This lack of dialogue led to all kinds of interpretations of policy decisions; at one point, 78 notifications were issued to schools in a short period of nine months.

The low status and morale of teachers was also high on the list of complaints. According to the Singapore Teachers' Union, resignations of teachers and principals were consistently high in the early 1970s. In 1973, there were 379 resignations (2.1 percent of the teaching force); in 1974, there were 350 resignations (1.9 percent); and in 1975, there were 306 resignations (1.7 percent).[5]

The year 1978 was a watershed in Singapore's educational development. To support its broad catch-up economic strategy, and working on the premise that senior servants and talented bureaucrats should assume major roles in decision making, spearheading changes, and managing large government enterprises, the government introduced a technocratic ethos in its education framework. A high-level reviewing committee, led by Dr. Goh Keng Swee (the then–deputy prime minister) and his team of systems engineers, reviewed the education system and totally overhauled it. Its report (popularly known as the *Goh Report*) brought to light the education doldrums embedded in the system as reflected in two sets of statistics: education wastage and the literacy level of the students. Education wastage—failure to achieve the expected standards and premature school leaving—for the years 1971 to 1974 was high. Out of 1,000 pupils entering primary one, on average 206 dropped out of school nine years later, without acquiring any useful qualification or skill. It was recommended that those pupils who did not have the ability to proceed satisfactorily in the academic stream would be screened out and prepared for vocational careers.

The low education standard in the 1970s was also reflected in the poor literacy level, in terms of proficiency in the English language. Among pupils who passed their PSLE and young national servicemen with educational levels ranging from no formal education to secondary three, an average of 40 percent passed the O-level Cambridge Schools Examinations in the 1970s. This was despite the fact that the nation's literacy rate increased from 72.7 percent in 1970 to 77.6 percent in 1978 (*Straits Times* Aug. 11, 1978). The low English proficiency resulted in the overall low education standard.[6] Out of 1,000 pupils entering primary one, only 440 reached secondary four after 10 years. Of this number, only 106 obtained three or more O-level passes in the Cambridge Schools Examinations.

By the mid-1970s, the adoption of the EOI strategy had enabled the country to enjoy full employment. However, it was apparent to the political leaders that to sustain robust growth rates, the people must develop competencies in science and technology. British colonialism did not leave behind a legacy of a well-planned education system that emphasized the development of technical and vocational skills. The earlier-than-expected British military withdrawal in 1971 also created the pressing need for the supply of skilled labor resources. The long time lag to develop technical and vocational skills had made it difficult for the government to introduce measures to quickly close the technological gap. The problem was compounded by the severe shortage of local expertise in the field of science and technology who could have contributed to the development of science and technical education in schools. A study report in 1970 by Dutch economist Albert Winsemius highlighted the deficiency in terms of the shortage of skilled workers, such as engineers, management personnel, and technicians.[7] Whatever limited pool of engineers the country had was largely taken up by the multinational corporations (MNCs) that dominated the fast-expanding manufacturing sector (Goh 1972, 275). The Singapore government had adopted an aggressive open-door policy to attract MNCs and foreign expertise into the small city-state to provide the impetus for an industrial takeoff and to close the technological gap. As explained by Goh Keng Swee, then the deputy prime minister, in his 1970 budget speech, "When foreign corporations bring their expertise, what we experience as a developing nation is a brain-drain in reverse. . . . In the long term the scientific know-how and technological processes which we now borrow from abroad must in course of time develop on an indigenous base at our institutions of higher learning" (Parliamentary Debates 1970).[8]

Although new governmental institutions were set up to deal with science and technology policy problems, quite often the measures recommended did not endure for long. Instead, there was a bewildering succession of ad hoc committees, councils, and agencies, each of which sent out different signals and directions. The confusion was further reinforced by the ineffectiveness of the Ministry of Science and Technology (set up in 1968), which suffered from a shortage of high-level administrators and having to oversee a wide range of activities, from coordination of technical education to the promotion of research work (*Straits Times* Feb. 18, 1981). Eventually, on April 1, 1981, 12 years after it was formed, the ministry was dissolved. As explained by Goh Chok Tong (the former prime minister and now Singapore's senior minister), "the defunct Ministry of Science and Technology had only a budget of $100,000 to disburse as research grants. . . . We did not have a research and development policy until now [1981], because research and development was not critical to our economic growth strategy in the last decade" (*Straits Times* Jun. 8, 1981). Young Singaporeans' indifferent attitudes toward blue-collar jobs persisted. The magnitude of the problem was seen in some shocking statistics in 1976—of the 150,000 clerical and related workers, only 2 percent were work permit holders; but of the 1,600 metal process workers, 46 percent were work permit holders, and the figure was 56 percent for the 4,700 woodworkers and a staggering 60 percent for the 55,000 building construction workers (*Straits Times* Aug. 9, 1976).[9] Recognizing the backwardness in the development of science and technology in the country, the Singapore government adopted in the 1980s developmental strategies designed to push the economy and society higher up the technological ladder. With this vision, more educational changes were introduced to prepare the people for the "Second Industrial Revolution" in the 1980s.

SUSTAINABLE DEVELOPMENT THROUGH AN EFFICIENCY-DRIVEN EDUCATION, 1978–1997

By the end of the 1970s, social and economic indicators pointed to a rich and progressive Singapore in the midst of developing countries still battling with the problem of poverty. In 1980, after two decades of intensive expansion of the manufacturing sector largely through the aegis of foreign MNCs, the manufacturing sector contributed 28 percent of Singapore's gross domestic product (GDP), as compared with 12 percent in 1960. However, to achieve sustainable development, it became clear that as countries in Southeast Asia began to compete effectively for foreign investments in low-skilled, labor-intensive industries, Singapore's previous comparative advantage in labor-intensive manufactured products was gradually being eroded. The emphasis shifted to a strategy that could accelerate Singapore's transition from a "third-league," labor-intensive, industrializing country to a "second-league," capital-intensive economy. Thus, the Second Industrial Revolution was launched in 1981 to accelerate Singapore's transition to a more sophisticated technological base, thereby taking it out of competition with the lower-wage countries and lessening its reliance on labor expansion for economic growth. There were two main strategies of the restructuring program: the continual task of attracting MNCs to invest in high-technology operations, and the promotion of science and technology, such as activities in research and development.[10] To provide a stock of basic education, skills, and attitudes required for industrialization, the government revisited the education system to use it as a major vehicle in nation building, with the state acting as a strategic player not only in manpower planning, but also in the wider process of economic development. The ability of the state to successfully manage supply and demand of education and skills was and continues to be a major source of Singapore's competitive advantage.

After two decades of rapid expansion of educational opportunities for all young Singaporeans, during which universal primary and lower secondary education was achieved, the government decided to shift its focus from the fulfillment of mere quantitative demands to quality. The emphasis was on upgrading and providing quality education. Survival-driven education was structured on the premise that children of different levels of intelligence and learning ability were expected to progress at the same rate. With the pace of teaching pegged to the average pupils, the very intelligent would find schooling a boring experience and, at the other end of the spectrum, those with learning difficulties would find it difficult to keep pace with the rest.

To support the drive toward sustainable development and reflect the economic restructuring strategies, education was revamped with an emphasis on efficiency. Aimed to reduce educational wastage, a New Education System (NES) was introduced in January 1979 (see figure 1.1). The NES provided for three streams in both primary and secondary school, to allow pupils to progress at a pace more suited to their abilities.[11] Slower primary pupils were allowed up to eight years to complete primary education, while secondary pupils could take up to five years to acquire the General Certificate in Education (GCE) O level and a further three years for the advanced (A) level. A new lower-level secondary school leaving certificate, the GCE Normal (N) was introduced. In manpower terms, the effect of the NES was to enable each pupil to go as far as possible in school, and thereby achieve the best possible educational takeoff for training and employment.

By the early 1980s, the key features of the efficiency-driven education system were in place: a national curriculum with a stress on bilingualism and moral, civics, science, mathematics, and technical education; tracking, with regular student assessment regulated by the Ministry of Education's Research and Testing Division;

Figure 1.1 The New Education System, 1979

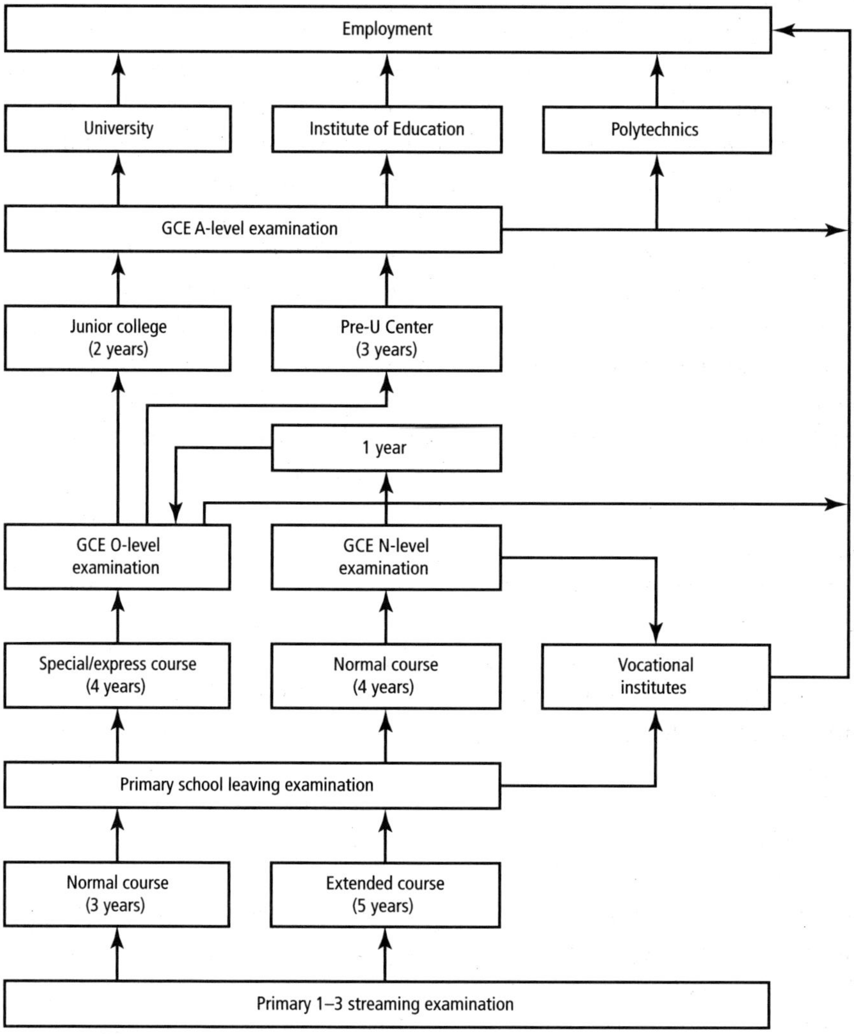

Source: Authors.
Note: GCE = General Certificate in Education.

curriculum materials to fit the school syllabuses and produced by the Curriculum Development Institute of Singapore; clear lines of progression to the university, polytechnics, and vocational institutes; and, by 1984, a systematic and year-long professional training for principals and heads of departments. Primary streaming (at primary three) and secondary streaming (at secondary two) began in 1979 and 1980, respectively, and second language was made compulsory for university entrance from 1980.

On the whole, the NES saw improvements in academic results. Prior to the implementation of the new system, more than 60 percent of the pupils who sat for the PSLE and the O-level examination failed in one or both languages. By 1984, the overall percentages of pupils passing the PSLE in English and the second language were 85.5 and 98.7 percent, respectively. For O-level English, the percentage jumped to more than 90 percent. At the same time, the high attrition rates at the primary and secondary stages of education noted in the *Goh Report* of 1978 declined sharply. In 1986, for example, only 3,772 pupils (or less than 1 percent of the total school population below 16 years of age) left school without having at least 10 years of education. The success in reducing educational wastage provided the city-state with an educated workforce able to cope with the demands of a rapidly expanding economy. As in the previous decades, education in Singapore in the 1980s and beyond, being both a public and merit good, was (and is) heavily subsidized by the government. In 1989, private expenditure on education was only 0.55 percent of GDP (as compared with 0.86 percent in 1960) (Low, Toh, and Soon 1991, 135–138).

However, within the education system, there were still teething problems. The strictly top-down approach in planning, disseminating, and enforcing educational changes was a clear reflection of the Singapore government's paternalistic style of rule. In the process, it produced three unhealthy trends.

First, it generated the "yes-man" syndrome and the acceptance of change without question by those below. Second, it inculcated an overreliance on the top leaders for direction. Third, it nurtured a spoon-feeding culture. The end result was an education service that lacked autonomy and initiative and had a general sense of detachment from the policy makers. Within schools, teachers and children alike were mechanically fed by a bureaucratically designated and rigid curriculum. The double-session system imposed constraints on schools by restricting the availability of physical facilities and imposing severe inconveniences on teachers. Not surprisingly, even by the mid-1980s, principals and teachers alike suffered from low morale and lacked the deep commitment to implement effectively the changes emanated from the top. Teachers also had to endure a poor social status, ineffective supervision and guidance, and bleak promotion prospects, especially for the nongraduate teachers.

With the appointment of Dr. Tony Tan Keng Yam as minister of education in 1985, the pressing problems in the education system were tackled with great vigor. The guiding philosophy for Singapore's education system in the 1980s was explicitly expressed by the former banker who answered the call of duty to serve in the cabinet:

> I would say that our education system in the 1980s should be guided by three considerations: Firstly, preparing the child for work in a Singapore which is rapidly becoming a modern centre for brain services and technological industries.

> This means that he will need to have a sound knowledge of English. Secondly, equipping him with a sufficient knowledge of his mother tongue so that he will retain a link with his cultural origins. This is the rationale for our policy on bilingualism. Thirdly, inculcating in the child an awareness of the necessity of moral and traditional values so that he will grow up to be a responsible adult, conscious of his obligations to himself, his family, his neighbours and his nation (*Business Times* Jul. 8, 1980).

Unpopular policies such as the *pinyin* names and graduate mother schemes were abolished. The former relates to the policy of expressing names of Chinese school children in *pinyin* or simplified Chinese. It was perceived in some quarters as a "politically correct" move to affirm Singapore's close relations with China. The graduate mother scheme (aimed to reverse the declining reproductive rates of mothers with university degrees) was another polemic policy measure that led to wrath on the part of many Singaporeans. It gave graduate mothers priority for registering their children in primary schools. From 1985 to 1991, a series of well-planned educational changes were introduced that reduced wastage, increased flexibility within the school systems, gave greater autonomy to schools, and provided greater access to higher education. All pupils leaving the primary school system were placed in the appropriate secondary school courses that would match their learning pace, ability, and inclinations. A gifted education program was started in 1985, English was made the main medium of instruction in all schools, a pastoral care program was started in 1987, and all secondary schools were to have only single sessions starting in 1989. Changes were also made to tackle the issue of the shortage of teachers. In the words of Dr. Tony Tan, "The basic solution to the problem of attracting high-quality people to join the teaching profession is to pay them sufficiently" (*Straits Times* Jul. 8, 1980). Training programs at the then–Institute of Education were revamped, and full-time training for nongraduate and graduate trainee teachers was started in July 1980.

One critical issue that did not receive much governmental attention was the failure of the education system to inculcate positive values and attitudes toward technical training and blue-collar jobs.[12] Until the early 1990s, little effort was made to upgrade vocational and technical education. Vocational training was (and is) specifically aimed at providing a form of continual education for the less academically inclined pupils. Before 1992, those who failed their PSLE and the examination at the end of their secondary two were channelled into vocational institutes. Unlike in South Korea, where vocational and technical training is held in high esteem, the Singapore system failed to project the same image. Vocational institutes became "dumping grounds" or "catch-nets" for those who failed to measure up to the requisite academic rigor.

The negative perception of vocational and technical training was not tackled seriously by the Singapore government until the late 1980s. As the young continued to show an aversion toward blue-collar jobs, the danger of the country not possessing a sufficient pool of technically skilled local workers became obvious. This scenario prompted a serious warning by Lee Yock Suan, the minister of education, in June 1994: "Singapore will be poorer if everyone aspires to and gets only academic qualifications but nobody knows how to fix a TV set, a machine tool or a process plant. We need a world-class workforce with a wide variety of knowledge of skills to achieve a world-class standard of living" (*Straits Times* Jun. 14, 1994).

Several institutional changes were introduced in recent years to enhance the image of technical and vocational education in Singapore. In 1992 the VITB was totally revamped and renamed the Institute of Technical Education (ITE). Sprawling ITE campuses, with excellent educational and sports infrastructure and cutting-edge technological support, were built in several locations throughout the island. Beginning in 1992, pupils who did not fare well at the end of the primary education were channelled to a new Normal Technical secondary stream before gaining admission to the new postsecondary institutes of ITE. There the students would be given the necessary time to master basic skills, especially proficiency in the English language. Scholarships were also made available for top ITE graduates to pursue diploma courses in the polytechnics (*Straits Times* Dec. 30, 1993).[13] Beginning in August 1994, the ITE launched its attachment programs for secondary two Normal Technical stream students. The objective was to familiarize students with the state-of-the-art campuses and, more important, to "remove any fears of machinery and tools or hang-ups about blue-collar jobs" (Chiang 1998, 64). Market demand for the well-trained ITE graduate, especially by some 650 participating companies under ITE's apprenticeship scheme, led to a rise in their starting salary, from an average of about S$700 per month in 1994 to about S$1,200 per month in 2005. There were also many success stories, highlighted in the newspapers, of ITE students making it to the polytechnics and eventually acquiring university degrees. In short, although enrollment into these training schools is still limited to those who find it difficult to go the academic route, the image of vocational training has totally changed for the better.

At the tertiary level, in line with the government's effort to enlarge the pool of scientific and technical manpower and its overall economic vision to transform Singapore into a developed nation, total enrollment in local degree and diploma courses increased by more than 200 percent: from 20,305 students in 1980 to 62,683 students in 1992.[14] Increasing university enrollment, however, did not hide the fact that Singapore was critically short of university graduates to drive economic growth. In 1980, only about 5 percent of the annual cohort of students entered universities and 8 percent entered polytechnics (compared with 20 percent in Taiwan and 40 percent in Japan for universities and polytechnics combined). Admission was (and is) highly competitive, and too few places were available. There were also restrictions in the form of quotas of enrollment for the various faculties (such as law and medicine), although these were determined as part of national manpower planning.

Though the increasing number of polytechnic and university graduates did help to change the profile of the workforce, the government recognized that, to become a technologically advanced city-state, the country needed a sustainable supply of indigenous scientists and engineers. For Singapore to develop its own indigenous technological capability, the lion's share of the supply of scientists and engineers had to come from native-born students educated and trained in local universities and polytechnics.[15] In 1990, out of every 10,000 Singapore workers, 114 were engineers by qualification, but only 29 were research scientists and engineers.

Concerted efforts, including better employment prospects and higher baseline salaries, were made in the public and private sectors to entice young Singaporeans to take up science and engineering disciplines in the universities. This resulted in an increase in the output of science and engineering graduates during the 1980s, as seen in table 1.4.

The increase in the number of graduates in science and engineering was sustained throughout the 1980s. Most significant: The number of engineering graduates doubled between the periods 1980–85 and 1986–89. This was an indication of the success of the government manpower planning "in meeting the needs of the economy for trained personnel at all levels" (Parliamentary Debates 1988, col. 1503). However, the government confirmed that "the major constraint on the expansion of technical education has been the number of qualified trainees, not the demand for graduates or the availability of places. . . . [T]he Engineering faculty at the University, which expanded rapidly, had difficulty in filling its places, and admitted some marginal students, and then suffered high failure rates in its five-year examinations" (Parliamentary Debates 1988, col. 1504). The shortage of able students doing engineering was compounded by the fact that "[t]he biggest misallocation in our tertiary education is the very low proportion of girls doing engineering" (Parliamentary Debates 1988, col. 1505). Girls, some of whom even outperformed the boys at A-level examinations, were more interested in courses

Table 1.4 Number of Degrees Awarded by Singapore Universities, 1981–89

Courses	1980–85	1986–89
Arts	3,792	4,542
Science	3,180	4,105
Engineering	2,467	5,005

Source: Calculated from tables 15.12 and 15.13, *Yearbook of Statistics* (Department of Statistics 1989, 304–5).

Table 1.5 Research Scientists and Engineers (RSEs)

Year	Number of RSEs	Labor force (thousands)	RSEs per 10,000 labor force
1978	818	975	8.4
1981–82	1,193	1,128	10.6
1984–85	2,401	1,188	20.2
1987–88	3,361	1,252	26.8
1990	4,329	1,516	28.6
1991	5,218	1,554	33.6
1992	6,454	1,620	39.8

Source: National Science and Technology Board 1992.

such as accounting and business administration because "they think [that in engineering] they may get their hands dirty" (Parliamentary Debates 1988, col. 1505).

In terms of research and development (R&D) manpower needs, the increase in the number of science and engineering graduates contributed to a steady rise in the pool of research scientists and engineers (RSEs). This is shown in table 1.5.

It was also in the mid-1980s that Singapore launched its National Information Technology (IT) Plan, which marked the development of a "wired" nation. Although measures were introduced in schools to promote computer literacy, the buy-in was slow, and it was not until the IT Master Plan of 1997 that strong and concerted efforts were made.

TOWARD A KNOWLEDGE-BASED ECONOMY THROUGH AN ABILITY-DRIVEN EDUCATION, 1997–PRESENT

Globalization, powered by rapid technological advances, has redefined the competitive framework of nations. In the new economic era, national wealth is increasingly determined by discovery and application of new and marketable ideas. The transition to a knowledge-based economy (KBE) shifts the emphasis of value away from production toward innovation and creativity. For Singapore and Singaporeans, the faster the Singapore economy changed, the harder it was for the citizens to be confident of their skills and employability. In short, the new economy carried a steep price: more frenzied lives; less security; more economic and social stratification; and the loss of time and energy for family, friendships, community, and self. These trends required Singapore's education system and structure to be redefined and realigned to meet the challenges of the new century. Stakeholders, especially the parents and the community at large, became actively engaged. Singapore and its education system entered into an ability-driven phase to meet the demands of the KBE.

By 1995, efficiency-driven education was producing positive outcomes. Singapore's youth performed exceptionally well in international mathematics and science tests (TIMSS 1995 and 1999). The 1995 research compared mathematic and science test scores of 13-year-olds in 41 countries. The international average score was 500. At the top of the list was Singapore with 643, followed by South Korea, Japan, and Hong Kong. This feat was again achieved in 2003. While Asian values were cited as success factors, the Singapore policy of streaming students according to academic abilities helped teachers to be more focused in their teaching. The pupils also benefited from major changes to the mathematics syllabus in 1990 and from the 1985 shift in the method of teaching science that placed more emphasis on thinking skills and understanding of concepts, rather than on rote mastery of content. Attrition rates for secondary schools decreased significantly, from 19 percent in 1980 to 3.5 percent in 1999.

The next milestone was the June 1997 shift in strategic paradigm, from an efficiency-driven education to an ability-driven one, encapsulated in the vision "Thinking Schools, Learning Nation" (TSLN).[16] The vision of TSLN hinges on the premise that, devoid of natural resources, the future sustainability and wealth of the small city-state depends on the capacity of its people to learn—and to learn continuously throughout their lives. The decision to make a radical shift toward ability-driven education in the late 1990s was timely and imperative. Undoubtedly, for nations to survive and prosper in the 21st century, the quality of education would be a critical factor for success and would differentiate the wealth of nations. Singapore's leaders learned much from the examples of the United States, Great Britain, and Japan. While the Americans were (and are) unsurpassed in producing highly creative and entrepreneurial individuals, there were serious concerns about the low average levels of literacy (including technological literacy) and numeracy among young Americans. Similar trends were also experienced by young British students. The Japanese also acknowledged the limitations of its mass-oriented school system with its government-controlled curriculum, but they consistently revisited and refined their educational system, from primary to postgraduate education, to sustain its standing as one of the most innovative and competitive nations in the world. Like Japan, Singapore seeks to keep the best of the old in the education system while forcing through needed changes.

Ability-driven education would give all youth 10 years of general education, including six years of compulsory education at the primary level, during which they could participate in a variety of programs according to their ability (see figure 1.2). The school system features a national curriculum, with major national examinations at the end of the primary, secondary, and junior college years. However, the ability-driven education provides greater flexibility and choice. Upon leaving primary school, the young Singaporean now can choose from a range of educational institutions that cater to different strengths and interests. For example,

Figure 1.2 Ability-Driven Education System, 2007

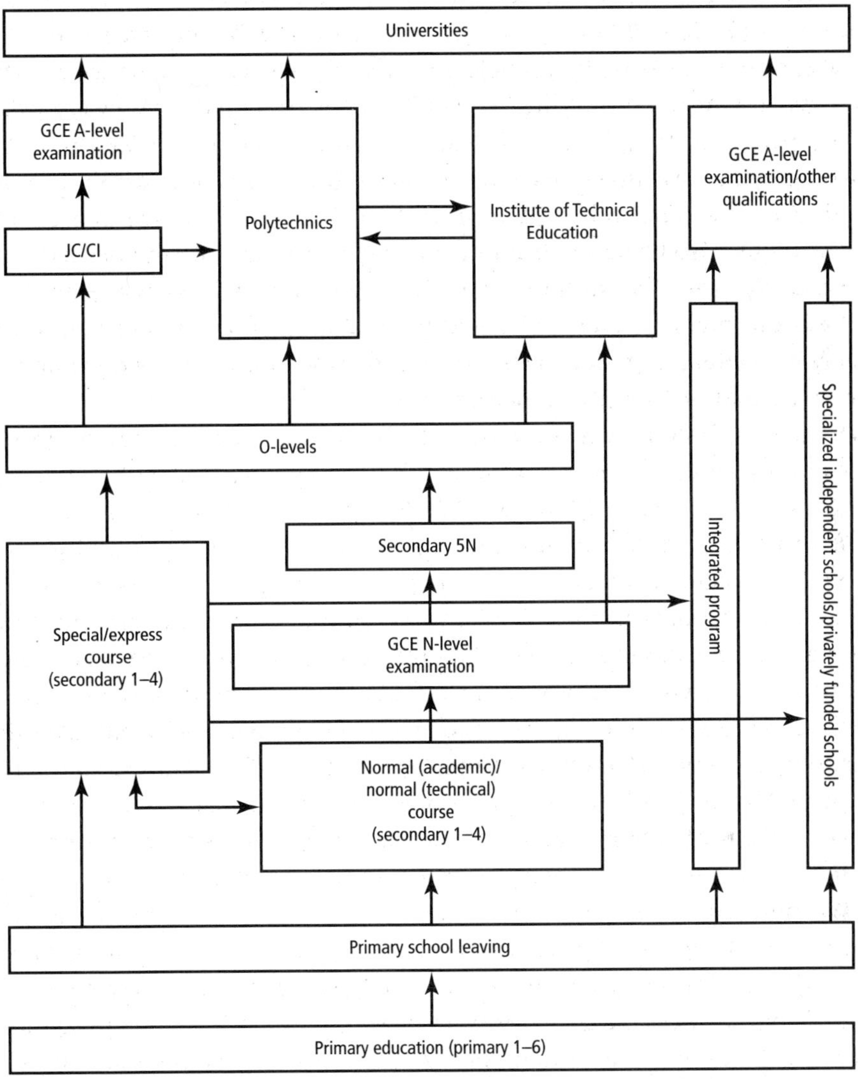

Source: Authors.
Note: JC/CI = junior college/centralized institute.

brighter students can apply to join the Integrated Program, a new component in the education system that spans secondary and junior college education, without the GCE O-level examination at the end of secondary school.

A responsive education structure was developed. The overall objective was to motivate Singaporeans to continually acquire new knowledge; learn new skills; gain higher levels of technological literacy; and develop a spirit of innovation, enterprise, and risk taking without losing their moral bearings or their commitment to the community and nation (Gopinathan 1999).[17] To achieve a quantum improvement in Singapore's whole process of education, the government launched several major initiatives, including revamping career paths for teachers, teaching creative thinking, introducing collaborative learning strategies, stressing national (or citizenship) education, making more use of new technologies in teaching and learning, and giving schools more resources and greater autonomy. In essence, ability-driven education has two key features:

- Maximal development of talents and abilities. Ability-driven education is premised on the belief that every child has some talent or ability. The scope and scale of talent within each student differs, but everyone should excel according to the combination of talents and abilities he or she possesses.
- Maximal harnessing of talents and abilities. Education must inculcate the appropriate national values and social instincts so that young Singaporeans can be committed to Singapore and actively contribute to the growth of the nation. Ability-driven education also offers opportunities to harness the talents and abilities of all teachers and leaders, both in schools and at the Ministry of Education.

Schools were strongly encouraged to take ownership of their curriculum and cocurricular activities to identify talents and abilities and to develop customized programs to meet individual students' aptitudes and skills. These specialized programs include the Music and Art Elective Programs, Gifted Education Program, and specially designed physical education and Chinese classes. As mentioned earlier, vocational training under the ITE was also given a strong boost. Government recurrent per-student expenditures on technical and vocational education increased from S$4,883 in 1991 to S$8,018 in 2004. Infrastructure, facilities, and technical equipment are consistently upgraded to ensure they match industrial needs.[18]

All these structural changes and education initiatives were matched with changes in education funding. During the past two decades or so, several new moves related to the financing of education were created by the Ministry of Education. In 1991, an innovative scheme, known as the Edusave Scheme, was announced. It offered grants to each child between 6 and 16 years of age to meet specified education expenses, such as the costs for educational visits to other countries and enrichment programs outside the formal school curriculum. Hence, the Edusave financial provision incorporates an element of choice in the use of funds, serving to customize the use of education facilities according to needs. An endowment fund was also established with a capital sum of S$1 billion to be increased yearly up to a total of S$5 billion. Government recurrent expenditures on education increased from S$2,013 per primary student in 1991 to S$3,541 in 2005, and

S$2,843 per secondary student in 1991 to S$5,390 in 2005 (Ministry of Education 2005, 49). On the whole, government spending on education averages about 4 percent of GDP.

Singapore is perhaps one of the few countries in the world to provide a generous employment package for the teaching profession to retain teachers and maintain a high-quality teaching force. Besides remunerations that are comparable (or even better) to those for beginning lawyers, engineers, and even medical doctors in the government service, each teacher is entitled to 100 fully paid hours of professional training per year. A Connect Plan, which provides monetary rewards for teachers who stay in service after a certain number of years, was also introduced. Finally, in the spirit of lifelong education, school leaders and teachers are encouraged to take sabbatical leave to pick up new knowledge and skills—and not necessarily in an education institution, but in other sectors as well, such as the hospitality industry.

It was also during this period that information and communication technology (ICT) took off in Singapore's schools and tertiary institutions. In the first Master Plan of 1997, the underlying rationale was that ICT could be integrated into the "thinking curriculum" to motivate students to be creative and independent learners. S$2 billion (for the period 1997–2002) funding was set aside to introduce ICT in schools and to have pupils spend 30 percent of curriculum time learning with, or through, computers. The Ministry of Education provided the initial training and infrastructure expenditures, after which principals were given the funds for upgrading courseware and professional development programs. The second Master Plan continued this rationale of adopting ICT as a key enabler in making student-centered learning and assessment a reality, and in helping Singapore to reach the objectives of ability-driven education and the vision of TSLN. The second Master Plan adopted a systematic and holistic approach by integrating all key components in the education system—curriculum, assessment, pedagogy, professional training, and culture.

CONCLUSION

As with OECD countries, Singapore has entered what Robert Reich describes as the "Age of Terrific Deal," where choices are almost limitless and it is easy to switch to something better (Reich 2001, 13). Social and economic forces are exerting themselves strongly for educational change, the outcomes of which, in turn, affect every aspect of Singapore society. Pragmatic Singaporeans are becoming better educated and more well traveled. But income disparities are widening. As the stakes in getting a good education continue to rise and with meritocracy consistently emphasized, wealthier and more ambitious parents more aggressively resort to "school sorting" and seek the best education they can afford for their children. At the other end of the spectrum are socially and economically dysfunctional families whose children are likely to form the bulk of school dropouts each year.

In the years ahead, the Singapore government will be constantly planning and reviewing educational policies and changes that are aimed to

- Prepare young Singaporeans for the KBE and, in the process, sustain Singapore's competitiveness
- Strengthen national identity, values, and social cohesion and, in the process, sustain Singapore's society regardless of race, language, or religion

The task at hand is not just to deal directly with pupils, teachers, and schools. More significant is the fact that a proactive approach toward engaging parents and the community as "partners in education" will be adopted.

Education provides the city-state of Singapore with the strong fundamentals to sustain its competitiveness. With no natural resources to exploit, the development of the country's manpower resources through a sound and robust education system is crucial. Singapore's case study has shown that strong political leadership and will have guided the overall education development and produced a structure and system that is relevant and responsive to the ever-changing economic and social landscape. Singaporeans recognize the importance of a good education in order to enjoy economic independence and good standards of living. It must be reiterated, however, that this drive toward attaining good education is sustainable because the nation possesses the economic and social environment that allows its citizens to reap the full benefits of their investments in educational pursuits. Indeed, when Singapore was in the throes of economic recession (as happened during the Asian financial crisis in 1997), Singaporeans continued to pursue their quests for academic excellence with the view that they would be more marketable or employable once good economic times returned.

NOTES

1. In the 1950s, frequent clashes and demonstrations against the government were held by Communist-infiltrated trade unions and Chinese schools. The British soon decided that the best political weapon against the Communist insurgency would be to grant national independence to Singapore. This would deprive the Communists of their role as champions of antifreedom movements and would nullify the justification for insurrection against the government. Therefore, the stage was set for the first democratic election of a self-governing Singapore in May 1959. The People's Action Party, under the leadership of Lee Kuan Yew, won convincingly. Lee became the first prime minister. At the same time, the state flag and national anthem, "Majulah Singapura," were adopted. About four years later, in September 1963, Singapore became part of Malaysia. But political differences soon reached an intolerable level. On August 9, 1965, under the leadership of Lee Kuan Yew, the

island of Singapore was formally separated from Malaysia and became a sovereign, democratic, and independent city-state.

2. The Malays were (and are) considered the indigenous people living in Singapore at the time the British founded Singapore in 1819. Hence, the Malay language became Singapore's national language. Singapore's national anthem is sung in the Malay language.

3. To some extent these privately supported secondary schools played a crucial shock-absorbing function, especially when the population of primary school leavers was bulging and the state's ability to fund the construction of secondary schools was progressively declining.

4. Vocational training and employer-based training constituted the twin strategies of skill-level manpower development. In this respect, the Skills Development Fund (SDF), administered by the Economic Development Board, was an invaluable source of funding for companies to promote employer-based training. This refers to customized training to meet production, restructuring, and specific development needs, undertaken directly by employers as a part of their investment in manpower resources. The SDF worked closely with VITB in promoting vocational skill training and awarded grants to employers to sponsor (up to 90 percent) employees for VITB's skill courses and apprentices.

5. Objectively, the resignation rates of 1.7 to 2.2 percent for this period were not particularly high. The rates today remain more or less in the same range as they were in the 1970s.

6. Since the 1950s, more and more parents sent their children to English stream schools. In 1960, 49 percent of all students were registered for the English stream, and by 1970, 66 percent were. In 1982, the figure went up to 90 percent. The reason behind this trend was an economic one. Singapore's economy was inextricably tied to the outside world, especially developed nations where the international language for business and trade is English. Moreover, all multinational corporations (where employment was highly sought) in Singapore used the English language.

7. Dr. Albert Winsemius was the leader of a United Nations Industry Survey Mission to Singapore in 1961. The *Winsemius Report,* as it became known, convinced the Singapore leaders that the traditional dependence on entrepot trade would not ensure the future economic survival of the small nation.

8. These statements reflected the optimism of a young but fast-developing nation. In fact, Goh's comments made in 1970 raised several significant, closely related issues concerning Singapore's quest for technological excellence in the 1980s and 1990s: the transfer and diffusion of technology and skill from MNCs, the lack of a critical mass, brain-drain of local expertise, the weak university–industry linkage, the lack of a well-planned science and technology policy, and the painfully slow development of R&D in Singapore's indigenous firms. Compared with the newly industrializing countries in East Asia and in Japan, Singapore in the 1970s suffered from low labor productivity growth. Between 1973 and 1978 "real productivity growth in Singapore averaged about 3 percent per annum, compared to an average of 7 percent for Hong Kong, Taiwan, and South Korea," according to Goh. These labor-intensive industries do not require professional scientists or engineers; they only need to have experienced foremen or plant supervisors and imported managers. Hence, even within larger MNCs, transfer and diffusion of technology and skill was very rare. See also the speech by the Minister of Trade and Industry quoted in Lim Joo-Jock (1980, 279).

9. In Singapore's context, a work permit is a work pass issued to a skilled or unskilled foreigner earning a certain maximum monthly salary to work in Singapore. Currently, the monthly basic salary stands at not more than S$1,800.

10. However, the impact of an expanding manufacturing base through foreign enterprises on the general managerial and technical skill levels of the workforce was not easily seen. Local industrial establishments in Singapore during this period were characterized by their small size, low capital input, and use of simple technology. In 1969, 70 percent of manufacturing enterprises employed 10 to 39 workers, while only 10 percent had more than 300 workers. Though foreign investors were quick to take advantage of Singapore's open-door policy and the many incentives offered by the government, they were also rational in their technological choice and organization of work. The small domestic market and the scarcity of local managerial and technical know-how and expertise imposed a limit on the size of the foreign firm. Therefore, apart from the shipbuilding and repairing industry and the chemical–petroleum industry, industrial firms in Singapore were largely labor-intensive, low-wage, and low-productivity enterprises, requiring the mere repetition of simple operations along the assembly and production line.

11. Streaming—the separation of students into different categories or streams—is a prominent feature of the Singapore education system. The rationale behind streaming, which began in 1984, is to allow the system to best address the needs of each student according to his or her academic ability, preventing a scenario in which the best students are bored by a standard curriculum and the weakest students struggle to pass. Such reasoning makes perfect sense in Singapore's context, which stresses meritocracy. Although the virtues of streaming are much debated, it in many ways is one of the most successful features of Singapore's education system. Streaming has been blamed for inducing excessive and unnecessary stress in students. Vast amounts of tuition, "mugging" (a term used to describe repeated, excessive study), and the resultant stress are part of the lives of many students in the education system. Others see streaming as a form of social class stratification, where the brighter students go on to earn university degrees and polytechnic diplomas and the Normal-stream students end up with certificates of vocational training and work as nonprofessionals. In short, the streaming system is perceived to limit the students' potentials. Success stories featuring Institute of Technical Education (ITE) students eventually heading to university or becoming successful entrepreneurs often make the front page in the newspapers, adding strength to the argument that streaming is unnecessary. However, of the thousands in the Normal stream in each cohort, only a scant few make it to the university. From a national perspective, the streaming system is efficient: It allows the appropriate allocation of resources and adoption of the right teaching methods for the right students, and provides learning environments more suited to the individual student.

12. The African countries, too, are trying to break down the persistent stigma of vocational training schools being seen as second-best alternatives after failure to enter conventional academic secondary schools. In addition, the curricula of vocational training centers in most countries suffer from rigidity that ignores the signals in the market regarding changes in the skills needed.

13. Each year, about 400 out of 3,500 ITE graduates join the polytechnics for a diploma course. For a comprehensive understanding of the development of technical education in Singapore, see Mickey Chiang (1998).

14. Ministry of Education *Annual Report*, various years. In some OECD countries, enrollments in the higher education sector also increased during this period. In the Netherlands,

enrollments in the higher education sector increased by 13 percent from 1980 to 1988; in Japan, university undergraduate enrollments rose by about 9 percent between 1978 and 1989; and in Norway, the corresponding figure was 10 percent between 1979 and 1986. The main reason for increased enrollments is the stronger presence of women within the student population. See OECD (1992, 137).

15. This important prerequisite for technological self-reliance was mentioned by Hayashi in his analysis of Japan's experience in absorbing foreign technology. According to Hayashi (1990), "Foreign engineers and technologists can and should play only a supplementary role . . . In spite of the diachronic, trans-cultural nature of technology, it cannot function independently of the society and culture in which it is expected to function. Only members of that society can make the best use of a technology. In other words, only native engineers can adapt a foreign technology to their country's climate and history, can intermediate, stabilize, disseminate, and finally, root it firmly in their country."

16. The "Thinking Schools, Learning Nation" concept or vision was launched by then–Prime Minister Goh Chok Tong on June 2, 1997. See also Sharpe and Gopinathan (2002).

17. In line with these changes, the National Institute of Education (NIE) reviewed its teacher training curriculum to meet the objectives of TSLN. NIE ensured that its preservice training curriculum and professional development programs would stay relevant and responsive. One key factor for its successful role is the close and strong tripartite relationship between the Ministry of Education, schools, and the institution.

18. Many African countries have infrastructure and equipment for technical and vocational training that are, for the most part, obsolete and inadequate to cater to the needs of industries. The problem is compounded by the high costs of importing new equipment.

REFERENCES

Business Times. July 8, 1980.

Chiang, M. 1998. *From Economic Debacle to Economic Miracle: The History and Development of Technical Education in Singapore*. Singapore: Times Edition.

Clark, D. 1971. "Manpower Planning in Singapore." *Malayan Economic Review* 16 (2): 20–28.

Colony of Singapore. 1954. "Report of the Industrial Resources Study Groups." In Andrew Gilmour, *Official Letters, 1931–1956*, Mss. Ind. Ocn. s. 154.

Colony of Singapore. 1955. *Annual Report*.

Department of Statistics. Various years. *Yearbook of Statistics*. Singapore: Department of Statistics.

Dixon, C. 1991. *South East Asia in the World Economy*. Cambridge, U.K.: Cambridge University Press.

Goh, K. S. 1972. *The Economics of Modernization*. Singapore: Asia Pacific Press.

Gopinathan, S. 1999. "Preparing for the Next Rung: Economic Restructuring and Educational Reform in Singapore." *Journal of Education and Work* 12 (3): 295–308.

Hayashi, T. 1990. *The Japanese Experience in Technology: From Transfer to Self-Reliance*. Tokyo: The United Nations University Press.

Lim, J. J. 1980. "Bold Internal Decisions, Emphatic External Outlook." In *Southeast Asian Affairs*, 273–91. Singapore: Institute of Southeast Asian Studies.

Low, Linda, M. H. Toh, and T. W. Soon. 1991. *Economics of Education and Manpower Development: Issues and Policies in Singapore*. Singapore: McGraw Hill.

Malaya Tribune. March 13, 1953.

Ministry of Education. *Annual Report*, various years.

Ministry of Education. 1966. *Progress in Education in Singapore, 1959 to 1965*. Singapore: Ministry of Education.
Ministry of Education. 2005. *Education Statistics Digest 2004*. Singapore: Ministry of Education.
National Science and Technology Board. 1992. *National Survey of R&D in Singapore*. Singapore: National Science and Technology Board.
OECD (Organisation for Economic Co-operation and Development). 1992. *Technology and the Economy: The Key Relationships*. Paris: OECD.
Pang, E. F. 1982. *Education, Manpower, and Development in Singapore*. Singapore: Singapore University Press.
Parliamentary Debates. 1970. Annual Budget Statement, March 9, Singapore.
Parliamentary Debates. 1988. *Official Reports*, March 28, vol. 50, col. 1503, Singapore.
Parliamentary Debates. 1988. *Official Reports*, March 28, vol. 50, col. 1504, Singapore.
Parliamentary Debates. 1988. *Official Reports*, March 28, vol. 50, col. 1505, Singapore.
Reich, R. B. 2001. *The Future of Success*. New York: Alfred A. Knopf.
Sharpe, L., and S. Gopinathan. 2002. "After Effectiveness: New Directions in the Singapore School System?" *Journal of Education Policy* 17 (2): 151–66.
Straits Times. September 26, 1965.
Straits Times. November 25, 1965.
Straits Times. March 24, 1976.
Straits Times. August 9, 1976.
Straits Times. August 11, 1978.
Straits Times. July 8, 1980.
Straits Times. February 18, 1981.
Straits Times. June 8, 1981.
Straits Times. December 30, 1993.
Straits Times. June 14, 1994.

CHAPTER 2

Strategic Management of Educational Development in Singapore (1965–2005)

David NG Foo Seong

INTRODUCTION

Singapore was described as a "somnolent, swampy fishing village" back in the early 1960s (Neher 1998). With no natural resources, Singapore faced severe racial, religious, and political turmoil, intensified by its 1965 separation from Malaysia (Lee 2000). In a span of 40 years, the Singapore government has managed to eliminate persistent poverty, unemployment, and crime and grow its per capita income from US$530 in 1965 to US$24,560 in 2004 (Department of Statistics 2005).

The only significant resource Singapore had was (and is) manpower. Yet in the early 1960s, the population was divided by race, language, religion, culture, and lifestyle. The literacy rate was 57 percent. Local university graduates numbered a few thousand. However, by the end of the 1990s, 40 percent of eligible youths (compared with 5 percent in 1970) were enrolled in higher education. In 1965, only 51,959 persons were employed in manufacturing industries. By 1975, the number had climbed steeply to 218,096 (Chiang 1998).

In the area of education, Singapore has consistently performed well in international studies such as the Trends in International Mathematics and Science Study (TIMSS). TIMSS conducts its study once every four years, and Singapore has been ranked first in science and mathematics achievement since 1995.

The economic and educational successes of Singapore did not happen by accident. Strategic planning, a strong political will, and a stable government are key factors in charting the success of Singapore. This chapter discusses the parallel phases of the strategic industrialization and educational reforms in Singapore.

In education, the focus of the discussion is on primary, secondary, and technical education. The analytical framework employed in this study is from the strategic triangle alignment of core strategy, organizational design, and the external environment between the government and academic institutions.

BACKGROUND

Economic planning has played a very significant role in the development of Singapore's industrialization, education, and manpower needs. Since 1965, Singapore has undertaken four distinctive industrialization phases for its economic transformation. Table 2.1 summarizes the industrialization phases.

FIRST INDUSTRIALIZATION PHASE

The first industrialization phase began in the early 1960s with factories producing garments, textiles, toys, wood products, and hair wigs. But along with these labor-intensive industries, there were also some capital- and technology-intensive projects such as Shell Eastern Petroleum and the national iron and steel mills.

SECOND INDUSTRIALIZATION PHASE

The second industrialization phase began in the early 1980s, when Singapore moved into knowledge-intensive activities such as research and development (R&D), engineering design, and computer software services. In this phase, the flexi-wage system—in which pay hikes were related to a company's profitability—was first introduced to improve Singapore's competitiveness. The impact of the high-wage policy resulted in swelling wage bills as Singapore slid into a recession.

With the goal of selling Singapore as a total business center, the Economic Development Board (EDB)[1] set out to attract international service corporations in

Table 2.1 Timeline of Singapore Economy and Economic Policy

	1965–1973	1974–1985	1986–1997	1998–onward
Economic issues	Expulsion from Malaysia, British military withdrawal	Oil and commodity price shocks, labor shortages	High labor costs, overinvestment in real estate	Asian financial crisis, challenge from China, economic maturity, high land costs
Economic policies	Promotion of investment, promotion of labor-intensive manufacturing, wage restraint	Emphasizing capital-intensive industry, importing foreign workers, high-wage policy	Emphasizing services as second engine of growth, regionalization	Emphasizing knowledge-based economy, domestic entrepreneurship

the financial, educational, lifestyle, medical, information technology, and software sectors. The economy was to be supported by twin engines of growth: manufacturing and services. The promotion of local enterprises also became increasingly important.

THIRD INDUSTRIALIZATION PHASE

The third industrialization phase began in the 1990s, when Singapore built on its knowledge-based economy to meet the challenges of the new millennium. Knowledge, creativity, and innovation were the key determinants of long-term competitiveness. The development of a highly educated and flexible workforce was, therefore, very important. A wide pool of skilled knowledge workers was developed via strong industries dealing with innovation and technology.

EDB continued to play a prominent role in charting strategies to realize Singapore's vision for the 21st century, which was to be a relevant and competitive center for goods, services, and information. The strategies included:

- Strengthening industry clusters.
- Identifying and growing new clusters.
- Nurturing innovation-driven enterprises.
- Developing new geographies.
- Making Singapore's environment conducive and competitive for global business.

FOURTH INDUSTRIALIZATION PHASE

The ongoing fourth industrialization phase, which began after 1997, aims to make Singapore a developed nation. The manufacturing sector and service industry continue to be the twin pillars of growth. There is added emphasis on the development of services in health care and education. This new phase promotes entrepreneurship among domestic companies—encouraging people to be innovative, improving the ability of firms to develop new ideas and businesses, tapping new export markets, and broadening the economic base.

ACADEMIC INSTITUTIONS

The government has always been clear about the objective of education. The mission of the Ministry of Education (MOE) is to mold the future of the nation. Thus, MOE, which oversees Singapore's educational system, works closely with various other government ministries and agencies, such as the Ministry of Trade and Industry (MTI), Ministry of Manpower (MOM), and the EDB, to formulate and implement education policies.

There are three tiers in the Singapore educational system:

- Free,[2] compulsory primary education for up to six years, leading to a common national examination, the Primary School Leaving Examination (PSLE).[3]
- Heavily subsidized (monthly school fees of S$5), noncompulsory secondary education for up to five years. The academic stream leads to the Singapore-Cambridge General Certificate of Education at the Ordinary (O) level, and the technical stream leads to the Certificate at the Normal (N) level.
- Highly subsidized tertiary education at a university (following two years of pre-university education), polytechnic, or technical institute.

The medium of instruction is English for most subjects. Students take the national examination administered jointly by the Singapore Examination and Assessment Board and the Cambridge University Local Examinations Syndicate at the end of secondary education. With this well-regarded qualification, students can apply to tertiary institutions worldwide.

The government has invested heavily to enhance the quality of the school system through recruitment of more teachers and improvement of the physical and information communication technology infrastructures. Table 2.2 shows the government's expenditure on education from 1965 to 2005.

The government, in consultation with employers and academia, lays down educational policies, provides the funds for their implementation, and sets up the relevant institutions where necessary. Employers' representatives sit on the policy-making committees of education and training institutions. Industry advisory committees made up of industry representatives have been set up to ensure that courses are relevant and up to date.

Table 2.2 Government Expenditure on Education (S$ thousands)

Year	1965	1975	1985	1995	2005
Total	130,211	391,264	1,775,580	3,443,857	6,102,849
Recurrent expenditure	112,805	339,870	1,388,325	2,682,419	5,233,588
Primary	65,144	129,351	422,806	694,703	1,148,491
Secondary and pre-university	24,923	88,900	431,866	831,401	1,591,752
Institute of Technical Education	2,822	43,243	80,294	109,670	203,992
Polytechnics	2,400	12,330	110,434	338,960	624,794
National Institute of Education	1,999	6,487	22,979	40,922	85,641
Universities	10,337	41,048	253,811	520,289	1,012,860
Others	5,180	18,511	66,135	146,474	566,058
Development expenditure	17,406	51,394	387,255	761,438	869,261

Source: Ministry of Education 2006.

While employers' immediate training needs are important, the future needs of the economy as defined by the government are equally important in determining the development of human capital. These definitions of human-capital development through education are elaborated in the rest of this chapter.

The government has further set a target of developing Singapore's universities into world-class institutions in part through collaborations with selected international institutions, including the Massachusetts Institute of Technology, the Georgia Institute of Technology, the Technical University of Eindhoven, and the Technical University of Munich.

The two comprehensive universities—National University of Singapore and Nanyang Technological University—play a major role in the public sector R&D effort in conjunction with the Agency for Science, Technology and Research (A*STAR)[4] research institutes. In January 2000, a third institution, the Singapore Management University, was established. The new university explicitly adopted a North American educational model.

In technical education at the tertiary level, five polytechnics offer diploma programs in a range of disciplines, from engineering to business and media. The Institute of Technical Education (ITE) provides tertiary-level vocational education. It consists of three colleges that provide both full-time education and part-time training in support of continuing education and training initiatives of other ministries.

Tertiary-level enrollments have been carefully regulated to ensure a balanced mix of graduates, in line with the manpower estimates based on projected gross domestic product (GDP) and productivity growth.

In particular, the Singapore government has always exhibited a bias toward science and engineering education because of the economic policies and industrialization needs. In each industrialization phase, manufacturing has always been one of the twin pillars for economic growth. An interministerial committee[5] of the MOE, the MOM, the MTI, and the EDB, chaired by then–Minister of State (Education and Manpower) Ng Eng Hen, reiterated the need for this slant to avoid shortages of technical manpower experienced by other developed countries (Ministry of Education 2003).

FIRST INDUSTRIALIZATION PHASE AND EDUCATIONAL REFORM (1965–78)

CHALLENGES FACED BY THE GOVERNMENT

In August 1965, the separation of Singapore from the Federation of Malaysia posed three main challenges. Prior to the separation, Singapore had decided on an import-substitution strategy to build its economy. The immediate challenge caused by the separation resulted in the abortion of the import-substitution strategy because regional markets such as Malaysia were raising barriers against imports. The second challenge was the confrontation with Indonesia that threatened Singapore's role as a major trading port for the region. In addition, the planned withdrawal of British bases within five years added worries that the high unemployment rate that was estimated at about 10 percent would increase even more. British bases in Singapore then were employing around 40,000 workers.

ECONOMIC STRATEGY

The EDB was set up in 1961 to develop a strong manufacturing sector that would solve the unemployment problem in Singapore. It was given a broad mandate to attract foreign investment in manufacturing and thereby create jobs.

From 1965 to 1978, Singapore's drive toward industrialization was focused on attracting foreign multinational companies (MNCs) to manufacture in Singapore and export to global markets. EDB began to aggressively promote Singapore as a low-labor-cost base for MNCs.

To attract MNCs, Singapore had to improve the labor and investment climate quickly. The Employment Act was enacted in 1970 to lay down standards of employment to help resolve industrial disputes. In addition, the National Trade Union Congress (NTUC)[6] and National Wages Council (NWC)[7] were also formed in 1972 to help promote better labor-management relations. The NTUC and the People's Action Party (PAP) started off as a symbiotic relationship. A tripartite alliance with NWC quickly developed, however, after the labor movement chose, in 1969, to adopt a cooperative, rather than confrontational, policy toward employers. Indeed, tripartitism between the government, the employers, and labor is the driving force behind Singapore's economic and social development.

Union leaders and employers serve on key institutions such as the NWC, the EDB, the Central Provident Fund (CPF),[8] and the Singapore Productivity and Standards Board (PSB).[9]

Government and employer representatives also give the benefit of their experience to the labor movement by serving on the boards of cooperatives, business ventures, and other organizations affiliated with the NTUC.

At the same time, Singapore invested heavily in key infrastructures, including the establishment of the Jurong Town Corporation (JTC). JTC provided manufacturers with their choice of industrial land sites on which they built their factories or provided ready-built factories for the immediate start-up of manufacturing operations.

In this first reform, the economy grew by an annual average of 10 percent. The steady increase in the manufacturing sector's share of GDP was evident. The manufacturing sector grew from 14 percent of GDP in 1965 to 24 percent by

1978. As the economy grew, unemployment fell to a low of 3.6 percent in 1978 (Department of Statistics, various years).

FIRST EDUCATIONAL REFORM

The young nation of Singapore took stock of its reality. With people as its most valuable resource, the government needed to look at the quality and relevance of the output from the school system.

Education prior to 1965 was decentralized and based on vernacular and ethnic lines of Chinese, Malay, and Tamil schools. It provided a chaotic and challenging situation for the newly elected PAP government in 1959. Socially, the main races that made up the multiracial society of Singapore (with ethnic Chinese accounting for 76 percent of the population, Malays 15 percent, and Indians 7 percent) (Department of Statistics, various years) had been exhibiting different loyalties and cultural affinities outside of the country. The Chinese schools, for example, had been established and maintained by the local Chinese community. Such schools were highly politicized and showed a strong China orientation.

An integrated educational system was needed, but creation of one posed difficult challenges because of the ethnic affinities. This decision to integrate the educational system was important as the survival of the country was at stake. In addition, the direction set by the economic policy to attract MNCs to set up manufacturing bases in Singapore magnified the importance of a workforce that could meet the needs of foreign corporations. It required a workforce that was able to understand and communicate in English. These MNCs and industries also required a substantial amount of skills at all levels from the machinist working on machine tools to professional engineers with a wide range of backgrounds. The following strategies were formulated to create an integrated educational system.

Strategy 1: Centralization of the Primary and Secondary Educational System. The first step of integration was to move the educational system from decentralized to centralized. A Five-Year Plan in education was introduced. The main features of this plan were:

- Equal treatment for the four streams of education: Malay, Chinese, Tamil, and English.
- Emphasis on the study of mathematics, science, and technical subjects.
- A common syllabus for all school subjects in the four languages.
- Compulsory bilingualism in all schools.
- A common national examination system for the primary schools.
- Universal free primary education.

To achieve the plan, expenditures on social development constituted 40 percent of the total development expenditures despite the priority given to industrial

Table 2.3 Social Development Expenditures (1961–65)

	S$ millions	Percentage
1. Health	35.80	10.23
2. Education	94.48	27.00
3. Social welfare	1.77	0.51
4. Housing	153.60	43.90
5. Sewerage	47.36	13.54
6. Community services	6.07	1.73
7. Culture	10.80	3.09
	349.99	100.00

Source: Department of Statistics, various years.

expansion. Education constituted 27 percent or US$61 million of the social development expenditure (see table 2.3).

In 1960, the PSLE was conducted in all four official languages. By 1966, the PSLE was conducted for all language streams by the MOE at both the School Certificate and Higher School Certificate levels (Doraisamy 1969). These examinations provided a means to evaluate the quality of school output.

Standardizing the examination system naturally provided the means to introduce a uniform curriculum (Wee and Chong 1990). From 1966, the study of a second language was made compulsory in all secondary schools. By 1968, science and arithmetic were being taught in English in most non-English medium primary classes.

In 1969, the government decided that second language papers would be set and marked at a level two years below that of the student's first language. From that year, the second language was a compulsory subject in examinations at the School Certificate level. Woodwork, metalwork, and basic electricity were taught in English, Malay, and Tamil in secondary one classes.

In 1972, the MOE began planning a program to strengthen bilingual education. By 1974, equal weighting was given to the first and second languages in the PSLE. In 1974, a new subject, Education for Living, which integrated civics, history, and geography, was taught entirely in the mother tongue (Gopinathan 1974).

Strategy 2: Growth of Technical Education. The tumultuous years (1962–1966) saw an aggressive plan to develop skilled manpower for the needs of the first industrial phase. In the first industrial phase, the urgent need to develop a strong manufacturing sector to solve the unemployment problem and to attract MNCs was instrumental in the aggressive plan to develop skilled manpower. Twelve vocational schools and seven technical schools were built and equipped (Chiang 1998). The technical schools introduced courses such as mechanical engineering practice, electrical fitting, electrical installation, and radio servicing, among others. These courses were designed to meet the skilled manpower needs of industrialization.

The phenomenal growth of technical and vocational education in Singapore required much coordination and management. The Technical Education Department (TED) was created within the MOE. All the technical and vocational schools and industrial training centers came under the coordination and management of the TED.

It was through the TED that basic workshop subjects such metalwork, technical drawing, and basic electricity were made compulsory for all male students and 50 percent of girls in their first two years in secondary schools. The other 50 percent of girls took courses such as home economics (Chiang 1998). It was not possible to provide every secondary school with workshop facilities. Centralized workshops, strategically located near most of the secondary schools, were set up to give students hands-on training in the use of basic tools and materials. As a result, every morning and afternoon, thousands of students traveled a few kilometers to the nearest centralized workshop.

In 1969, the TED made several changes to technical education based on recommendations from the MOE, MTI, and MOM. These policy changes once again reflected the interministerial collaborative working relationship. The vocational stream in secondary school education was discontinued. This vocational stream, introduced in 1964, was a stop-gap measure to keep those who failed primary six and primary school dropouts off the streets in the early turbulent and politically volatile days. With the economy growing, the need in the industrial sector changed from unskilled or semiskilled labor to technically trained workers. To meet the new challenge, the TED converted four vocational schools into industrial training centers. Six other vocational schools were amalgamated with secondary schools adjacent to them.

Strategy 3: EDB Training Centers. Singapore's success in establishing a thriving manufacturing sector surfaced an increased demand for more skilled manpower. There was a need to meet this demand immediately, and the time taken for students to complete their secondary education and then proceed to technical education was too long. The EDB's response was to set up training centers. This was achieved with technical and financial assistance from the United Nations Development Programme (UNDP).[10] By 1968, six EDB training centers were set up (Chiang 1998).

These centers were very different from the workshops that provided basic hands-on knowledge to secondary school students. The centers provided direct training for workers through the production of actual components or parts needed by manufacturing companies in Singapore. The training was therefore relevant and up to date, and graduates could go directly into new factories and be productive in a very short time with minimal on-the-job training.

Strategy 4: EDB and Company-Based Training Centers. The success of the first industrialization phase resulted in a continuing need for specialist training that could not be provided through the technical schools or the training centers. Thus, the EDB began working with large industrial companies to set up facilities to train personnel for the industries' needs. As an example, the Tata Group of India, which was the largest engineering company in India, set up a precision engineering plant in Singapore. EDB helped Tata to set up a training facility to prepare sufficient numbers of workers for the Tata plant. In the process, the number of extra workers trained doubled the number required by Tata, and these extra workers could meet similar manpower needs of other factories (Chiang 1998).

The Tata experience was a prototype for other cooperative projects between the EDB and other MNCs. EDB provided facilities for the MNCs to set up their own training process for the type of workers required. These company-based training centers gave Singapore a jump start in training skilled workers for the precision engineering, optics, and electrical appliances industries who would otherwise not be able to be trained through the technical schools.

The EDB training centers did not duplicate the training provided by technical schools. EDB training complemented the efforts of the technical schools and sought to provide technical education faster and aligned with the needs of the industries in the first industrialization phase. Therefore, through cooperation with MNCs, centralized workshops, and technical and financial assistance from the UNDP, EDB adopted multiple approaches to train and produce the technical workers needed for the industrialization phase.

EDUCATIONAL ACHIEVEMENTS

The first educational reform resulted in a systematic increase in student enrollment, particularly in the secondary schools. Partially contributing to this increase was the provision of universal free primary education.

The process of standardizing school output was spearheaded by a common examination system and a uniform curriculum. The common national examination became an important measure of the changing quality of the output from the school system. The quality of the output of the school system saw a steady improvement in this first phase of reform.

The PSLE results improved gradually from 61 percent of the candidates passing the examination in 1965 to 83 percent in 1980. In the General Certificate in Education (GCE) O-level examination, the percentage of students obtaining at least three O-level passes (or credits) increased from 53 percent in 1965 to 69 percent in 1980. If a more stringent criterion is used, the percentage of students with at least 5 O-level passes increased from 9 percent in 1965 to 40 percent in 1980.

Table 2.4 Student Enrollment and Total Population (1965–74)

Year	Primary schools	Secondary schools	Total Singapore population
1965	357,075	114,736	1,886,900
1966	364,846	132,088	1,934,400
1967	368,654	144,448	1,977,600
1968	371,970	150,641	2,012,000
1969	366,881	147,981	2,042,500
1970	363,518	145,740	2,074,500
1971	357,936	153,522	2,112,900
1972	354,746	161,371	2,152,400
1973	345,284	173,109	2,193,000
1974	337,816	174,177	2,229,800

Source: Department of Statistics, various years.

Table 2.5 National Examination Results (1965–80)

		% GCE O-level candidates	
Year	% PSLE candidates passed	Obtaining 3 O-level passes	Obtaining 5 O-level passes
1965	61	53[a]	9[b]
1971	53	53	28
1980	83	69	40

Source: Ministry of Education 2006.
Note: GCE = General Certificate in Education; PSLE = Primary School Leaving Examination.
a. School Certificate (Divisions 1, 2, and 3) Malaysia Certificate of Education
b. School Certificate (Division 1 only)

SECOND INDUSTRIALIZATION PHASE AND EDUCATIONAL REFORM (1979–84)

CHALLENGES FACED BY THE GOVERNMENT

The 1980s saw Singapore embark on what the government called the "Second Industrial Revolution," a move into knowledge-intensive activities such as R&D, engineering design, and computer software services. In his 1981 budget speech, then–Minister of Trade and Industry Goh Chok Tong said, "The prime objective of the plan is to develop Singapore into a modern industrial economy based on science, technology, skills and knowledge."

In the region, many other countries were also moving into industrialization. These countries had a comparative advantage in terms of land and low-cost labor and had become strong contenders for MNC investments. Success in the economies in these countries resulted in a tight labor market. The government's view was that there were economic and political costs in trying to sustain high economic growth through labor force expansion. There was a need to restructure the economy toward higher-value-added activities and move away from labor-intensive to capital-intensive production.

ECONOMIC STRATEGY

To resolve the contradiction between labor-intensive and capital-intensive production and address the rapid intake of foreign labor, Singapore embarked on a wage correction policy. The purpose of this strategy was to induce efficient use of labor and to accelerate Singapore's transition to a more sophisticated technology-based economy.

The government intervened to raise wage costs to discourage low-skill, labor-intensive investments. Tariff revisions and restrictions on imported labor were put in place. Simultaneously, a range of initiatives was introduced—such as generous tax and fiscal incentives and expansions and improvements in social and physical infrastructure—to attract capital-intensive investments.

As the government set the directions for economic restructuring—moving into the higher-value technological-based economy—Goh Chok Tong stated, "Higher wage increase is, however, only one policy instrument for economic restructuring. . . . [T]raining must be stepped up to enable our workers to acquire new skills and refine old ones" (MTI 1981).

This emphasis on training and development of manpower resulted in the government's efforts to expand education at all levels, particularly at the technical and tertiary levels. Government development expenditures on education rose from US$21.45 million in 1978–79 to US$245.38 million in 1982–83, an increase of 1,044 percent (Department of Statistics, various years). Manpower development was closely tailored to the needs of private companies engaged in, or moving toward, higher-value-added production.

Efforts to produce a generation of skilled labor prompted the government to produce more engineers. Total enrollment of students rose by 49.4 percent in universities and polytechnics and 7.5 percent in technical and vocational institutes from 1979 to 1983 (Department of Statistics, various years).

In this second industrialization phase, the economy grew at an annual average of 7.3 percent. The measure of nominal value-added per manufacturing worker grew from US$12,050 in 1979 to US$17,680 in 1985. The government had assumed a crucial role in raising workers' skills to accelerate industrial restructuring. As a result of implementing part-time certification and foreign company participation in institutes of technology, the goal of producing skilled manpower for the industries was realized. Skilled manpower employed as a share of total employment doubled from 11 percent in 1979 to 22 percent in 1985 (Department of Statistics, various years).

SECOND EDUCATIONAL REFORM

Increasing stability in the school management environment throughout the first phase led to the next phase of educational reform. There was greater openness involving the general public in discussions on various aspects of education. Though the first phase of educational reform established authority in the school system, there were weaknesses in the system. In particular, the ineffective bilingual policy, low literacy levels, and high wastage in the system raised concerns. The need to reduce such wastages and improve the quality of education was urgent.

A review of the educational system led to recommendations for a New Education System (NES) in the *Goh Report* (Goh 1979). The following areas were highlighted for reform in the report:

- The structure.
- The curriculum.
- The organization and procedures within the MOE.
- The management of schools.

Strategy 1: Standardizing School Work Procedures and Processes. The weaknesses identified from the first educational reform were linked to a lack of emphasis on the quality input of the educational process. In the first reform, the focus was on the supply side of the educational equation. Issues critical and central to the quality aspect of education, such as pedagogy, content knowledge, assessment, and learning, were not given sufficient emphasis in the first reform. These quality issues were linked to a lack of professional management of the schools (Wee and Chong 1990).

To implement the NES, there was an urgent need to upgrade and consolidate the management mechanism of schools. Borrowing the concept from business organizations, the MOE felt that systematic performance of work was obtainable when work procedures and processes were standardized.

In January 1979, the MOE headquarters was reorganized. The Systems Branch in the Planning and Review Division was created. This division was in charge of planning policies and developing programs, improving the information system, and identifying and developing feedback mechanisms to monitor critical areas in the education system. It also assisted the Schools Division in implementing programs for improvements. This reorganization also resulted in the establishment of the Curriculum Development Institute of Singapore (CDIS). The previous emphasis on work procedures shifted to work processes in schools (Wee and Chong 1990).

Procedures were put in place for assessing the work of education officers for the annual *Staff Confidential Reports,* confirming appointments, and crossing efficiency bars. Principals and vice principals were responsible for assessing and reporting on all teachers in their schools.

In 1979, the Pupil Data Bank was introduced as part of the computer-based management information system for prompt and accurate decision making, planning, and control. Besides the production of the necessary statistics, the data bank could also retrieve data on individual pupils for research or other purposes. These statistics were extracted from the pupil record card and updated annually. Schools had ready access to pupil data for planning and monitoring purposes.

In July 1979, guidelines and format for the School Rolling Plan were distributed to principals. From 1980, schools have been writing formal plans for school improvement and incorporating them into the School Rolling Plan, thus ensuring that the processes of planning, reviewing, and monitoring are put in place. These plans were also used for annual internal appraisal by the schools themselves and external appraisals by the MOE's Schools Division every few years.

By the early 1980s, the process of consolidation and development of the management mechanism for standardizing school work procedures and processes had been put in place. In 1981, the MOE published the 252-page *Principals' Handbook.* It contained a comprehensive reference to policies, administrative procedures, and guidelines to help principals in the day-to-day running of their schools (Wee and Chong 1990).

Through standardization of the work procedures and processes, schools could systematically work toward school improvement. Some examples of the standardization include common national examinations, annual staff appraisals by vice principals and principals, annual internal school self-appraisals, and external school appraisals by the Schools Division of the MOE. In addition, financial regulations, procedures, and processes were emphasized, thus enabling better management control through financial audit.

By the end of this phase of the development of the school management system, the mechanisms for standardizing school output, work procedures, and processes had been put in place, heralding an increasing measure of decentralization of school management by the MOE.

Strategy 2: Setting Up the Curriculum Development Institute of Singapore. An important development in 1980 was the establishment of the CDIS. The CDIS took over from the Education Development Division the major function of developing all curriculum and teaching materials.

The CDIS's goal was to improve the teaching–learning process through the provision of quality curriculum packages, which included printed materials (coursebooks, workbooks, and teachers' editions) and audiovisual materials (picture cards, audiocassettes, charts and slides, three-dimensional teaching aids, games, multimedia kits, and even puppets, masks, and wigs). Among the priority projects undertaken by the CDIS were improving the mathematics and science curricula in both the primary and secondary schools.

One successful outcome of standardization of work procedures and processes in schools was the competence demonstrated by school principals in school management. The drive toward excellence in the management of work processes in schools was best demonstrated through the schools' appraisals since 1980.

The basic principle of management adopted by the MOE since 1980 was to give school principals as much autonomy as possible in running their schools. At the same time, the ministry holds the principals accountable for the quality of education they provide for the students. School appraisal was both an accountability exercise and a process to help schools evaluate their effectiveness and to identify areas for improvement. School appraisal consisted of two components: a self-appraisal conducted annually by the schools themselves, and an external appraisal conducted every four to five years by an external team of inspectors from the MOE.

Self-appraisal was an annual exercise carried out by all schools in four main areas:

- Management and organization of the school.
- Instructional programs.
- Extracurricular activities (ECAs).
- Pupil welfare programs.

Schools collected information on all four aspects and used this information to evaluate how well they had achieved set targets and objectives. They identified strengths and weaknesses in their programs and decided on strategies and resources to achieve desired outcomes. This cycle of planning, implementing, monitoring, and reviewing helped a school to assess itself critically and thus gradually increase its effectiveness. Where necessary, the schools requested professional assistance from the MOE and the CDIS.

The MOE did an external appraisal of a school every four to five years. It was conducted by a team of MOE officials consisting of inspectors of schools, specialist inspectors, and guidance officers. Every aspect of the school was thoroughly examined and the effectiveness of the whole program evaluated. Table 2.6 provides a summary of the number of schools appraised between 1980 and 1990.

In the 10 years since school appraisal was introduced, school appraisal reports have indicated that schools improved noticeably in their organization and management; in the delivery of instruction, ECAs, and student welfare programs; and in administrative efficiency. This improvement occurred because schools have consciously focused on specific desired outcomes that they have set for themselves in their action plans.

Table 2.6 Number of External Appraisals Conducted 1980–90

Number of times appraised	Number of primary schools	Number of secondary schools
Appraised once	296	136
Appraised twice	108	60
Appraised three times	1	0
Total appraisals	405	196

Source: Ministry of Education 2006.

Strategy 3: Certification through Part-Time Training in Technical Education. The increasing importance of technical education could be seen from the fact that the percentage of workers employed in the industrial sector had doubled to 28.3 percent between 1963 and 1973. The TED built a firm foundation for technical education by being under the MOE, but it was not ideally placed to bring industry and labor together.

The formation of the Industrial Training Board (ITB) in 1973 as a statutory board was intended to centralize, coordinate, and intensify industrial training (Chiang 1998). The TED was still involved actively in technical education under the MOE. However, there was a need to respond rapidly to new, emerging needs of industries for technical manpower. As a statutory board, ITB had much greater autonomy and flexibility in its operations than did government departments.

The ITB made a major change in 1973 by implementing the National Trade Certificate (NTC) and the Public Trade Test System. This system enabled workers who did not go through formal education courses, but picked up skills through on-the-job training and other means, to be certified through a standardized system of public examinations and be awarded NTCs. These certificates were awarded at three levels: semiskilled, skilled, and master craftsman, With common standards set and understood nationwide by employers, workers, and students, the NTCs quickly became recognized by employers. Thus the formation of ITB as a statutory board allowed it to implement the NTC program more rapidly than would have been possible through the bureaucracy.

The Vocational and Industrial Training Board (VITB) came into existence in 1979 through the amalgamation of the ITB and the Adult Education Board (AEB). The VITB had tripartite representation from government, employers and business, and the workers and unions, thus ensuring that the training was relevant and responsive to the demands of industries and employers. The AEB had been established to provide "second chance" academic education to adults who, for various reasons, did not have a secondary education up to the GCE "O" or "A" level. The VITB was set up to provide greater involvement of the industries and the government to meet the growing national need for technical and skilled manpower. Thus adult workers seeking to upgrade themselves could now do it through the VITB (Chiang 1998).

Under the VITB, technical education was promoted across a broader front. The use of media helped put the public limelight on technical education. Through popular new training programs aimed at mature workers with little education or technical training, the VITB was able to certify some 112,000 workers—up to 9 percent of the existing Singapore workforce.

Strategy 4: Foreign Company Participation in Institutes of Technology. In 1979, the EDB moved into a new phase in its training efforts when the Japan-Singapore Training Centre was established. This was the beginning of government-to-government technical institutes. These institutes of technology were different from the local polytechnics because they were established with the financial and technical assistance of foreign governments under renewable five-year agreements. The intent was to provide efficient and effective training quickly.

These institutes were offering two-year, full-time diploma courses as compared with the three-year diploma courses offered by the polytechnics. This training was more intensive, and it also provided a unique transfer of learning. The EDB's partnership with Germany to set up the German-Singapore Institute was an example of how locals could tap into the expertise and teaching systems and then adapt the learning to the local context. This approach gave rise to a new training concept that was uniquely Singaporean: the Teaching Factory Concept. This practical and application-oriented training approach became the hallmark of the EDB technical institutes (Chiang 1998). Trainees learned in a realistic and relevant learning environment. Thus, manufacturing took place while learning was going on.

Once again, the EDB supplemented and complemented the local technical institutes and training centers to produce the skilled manpower needed by industry.

THIRD INDUSTRIALIZATION PHASE AND EDUCATIONAL REFORM (1985–97)

CHALLENGES FACED BY THE STATE

When Singapore first began industrializing in the 1960s, developing countries were competitors. By the 1970s, the Asian newly industrializing countries became Singapore's prime competitors. In addition, competition from developed countries, especially in attracting MNCs, became more intense. MNCs seeking investment locations were comparing Singapore with Great Britain, Spain, and even some states in the United States.

In 1985, the Singapore economy was hard hit by the global recession. The high average economic growth of the 1970s could no longer be expected. The impact of globalization and the volatile world economy were external factors over which Singapore had no control.

As Singapore strived to meet these challenges, the need to find new niches and to sustain competitive advantage became increasingly important. In addition, the goal of achieving a developed-country status required focusing on other aspects aside from per capita gross national product and the standard of living. The intangibles such as an international mind-set, a strong work ethic, business creativity, and national teamwork become even more important determinants of the quality of the workforce and the development of the country. The quality of education took on a new significance in the 1990s as never before.

ECONOMIC STRATEGIES

The government took the lead in catalyzing the development of technology, deepening the technology base. In the process, the government invested S$2 billion from 1991 to 1995 under the National Technology Plan and another S$4 billion under the National Science and Technology Plan from 1996 to 2000 (National Science and Technology Board 2001).

Industrial strategy was refined to leverage synergies at the firm and industry levels. Mutually supporting industries were identified and developed to entrench entire cluster niche areas, such as electronics, petrochemicals, and engineering. By competing on the basis of clusters, Singapore could formulate cluster development plans with emphasis on core capabilities that were common to industries within the cluster.

Services were promoted as one of the twin pillars of the economy to diversify the sectoral and market dependency, reduce vulnerability, and promote a broader base for the economy. For this purpose, many incentives were offered for manufacturing investments—such as pioneer status, which provided tax exemptions and allowances to foreign companies for a certain number of years—and allowances were also extended to investments in service sectors.

In the area of education, providing quality education through quality staff to educate the population to its fullest potential became very important. It was the only way to mobilize the talent available to the nation.

In this third industrialization phase, the GDP grew at an average of 8.6 percent per annum. This rate was remarkable considering that many developed nations were growing incrementally at a much lower rate. The share of financial and business services sectors in total GDP grew from 21 percent in 1986 to 26 percent in 1997, signifying the success of stimulating the service component as the second pillar of economic growth. The number of research scientists and engineers grew from 3,361 in 1987 to 11,302 in 1997, thus ushering Singapore into higher-value-added research and development of products (Department of Statistics, various years).

THIRD EDUCATIONAL REFORM

According to the 1986 Report of the Economic Committee, Singapore was expected to be a developed country by the 1990s, with education being one of the fundamentals of economic growth. It further suggested that "the only way to mobilize the talent available to the nation and apply it to productive use" is for our population to be educated and trained to its fullest potential (Economic Committee 1986).

By coupling school management with the growing economy, the environment of school management was expected to be very dynamic. The school principal was expected to be an important contributor to economic growth. School leaders and staff were tasked to educate students holistically and to develop a creative, thinking, and innovative Singapore society, complete with flexible skills (Wee and Chong 1990).

The following recommendations were put forward by the Economic Committee report:

- Upgrading the median educational level of the Singapore workforce (60 percent of which, in 1979, had only primary or no education, and only 3 percent of which had tertiary-level education).
- Providing continuous training and retraining for the workforce.
- Expanding and improving education at the postsecondary and tertiary levels.
- Providing broad-based education aimed at the development of the "whole person."

Strategy 1: School Leadership Training and Development. In 1985, the minister of education suggested that "the key factor which will determine the success of our educational system is the quality of our principals and teachers" (Tan 1985). An in-service program in educational administration for incumbent principals, vice principals, and professional officers in the ministry headquarters was first implemented in 1982 with the assistance of the UNDP (Jacobsen 1983).

The Institute of Education, in collaboration with the MOE for the first time, conducted a one-year full-time course in 1984 for potential school principals, leading to the award of the diploma in educational administration. In this program, participants learned the theories and practices of school management. They also learned the technique of action research—applying what they learned to solve a real problem in a school together with the principal.

In 1983, a pilot project was implemented to prepare prospective heads of departments in the schools with the aim of developing competent administrative and professional teams. Initially, heads of departments went through a part-time training course. This was replaced by a one-year full-time training program. The pilot project was successful and was incorporated as a compulsory program for department heads. The program was later shortened to nine months of full-time training. All schools were targeted to complete organizational restructuring to introduce heads of department positions by 1994, thus giving principals a trained and competent management team to help in managing their schools (Wee and Chong 1990).

Strategy 2: Excellence in Education through Quality Schools. In pursuit of this goal of excellence, a pilot project converted nine primary and secondary schools that had double sessions into single-session schools. Double-session schools faced issues with scheduling and use of their facilities. Conversion to single sessions allowed greater flexibility in scheduling and program organization. A greater variety of programs could be offered to provide more opportunities for students and to meet their needs and interests.

The pilot project got a positive reception from principals, staff, students, and parents. On the basis of the reported success, the minister of education announced that by 1994, all secondary schools would be converted into single-session schools. This strategy required building an additional 50 schools over and above the 25 schools already planned under the ministry's existing school-building program.

To realize the goal of excellence in education, some of the well-established schools were allowed to become independent. Independent schools have greater autonomy in determining school fees, staff recruitment, and student admission. In 1988, 3 schools became independent, and by 1997, 10 schools were granted independent status. From 1988 to 1997, these independent schools had performed well, introduced several innovations in their curriculum, and provided their pupils with a wider range of cocurricular enrichment and enhancement programs.

Learning from the experience of the independent schools, the ministry set up 18 autonomous schools, which were given funds to buy enrichment and support services at their discretion. School clusters[11] were set up to facilitate the use of funds and resources to innovate and implement programs. Through these means, MOE encouraged all schools to introduce strategies and programs tailored to the needs of their pupils.

Strategy 3: Setting Up Institutes of Technical Education. Both the ITB and VITB played important roles in meeting the manpower needs of the fast-paced first and second industrialization phases. In 1992, it was clear that trainees with only primary education were not very successful. The need to have secondary education became paramount for moving into higher-value-added skills of the third industrialization phase.

The education authorities decided to give every student in Singapore at least 10 years of general education. Those who were more technically inclined were channeled into a new Normal (Technical) stream in secondary schools. There, they were prepared for entry into postsecondary technical institutes. This meant the VITB would have to be upgraded and converted into a postsecondary institution, awarding its graduates at least a semiskilled certificate. Thus the VITB was restructured to become the ITE.

Between 1992 and 1998, 10 ITEs were built or upgraded from the previous technical institutes all over Singapore. These ITEs introduced the New Apprenticeship Scheme through partnership with industries. This scheme required the employers to provide on-the-job training to the apprentices. For its part, the ITE tested and certified the apprentices and made available some 90 part-time courses to give them a strong theoretical foundation. These courses were conducted at ITE campuses or at company training centers that had Approved Training Centre[12] (ATC) status. By 1996, some 60 major companies and industrial organizations had been recognized as ATCs and were offering some 70 apprenticeship courses (Chiang 1998).

Strategy 4: Total Training Concept in ITE. To succeed in the modern workplace, a worker needed more than just technical knowledge and skills. This was even more crucial because Singapore products were competing in the international market. Recognizing this, the ITE complemented technical training with the inculcation of positive work values, social responsibility, and leadership qualities. This ITE training philosophy was called the Total Training Concept.

The establishment of the ITE brought about one of the most significant developments in technical education in Singapore. Previously, primary school leavers who did not perform well on the PSLE were channeled into the vocational schools under the VITB. These vocational schools were viewed negatively by parents and students because they catered to those who failed to make it into the mainstream secondary schools. Their graduates could not go further up the educational ladder. After the ITE was upgraded to a postsecondary institution, progression paths were provided for students who did well in ITE. These students could go on to polytechnics and, if they continued to do well, could proceed to university.[13] In 1995, some 1,300 students or about a third of those who graduated from the ITEs progressed to full-time and part-time polytechnic courses. What has astounded educators was that a fifth of such students graduated from polytechnics with Certificates of Merit, and some have won prizes as outstanding graduates.

EDUCATIONAL ACHIEVEMENTS

Through the implementation of the above strategies, the student intake enrollment increased significantly. Tables 2.7 and 2.8 provide comparisons of the intake of ITE students for 1997 and 2000 (Ministry of Education 2006).

Table 2.7 ITE Intake, Enrollment, and Output (Full Time), 1997

Courses	Intake total	Intake female	Enrollment total	Enrollment female	Output total	Output female
Engineering	1,402	143	2,350	252	915	100
Business and service skills	1,419	1,094	2,010	1,566	1,413	1,140
Technical skills	2,483	245	3,963	301	1,745	78
Total	5,304	1,482	8,323	2,119	4,073	1,318

Source: Ministry of Education 2006.
Note: ITE = Institute of Technical Education.

Table 2.8 ITE Intake, Enrollment, and Output (Full Time), 2000

Courses	Intake total	Intake female	Enrollment total	Enrollment female	Output total	Output female
Engineering	1,938	378	2,904	465	1,349	197
Business and service skills	2,395	2,004	3,073	2,530	2,091	1,752
Technical skills	5,439	866	9,997	1,348	4,210	480
Total	9,772	3,248	15,974	4,343	7,650	2,429

Source: Ministry of Education 2006.

The educational achievement in terms of O-level passes also saw a significant increase from 1991 to 2004, as shown in Table 2.9. These achievements were further strengthened when Singapore achieved international recognition in the TIMSS.

CURRENT INDUSTRIALIZATION PHASE AND SCHOOL REFORM (1997 ONWARD)

CHALLENGES FACED BY THE STATE

The Singapore economy was hit by the regional crisis that started with the devaluation of the Thai baht in July 1997. Although Singapore's financial and economic fundamentals were sound, the rapidly deteriorating external environment adversely affected Singapore because of its close linkages with the regional economies.

The Singapore economy contracted 1.4 percent in 1998, after achieving 8.3 percent growth in 1997. After positive economic growth in 1999–2000, Singapore was hit by another recession in 2001. The synchronized downturns in the major developed economies and the global electronics industry led to a sharp deceleration in global growth. The terrorist attacks on September 11 further aggravated the slowdown. As a result, the Singapore economy fell by

Table 2.9 Percentage of Pupils with at Least Five O-Level Passes

Year	Malay no. sat	% Malay passed	Chinese no. sat	% Chinese passed	Indian no. sat	% Indian passed	Others no. sat	% others passed	Overall no. sat	% overall passed
1991	3,207	45.0	29,772	74.0	1,866	55.0	299	58.0	35,144	70.0
1992	3,018	43.8	30,251	73.4	1,838	56.9	305	66.6	35,412	70.0
1993	2,940	45.9	29,345	74.3	1,771	58.6	296	64.5	34,352	70.9
1994	3,045	42.5	28,254	73.9	1,722	58.7	283	64.0	33,304	70.2
1995	2,865	46.0	28,172	76.7	1,747	61.1	291	63.2	33,075	73.1
1996	3,321	47.9	28,648	77.0	1,907	62.1	318	69.2	34,194	73.2
1997	4,344	46.0	30,114	77.7	2,284	59.1	399	63.2	37,141	72.7
1998	4,238	46.0	29,323	79.2	2,271	59.8	370	70.0	36,202	74.0
1999	3,934	49.0	26,555	81.2	2,151	65.5	416	72.4	33,056	76.3
2000	4,017	52.8	26,089	82.6	2,136	66.2	430	75.8	32,672	77.8
2001	3,990	56.5	26,943	84.3	2,133	70.3	466	74.7	33,512	80.0
2002	4,081	58.0	24,155	84.6	2,266	71.3	471	76.6	30,973	80.0
2003	4,083	59.0	26,351	85.9	2,376	73.5	523	80.9	33,333	81.6
2004	4,313	59.3	32,620	86.5	2,507	73.7	569	77.2	40,009	82.7

Source: Ministry of Education 2006.

2.3 percent in 2001, down from 10 percent growth in 2000 (Department of Statistics, various years).

The rise of large new players like China and India brought both challenges and opportunities. In addition, countries in the region began to aggressively attract foreign direct investment.

ECONOMIC STRATEGIES

Singapore aims to become a globalized, entrepreneurial, and diversified economy over the medium term. Following are its key strategies:

- Expanding external ties: embracing globalization through the multilateral trading framework of the World Trade Organization, regional cooperation, and bilateral free trade agreements.
- Maintaining competitiveness and flexibility: keeping the burden on the economy of taxes and the Central Provident Fund as low as possible, reviewing the labor market and wage system to make them more flexible, and pricing factors of production competitively.
- Promoting entrepreneurship and domestic companies: encouraging people to be innovative and improving the ability of firms to develop new ideas and businesses, tap new export markets, and broaden the economic base.

Table 2.10 Singapore Budget Allocations

	1997	1998	1999	2000	2001	2002	2003
Budget (US$ billions)	15.65	17.81	19.12	18.99	18.37	18.55	19.60
Percent to education	19.7	21.0	19.5	20.7	22.4	24.0	21.9

Source: Department of Statistics, various years.

- Growing manufacturing and services: upgrading these sectors by improving cost competitiveness, equipping the labor force with relevant skills, and developing new capabilities and industries.
- Developing human capital: investing in education, helping workers train and upgrade, and welcoming global talent to augment the indigenous talent pool.

Table 2.10 shows the commitment of the government to developing human capital through investing in education from 1997 to 2003. Despite the economy contracting by 2.3 percent in 2001, which was the largest decline in Singapore's postindependence history, the budget allocation for education increased in 2002 and 2003.

EDUCATIONAL REFORM

Singapore's survival as a nation depends on its ability to remain competitive and to anticipate change. In 1997, the MOE introduced a new reform called "Thinking Schools, Learning Nation." This concept is a step toward nurturing a creative and inquiring spirit and igniting a passion for lifelong learning.

The characteristics of Thinking Schools, Learning Nation are as follows:

- *Teacher's Role.* The teacher's role as facilitator, a guide on the side, is central to initiatives such as project work. Working on projects makes classroom learning applicable to life. The students draw the various strands of a topic together, obtaining a holistic view of the knowledge gained. The teacher encourages students to work in teams and emphasizes the importance of each member pulling his or her weight. The teacher also prompts students to be resourceful in gathering and processing information and in displaying the knowledge they have acquired.
- *Character and Leadership Development.* Education goes beyond textbook learning. Aside from instilling national values, teachers also play a role in character and leadership development. Character development takes place during the formal and informal curriculum—during civics and moral education lessons, the pastoral care and career guidance program, and cocurricular activities (CCAs). Through participation in CCAs, students are exposed to a wide range

of activities in uniformed groups, clubs, societies, and sports. They participate in programs to develop leadership skills and to acquire confidence and self-awareness. By engaging students in a meaningful way, teachers promote the acquisition and application of social and cooperative skills and instill in them a sense of social responsibility and commitment. The Community Involvement Program exposes students to a world that is different from theirs and helps them empathize with people from all walks of life.

This new educational reform gives more autonomy to school principals to lead and manage schools. There are fewer prescriptions of programs. Instead, school leaders and staff are encouraged to emphasize innovation and to instill greater professionalism in the management of schools.

Strategy 1: The School Excellence Model. To fulfill the purpose of Thinking Schools, Learning Nation, schools must provide an excellent teaching and learning environment. One of the ways to create such an environment is for schools to have an excellent self-appraisal system in order to continuously improve.

The School Excellence Model (SEM) was introduced in 2000 to guide schools in their self-assessments. SEM was adapted from the Singapore Quality Award (SQA)[14] model and the education version of the American Malcolm Baldrige National Quality Award (MBNQA) model.[15] The indicators and areas addressed in the model enable schools to pitch themselves against national benchmarks for organizational excellence. By measuring both outcomes and processes, schools are required to examine their practices as parts contributing to a whole. In doing self-assessment, every school must continuously question its current practices and established norms, thinking of more creative and effective ways of delivering the desired outcomes of education systematically and holistically.

As of January 2001, schools can apply to the MOE for external validation using the same model. A total of 53 schools—23 primary schools, 29 secondary schools, and 1 junior college—have applied and were externally validated. Of these, 5 schools received the inaugural Best Practice Awards: Anglo-Chinese School (independent), Paya Lebar Methodist Girls' School, Raffles Institution, River Valley High School, and Xinmin Secondary School.

Strategy 2: Singapore Quality Class Award. To ensure greater professionalism in the management of schools, schools are encouraged to participate in the Singapore Quality Class (SQC) Award. This award was established to provide organizations with a framework for achieving business excellence. To qualify for the award, organizations must score well in seven dimensions: leadership, planning, information, people, processes, customers, and results. SQC is based on the Singapore Quality Award Business Excellence Framework and is administered by the Standards, Productivity, and Innovation Board of Singapore (SPRING Singapore).[16]

For the first time since the SQC was instituted in 1997 to encourage organizations to work toward excellence, five schools attained the award, which traditionally has been given to business organizations. They were Raffles Institution, Anglo-Chinese School (independent), Xinmin Secondary School, River Valley High School, and Dunman Secondary School. The MOE, too, was awarded SQC status.

Strategy 3: ITE Breakthrough Plan. A new strategic plan—ITE Breakthrough—was formulated in 2000 to position ITE for the knowledge-based economy. The plan focuses on ensuring relevance and responsiveness of the ITE training system, strengthening its continuing education and training (CET) system to support national efforts in lifelong learning, developing a learning organization to enhance organizational capability, and further improving the image and profile of ITE in technical training. ITE's vision is to be a world-class technical education institution for a knowledge-based economy.

MEASURES OF SUCCESS

TECHNICAL EDUCATION

The improved image of ITE and favorable publicity on its successful graduates had generated greater interest in ITE training among secondary school leavers. In 2001, ITE's total intake was 11,342 students, surpassing the national intake target of 25 percent of the annual school cohort for technical education. Enrollment reached a high of 13,705 in 2005, an increase of more than 30 percent over the 2001 enrollment figure of 10,313 (Ministry of Education 2006).

Likewise, the CET programs for adult learners also saw positive growth. In 2001, a total of 58,989 adult learners attended training courses conducted by ITE, and another 131,401 participated in courses conducted by industry training partners under various ITE training schemes. The total number of training places taken up for ITE-conducted CET programs was 7 percent higher than the achievement in 2000 and 9 percent higher than the fiscal year 2001 target (Institute of Technical Education 2002).

EDUCATIONAL ACHIEVEMENTS

In the 2001 International Physics, Mathematics, Chemistry, Biology, and Informatics Olympiads, Singapore achieved the following rankings: It placed 10th out of 65 participating countries in the Physics International Olympiad, 29th out of 83 participating countries in the Mathematics International Olympiad, 9th out of 54 participating countries in the Chemistry Olympiad, 3rd out of 39 participating countries in the Biology Olympiad, and joint first with Slovakia out of 74 participating countries in the Informatics International Olympiad.

Table 2.11 Desired National Skills (%)

Skills profile	2000	Desired profile, 2008–2013
Skilled (postsecondary education)	55	65
Semiskilled (secondary education)	36	20
Unskilled (less than secondary education)	9	15
Total	100	100

Source: Ministry of Manpower 2000, 4.

In 2003, at the International Biology, Chemistry, and Mathematics Olympiads, Singapore students performed well at the following international competitions:

- International Biology Olympiad: one gold medalist and three silver medalists, with the team placing fifth out of 41 countries.
- International Chemistry Olympiad: one gold medalist, two silver medalists, and one bronze medalist, with the team placing 10th out of 59 countries.
- International Mathematics Olympiad: two bronze medalists and three honorable mentions, with the team placing 36th out of 82 countries.

As Singapore moves ahead in its economic and educational reform, the focus on human resource development will continue to take precedence. With the move into higher-value manufacturing and industries such as the life sciences, nanotechnology, and precision engineering, the desired national skills profile will need to be enhanced. Table 2.11 provides a comparison of the desired national skills needed for the new economy and the actual situation. The desired profile consists of 65 percent of the workforce in the skilled category, made up of 25 percent with degrees, 20 percent with diplomas, and 20 percent with postsecondary certification.

CONCLUSION

International competition has been the driving force of Singapore's economic development strategy since 1965. The evolution of the economic strategies has seen an emphasis from low-cost manufacturing exports to value-added manufacturing exports and services. Educational reforms have been carried out in parallel, based on the different needs according to the phases of industrialization.

In attempting to address the demands of the new world economy, Singapore's education landscape is being quite fundamentally overhauled to provide the broader-based intellectual foundation, critical-thinking skills, and creativity that the economy demands. An ability-driven education, allowing students' aspirations and interests to be better met, has evolved. This has broken the mold of a highly structured education system that characterized much of the first three educational reforms. This new phase emphasizes a system that values innovation, nurtures diversity, and encourages individuals with different strengths.

Singapore has invested heavily in the education and training of its people since its independence in 1965. Public expenditure on education as a percentage of GDP has been consistently high in relation to other expenditures. It grew from 3.1 percent in 1997 to 3.9 percent in 2004. The government played the lead role in the development of education and training in Singapore. It laid down the policies, provided the funds for their implementation, and continuously upgraded or built new institutions where necessary. The employers and academia were consulted in the formulation and implementation of these policies. The trends in government spending on human capital development are closely matched with the steady increase in gross national income and overall economic growth.

As with previous efforts at redefining the educational landscape in Singapore, the educational reforms continue to reflect Singapore's holistic approach. The 1960s and 1970s saw changes permeating schools and universities complemented by the work of vocational institutes, polytechnics, and joint technical training centers with MNCs.

Singapore is relatively well positioned to continue its agenda to upgrade the skills and educational attainment of its population. Today, the reforms at secondary schools and junior colleges are in step with changes at the universities, research institutes, and industry. The continuing emphasis on science and technology education remains for pragmatic reasons. However, the humanities are increasingly given importance to provide a broad-based and multidisciplinary education. Singapore is moving toward achieving a better equilibrium between developing an individual holistically and the country's need to stay economically competitive.

Five major lessons have been learned from the strategic management of educational reform in Singapore:

1. Align educational reforms with economic reforms through a consultative and collaborative working relationship among various government ministries and agencies. Inter-ministerial committees are important to provide greater coherence in the development of manpower needs for the nation.
2. Strategic educational reforms should be prioritized based on the capacity and ability of school staff. Putting in place excellent structures and processes and simultaneously developing the ability and capacity of school leaders and teachers is crucial before moving into greater decentralization, and a gradual move from centralization to decentralization is essential. Empowerment can only be appropriated when school staff have the ability and capacity to provide quality education through sound processes.
3. Employ a multiprong approach to meet current and future manpower needs. Upgrading skills and knowledge requires both a strong foundation of basic technical education and on-the-job training. Partnerships with business organizations, both locally and overseas, provide short-term measures to improve

technical expertise, while secondary and technical education institutions provide the future manpower needs.

4. Strategic planning for industrialization and educational reforms is characterized by flexibility in initiating required changes and responding to new challenges. The process of decision making is distinguished by efficiency, pragmatism, and a collaborative approach.
5. A strong social norm that values what education offers and job security through union agreements are important to sustain a long-term perspective of educational development.

NOTES

1. The EDB is a statutory board of the government of Singapore that plans and executes strategies to sustain Singapore as a leading global hub for business and investment. It was set up in 1961 with a budget of $100 million.

2. Primary and secondary education is free, although there is a fee of up to S$13 monthly per student that goes to the school to help cover miscellaneous costs.

3. The PSLE is administered by MOE. This nationwide examination tests students on the English language, mother tongue languages (Chinese, Malay, or Tamil), mathematics, science, and social studies.

4. A*STAR's focus is to conduct cutting-edge research in specific niche areas in science, engineering, and biomedical science. It consists of the Biomedical Research Council (BMRC), the Science and Engineering Research Council (SERC), Exploit Technologies Pte Ltd (ETPL), the A*STAR Graduate Academy (A*GA), and the Corporate Planning and Administration Division (CPAD).

5. Interministerial committees are set up to coordinate efforts to deal with national interests and concerns.

6. The NTUC is the sole national trade union center in Singapore. As of April 2005, it had 63 trade unions and 6 affiliates.

7. The NWC, as a government advisory body, recommends annual wage increases for the entire economy, ensuring orderly wage development to promote economic and social progress and assist in the development of incentive schemes to improve national productivity.

8. The CPF is a compulsory, comprehensive, social security savings plan. Working Singaporeans and their employers make monthly contributions to the CPF.

9. PSB focuses on three areas: domestic sector and small and medium enterprises, productivity and innovation promotion, and standards and conformance. As the national standards body, PSB helps to improve market access for Singapore's exports through its work on standardization. Standardization is also used as a major strategy to raise the productivity of industries, especially in the domestic sector. In 2001, PSB was repositioned to become SPRING Singapore.

10. The United Nations Development Programme is the United Nations' global development network, an organization advocating for change and connecting countries to knowledge, experience, and resources to help people build a better life.

11. Schools are grouped into clusters, and each cluster is facilitated by a cluster superintendent. The cluster superintendents develop, guide, and supervise the school leadership teams to ensure that schools are effectively run.

12. To participate in the scheme, the organization needed the following: a valid and structured training program endorsed by ITE as meeting national certification standards, adequate training facilities and equipment to conduct training and testing for the proposed ITE course, and professionally and pedagogically qualified trainers to conduct training and testing in the proposed ITE course.

13. To support the emphasis in technical education, two new polytechnics were established in the early 1990s: Temasek Polytechnic in 1990 and Nanyang Polytechnic in 1992.

14. SQA is the most prestigious award conferred on organizations that demonstrate the highest standards of business excellence.

15. MBNQA is given to businesses, education, and health care organizations that are judged to be outstanding in seven areas: leadership; strategic planning; customer and market focus; measurement, analysis, and knowledge management; human resource focus; process management; and results.

16. SPRING Singapore is a member of the Global Excellence Model (GEM) Council. GEM ensures that the award reflects the world's best validated management principles and practices.

REFERENCES

Chiang, M. 1998. *From Economic Debacle to Economic Miracle*. Singapore: Times Editions Pte Ltd.

Department of Statistics. Various years. *Yearbook of Statistics*. Singapore: Department of Statistics.

Doraisamy, T. R. 1969. *150 Years of Education in Singapore*. Singapore: TTC Publications Board, Teachers Training College.

Economic Committee. 1986. http://www.mti.gov.sgapp.mti.gov.sg/data/pages/885/doc/econ.

Goh. 1979. Ministry of Education, Singapore. http://www.moe.gov.sg.

Gopinathan, S. 1974. *Towards a National System of Education in Singapore, 1945–1973*. Singapore: Oxford University Press.

Institute of Technical Education. 2002. *Annual Report*. Singapore: ITE.

Jacobsen, G. S. 1983. *Report Prepared by UNDP Expert: Project Findings and Recommendations, Singapore*. Singapore: Ministry of Education.

Lee, Kuan Yew. 2000. *From Third World to First: The Singapore Story, 1965–2000: Memoirs of Lee Kuan Yew*. Singapore: Times Editions, Singapore Press Holdings.

Ministry of Education. 2006. *Education Statistics Digest*. Singapore: MOE.

Ministry of Manpower. 2000. *Report on Labour Force Survey of Singapore*. Singapore: Ministry of Manpower.

National Science and Technology Board. 2001. *Annual Report 2001*. Singapore: National Science and Technology Board.

Neher, Clark D. 1998. *Southeast Asia in the New International Era*. 3rd ed. Boulder, CO: Westview Press.

Tan, Tony K. Y. 1985. "Addendum to Presidential Address: Ministry of Education." In *Parliamentary Debate Singapore Official Report*, vol. 45, no. 1, Monday, February 25, 1985. In *Evolution of Educational Excellence*, ed. J. Yip and W. K. Sim. Singapore: Longman, 1990.

Wee, H. T., and K. C. Chong. 1990. "25 Years of School Management." In *Evolution of Educational Excellence*, ed. J. Yip and W. K. Sim. Singapore: Longman.

CHAPTER 3

Singapore's Textbook Experience 1965–97: Meeting the Needs of Curriculum Change

ANG Wai Hoong

INTRODUCTION

Before Singapore became an independent state in 1965, education was not available to everyone. The British provided education in English only for those able to gain admission to the few schools that were available then. Others who wanted an education went to vernacular schools that taught in their respective native languages (Malay, Chinese, and Tamil) as they were established by the different ethnic groups. The textbooks used during colonial days were from the migrants' homelands and tended to promote values that were not in line with those of a newly independent nation. The imported books were also expensive. Thus at independence, textbooks became an important tool in nation building as the government set about to provide education to all. Today, textbooks not only transmit knowledge and skills but can also influence and develop the thinking and values of students and, hence, affect their world view and attitudes. Thus, curriculum materials are very important as they can influence social cohesion and national development within a country. This chapter describes a period of textbook development in Singapore that has evolved since independence. Annex B at the end of the chapter describes the role of Singapore's commercial textbook publishers, highlighting the example of Panpac and its role in the United States and developing nations in textbook publication and marketing.[1]

PHASE I (1965–69) PREPARING FOR TEXTBOOK (CURRICULUM) DEVELOPMENT

TEXTBOOKS TO SHARE NATIONAL VALUES

When Singapore gained independence in 1965, there was an urgent need to inculcate shared civic values and responsibilities among the ethnic groups to achieve solidarity and racial harmony. While all the textbooks of other subject areas continued to be imported, the Ministry of Education hastened to develop a syllabus and textbooks for civics and created the Civics Training Subject Committee (1966–1973). The greatest concern was among the Chinese students at the secondary level who had revealed a strong orientation toward China.

After 18 meetings of the committee, the Chinese edition of the civics syllabus was distributed to all secondary schools in August 1967. Four textbooks were written by three textbook writers seconded to an editorial board at the University of Singapore. About one textbook was produced every four months. Schools were directed to buy and use them. These textbooks were translated into English, but the translations were never used because civics was taught in the mother tongues (Malay, Chinese, and Tamil).[2] In October 1971, the ministry made available a simplified version in Chinese for students in schools using English as a medium of instruction who studied Chinese as a second language.

TEXTBOOKS IN ALL THREE ETHNIC LANGUAGES

In response to the need to make inexpensive textbooks available, the Ministry of Education (MOE) established a publishing bureau (Education Publishing Bureau or EPB) in 1967. EPB was responsible for the development of textbooks for teaching the mother tongue languages (Malay, Chinese, and Tamil) and ensuring that all three ethnic groups could obtain textbooks at the same affordable price. Language textbooks not only teach the use of language but also transmit cultural understanding and values. It was critical that all ethnic language books promote the same values to develop a national identity. Students were required to buy their own textbooks from their school or other bookshops, which got them directly from EPB. Those who couldn't afford to purchase them could apply for free textbooks administered by the schools. Funds for these were provided by the MOE or other organizations that families could approach for assistance.

In October 1969, the Advisory Committee on Curriculum Development was formed to meet the urgent need to develop curricula (syllabuses and textbooks) more thoroughly and systematically so that the national educational objectives could be achieved as speedily as possible.

LEARNING POINTS IN TEXTBOOK DEVELOPMENT, 1965–69

A formal school curriculum consists of subject syllabuses. Each syllabus defines the topics of the content, the variety of teaching methods to be used, and the time to teach them. The type and the depth of knowledge selected are relevant to student physical, social, emotional, and cognitive development. In Singapore, another important consideration was how such curricula equipped students with knowledge and skills necessary for the national economic and industrial development. For example, mathematics, science, and technical subjects such as woodwork, metalwork, and electricity and electronics were important for industrial development. Mathematics and science were compulsory for all, and technical subjects were made compulsory for boys. Following are the salient features of Singapore's approach to curriculum development:

- The school curriculum was considered instrumental in achieving student and national development.
- A common set of civics textbooks was published in all three mother tongue languages to ensure that all students learned the same national values to develop a national identity.
- All students studying in non-English mediums of instruction were required to learn English as a second language, which was the common language for communication for all ethnic races in Singapore.
- Development of syllabuses and textbooks was a systematic and ongoing process. Syllabuses needed to be constantly updated in response to feedback from teachers, new findings in educational research, and changes in policy for national development.
- Textbook writers had to devote themselves full-time to their work. Writing effective lessons for textbooks required research, writing, and piloting in schools.
- Provision of textbook to the needy was built into the MOE budget to ensure that all students possessed their own textbooks.

PHASE II (1970–79) PIONEERING EFFORTS IN TEXTBOOK (CURRICULUM) DEVELOPMENT

TEXTBOOK DEVELOPMENT BY PART-TIME EDUCATION OFFICERS AND COMMERCIAL PUBLISHERS

In 1967, the Curriculum Development Committee was formed to identify curriculum needs and direct and coordinate the functions of 18 subject standing committees with their corresponding 18 subject working committees. The subject working committees were made up of education officers at MOE headquarters and schools. These committees formulated detailed subject topics, prescribed teaching methods, and specified standards of learning outcomes. Teacher workshops for implementation of the syllabuses were conducted, and feedback from schools was collated for refinement of the syllabuses. Unfortunately, all members of the Curriculum Development Committee had other duties, and the above functions were not fully carried out.

With the exception of the civics and education for living (EFL) textbooks, which dealt with national values and were developed by the Textbook and Syllabus section of MOE, all other syllabuses were made available to commercial publishers one year before implementation.

INTERDISCIPLINARY INTEGRATION ACROSS SUBJECTS

A few textbook (curriculum) projects were piloted by the MOE. An interdisciplinary integration across subjects was tried to reduce the number of subjects in an overcrowded curriculum. The thematic approach was also intended to make learning more meaningful. History, geography, and civics were integrated to form the subject "education for living." English, mathematics, and science were also combined in the Primary Pilot Project (PPP). Both of these projects were ultimately discontinued mainly as a result of insufficient teacher preparation.

A few projects were successful, however, and were continued into the next phase when the Curriculum Development Institute of Singapore (CDIS) was formed. These were the Lower Secondary Science Project to integrate physics, chemistry, and biology, and the PPP to teach oral skills before teaching reading and writing in the Chinese language. Table 3.1 provides descriptions of a few of the curriculum development projects undertaken by the MOE in the 1970s.

Five curriculum projects are summarized to show the different approaches to textbook development. Textbook writing is complex and in some cases, midway into the project, it was overtaken by events and shelved. Three areas are highlighted: origin of the project, innovative teaching methods, and bilingualism.

ORIGIN OF PROJECTS

Moral education, civics, and EFL textbooks were written in direct response to policy decisions. PPP was initiated by senior curriculum officers in the MOE to test alternative methods of teaching language. Lower secondary science was initiated jointly by the Science Teachers' Association of Singapore and the MOE.

Integration across subjects was advocated as the best way to acquire meaningful knowledge. The following subjects were integrated in the curriculum:

- EFL integrated civics, history, and geography.
- PPP integrated learning English with mathematics and science.
- Lower Secondary Science (LSS) integrated biology, physics, and chemistry.

Table 3.1 Summary of the Curriculum Development Projects in the 1970s

	EFL	Civics	Primary pilot project (English/ math/science)	Primary pilot project (Chinese language)	Lower secondary science project
Start–end	Jan. 1974–78	1967–78	Jan. 1971–73	Jan. 1974–76	Initiative: 1970–73 Trial phase: 1974–78
Grade Level	Primary 1–6	Secondary 1–4	Primary 1–3	Primary 1–3	Secondary 1 and 2
Purpose	• Replaced civics • For full-scale development and implementation • 3 versions in the Chinese, Malay, and Tamil languages	• Textbook development and revision • Use mother tongue, i.e., Malay, Chinese, and Tamil languages	• Pilot study to test alternative method of teaching English language (emphasis on oral skills)	• Pilot study to test alternative method of teaching Chinese language	• Trial approach to revise and replace the general science syllabus • ME-STAS collaboration in curriculum development
Curriculum Framework	11 themes to combine the moral values in civics with stories in history and geography	6 themes: individual, family, school, community, the nation, the world	Integrate mastery of English language skills in the learning of science and math content/concepts	Adopt the "speak" & "do" (oracy and literacy) approach to CL2 learning	1st generation materials based on 5 themes to integrate physics, chemistry, and biology
Curriculum Materials	• 12 booklets: 2 per level, 20–30 lessons per booklet • Teacher's manual • Support materials: EFL songs, games, wall charts, ETV, stories via radio	• Only 4 text-books, one per grade level (by 1967) • Compiled simplified version for CL2 students • No Malay or Tamil language textbooks until 1975	• 24 English pupil readers (12 readers for each grade [1 and 2]) • Pupil's worksheets • 10 × 3 (30) units EL for primary 1–3 • Teaching aids: shapes, plastics, flashcards, Handlens, 36 color slides, sound tapes, teaching charts	• Units of oral situations • Reading and writing materials • Pupil worksheets • Visual chart • Evaluation materials on listening, speaking, reading, writing	• Basic materials: – 5 units (thematics) of teacher's guides – Pupil's worksheets – 5 themes: exploring science, structure of matter, water and solution, energy, life and ecology • Supplementary materials: – Filmstrips (3 sets) – Keys to fauna/flora – Test items

(Continued on the following page)

Table 3.1 Summary of the Curriculum Development Projects in the 1970s (*continued*)

	EFL	Civics	Primary pilot project (English/ math/science)	Primary pilot project (Chinese language)	Lower secondary science project
Pedagogical approach	• Intended as moral and social education • Integrate three subjects into one subject	• Stories to illustrate "right conduct" • Didactic methods of teaching	• Adopt the "speak" (oracy/speech skills) and "do" (literacy skills in reading and writing) method to active language learning	• Premised on development of fluency in oral skills before mastery of reading, writing skills	• Basic foundation in science for *all* students • Acquire fundamental science knowledge, scientific skills, and attitudes
Decisions on policy	Report on Moral Education (1979) recommendation • EFL discontinued • Replaced by Moral Education Project (Good Citizen for primary and Being and Becoming for secondary)	• Civics textbooks scrapped • Religious knowledge introduced (1983)	• Stress on oral fluency discontinued because students were more fluent in oral skills and lacking in literacy (reading and writing) skills	• Under the NES, in March 1979, this project was renamed CLIPS (Chinese Language Instruction Materials for Primary School) for use in P1–P6 under CDIS	• Built on the 1st generation materials; revised LSS syllabus by 1981 • LSS was fully implemented with effect from 1983 under CDIS

Source: Yip and Sim 1990.
Notes: CDIS = Curriculum Development Institute of Singapore; CL2 = Chinese as a second language; EFL = Education for Living; LSS = Lower Secondary Science; NES = New Education System.

Termination of Projects. EFL, PPP, and civics were discontinued, a decision that was sometimes difficult for the project teams to understand. However, it could take several years to achieve positive results, and the projects lost their momentum. Priorities were reviewed as other more crucial needs became apparent.

The Chinese and LSS projects were carried over and continued to be developed under CDIS. After more than 10 years, Singapore students' science achievements were recognized in several international studies.

INNOVATIVE TEACHING METHODS

EFL, PPP, Chinese, and LSS advocated active participation by students for their own learning. EFL used small-group teaching through storytelling and songs (using audiotapes and TV) to inculcate moral values. These experiences were built into each lesson in the booklets.

Chinese and English adopted oral-aural skills and reading in the initial years. Writing skills were introduced later and were used to reinforce reading and listening skills.

BILINGUALISM

In Singapore's multilingual society, it was crucial to establish a common language among all races. Learning a second language was made compulsory in primary schools in 1960 and secondary schools in 1966. English was taught as a second language in the Chinese, Malay, and Tamil schools. However, the subject was poorly taught because of a lack of trained teachers and suitable textbooks.

In 1968, mathematics and science were taught in English in all primary schools. Subsequently they were also taught in secondary schools. It was felt that English was the most functional language for teaching mathematics, science, and technology, while mother tongue languages were essential for individuals to build up their cultural identity.

In 1976, mathematics and science were examined in English at the Primary School Leaving Examination (PSLE) taken by all primary school pupils at primary six. The curriculum time allocated to English was raised from 18 percent to 40 percent. The mother tongue as the first language and English as the second language were given the same weight in the curriculum and the PSLE to emphasize the importance of English. In English medium schools, the first language was English and the second language was a mother tongue.

Unfortunately, findings in 1979 showed that not only was there no improvement in results in English as a second language, but the science results in Chinese schools were negatively affected. Although teaching subjects in English increased exposure to the language, it was not useful because it required a high level of competence in English to learn the concepts, principles, and skills of the subject matter. Moreover, teachers who had been teaching mathematics and science in mother tongues had to switch to English to teach these subjects. Both the teachers and students were not sufficiently competent in English to cope with the sophisticated contents of the subjects. It was frustrating for both teachers and students.

Among the Chinese population there was another problem. Most were more conversant in dialects rather than Mandarin, which was designated as the official mother tongue in Chinese. For non-Mandarin-speaking Chinese students, Mandarin was a new spoken language, even though the written form was the same.

There was also a shift in the student population. More and more students were shifting to English-medium schools. From the mid-eighties, all students studied in English with the mother tongue as a second language.

LEARNING POINTS FROM TEXTBOOK DEVELOPMENT, 1970–79

- Individual subject committees initiated curriculum changes independently. Schools had difficulty responding to all the changes.
- The committee system created an overly complex hierarchy and a lack of continuity from the frequent changes in committee members.
- Textbook writing was not the core duty of the people developing the texts; hence, writers lacked time and focus to produce good textbooks.
- The Science Teachers' Association, a professional body, contributed expertise in syllabus and textbook development and provided peer teacher training. *This was a tremendous contribution as there was a shortage of trained science personnel.*
- Teachers generally relied on textbooks. Hence, textbooks needed to include additional materials to support various teaching strategies.

PHASE III (1980–95) INSTITUTIONALIZED INNOVATIONS IN TEXTBOOK (CURRICULUM) DEVELOPMENT

The original education system adopted from the British was to provide primary and secondary education, which led to pre-university and university studies. Many students who were not academically inclined did not fare well in such a course of study. Only 71 percent of the primary one cohort reached secondary school, and 14 percent reached pre-university level (Ministry of Education 2006). To reduce education wastage and promote more effective learning, the New Education System (NES) was introduced for primary schools in 1979 and for secondary schools in 1980.

TEXTBOOKS FOR THE NEW EDUCATION SYSTEM

Some students learn faster and some need more time to achieve a set standard. Those who are not academically inclined would benefit more from pursuing a nonacademic curriculum. Singapore introduced streaming to provide education that catered to all learners.

An extended course was introduced to provide an extra two years for students who needed further instruction before taking the national PSLE, which was normally taken after six years of primary education. Less academically inclined students were given this extra two years to pursue a different curriculum, focusing on one language instead of two, and to proceed to vocational training after completing primary school education.

Generally students sat for the General Certificate of Education Ordinary Level (GCE O) examination after four years of studies in the secondary school. Slower learners were given an extra year to take the newly developed General Certificate

Education Normal Level (GCE N) after four years. Those who qualified would proceed to sit for the GCE O after an extra year of studies. Those who did not qualify would proceed to technical and vocational training.

To implement the policy of 10 years of education for all students, the government made some adjustments to the educational system in 1994. The extra two years in primary school was abolished; all students would receive six years of primary school education. All students were given four or five years of secondary school education. The Normal (technical) course was introduced in secondary school to cater to the non-academically inclined students (14–16 percent of the student population between 1995 and 2005) (Ministry of Education 2006). To implement the NES, new syllabuses and new textbooks were urgently needed.

The MOE set up CDIS in June 1980 to meet this need. Its mission was to produce teaching materials of high quality, including textbooks and multimedia teaching materials. CDIS worked out a systematic developmental process that could be replicated for the different subject areas and disciplines. This process included pilot testing, systematic trialing, and design and publication of multimedia textbook packages. Formative and summative evaluations were conducted during the period of implementation. The feedback obtained at each stage in the process of development was used to refine teaching activities and, in due course, provide feedback for the next cycle of syllabus revision.

CDIS was set up with three textbook writing departments supported by a Division of Educational Technology (originally from the Education Technology Division in the MOE) and an Administration Department. Figure 3.1 shows the organizational structure and function of CDIS with respect to the development, dissemination, and diffusion of curriculum materials to schools.

THE ADMINISTRATION DEPARTMENT

The administrative staff worked with professional staff in project teams to chart time lines for each stage of the project and specifications for each set of materials, including the quantities to be produced. Details such as quality of paper, color separations, delivery dates, and pricing of textbooks were critical because textbooks, which parents had to buy, had to be affordable. Idealism needed to be tempered with reality. The administrative staff was constantly vigilant in keeping a watch on cost. The Administration Department was also in charge of negotiating for copyrights of materials, which could be quite complex and time consuming. Sometimes it was cheaper to pay for music and lyrics (for audiovisual materials) and illustrations made by local artists.

The manuscripts were prepared by CDIS officers and submitted to the Institute by MOE. Several factors determined the price of the textbook package offered by

Figure 3.1 CDIS: Structure, Functions, and Responsibilities

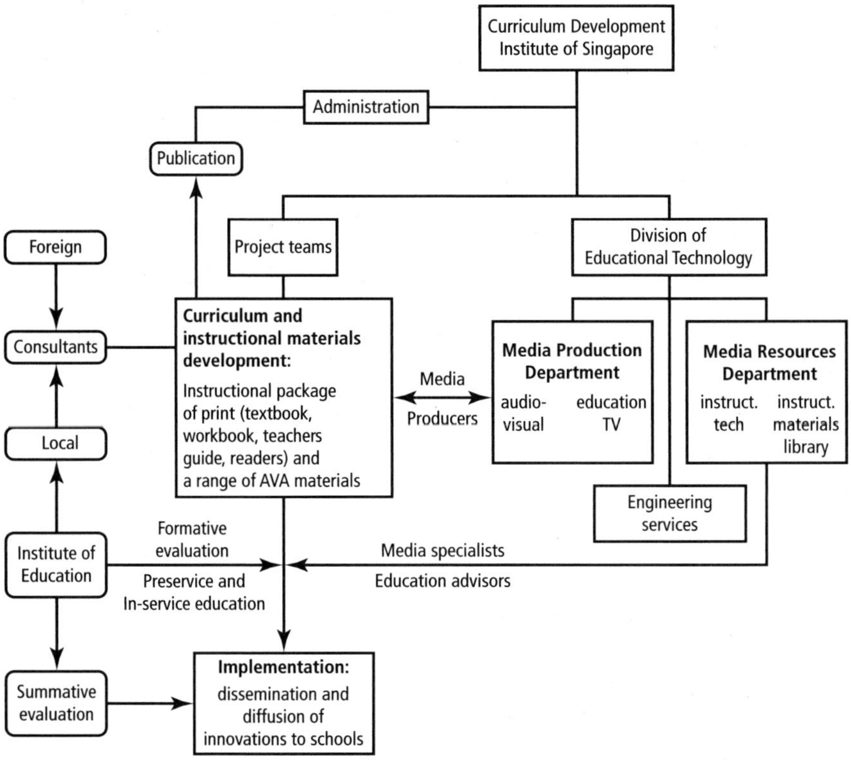

Source: Yip and Sim 1990.

commercial publishers, such as cohort in each grade, cost for production (editing, illustrating, and printing), shelf-life (number of years for guaranteed sales), and the commercial publisher's profit margin.

Bids from publishers were evaluated on a case-by-case basis. One important factor was the volume of sales. Generally, for textbooks, which had a high sales volume, CDIS negotiated a royalty for itself of 5–10 percent. The royalty depended on the range of services provided by the commercial publisher, such as illustrations, editing, mass duplication of teaching aids, and other services. The royalty was ploughed back into CDIS for training, research, and subsidizing non-commercially viable production. The MOE monitored CDIS operations.

Publishers also took care of the distribution of textbooks, teaching aids, and teachers' handbooks to schools. Generally CDIS collaborated with different commercial publishers to publish textbooks for different subjects via the tender system. Commercial publishers had an agreement with CDIS for a 10-year sale period with minor revisions arising from syllabus changes. This was another way of ensuring the prices of textbooks were affordable.

For materials that were not commercially viable, that is, materials with a low print volume, CDIS would cover the full cost of publishing. For example, the lowest ability group in the primary level (about 5 percent of the cohort) was streamed into a monolingual course from primary four to primary eight, and the Learning Activity Program teaching materials for the monolingual course were not profitable. Innovative and high-quality materials were designed for four levels of students in primary schools. Books for language arts, mathematics, science, domestic science, and technical studies in mother tongue and English were published by CDIS. These books were priced similarly to textbooks for students in other courses. CDIS had to subsidize printing and distribution cost.

Table 3.2 lists the core textbook packages and supplementary packages prepared by CDIS. The core projects were copublished with commercial publishers. CDIS had to cover the costs for publishing and distributing the supplementary packages.

CDIS PROJECT TEAMS

CDIS was located near the Botanical Gardens, away from the administrative bureaucracy at MOE headquarters, to provide a work environment conducive to creative efforts for textbook development. Small writing teams were formed from experienced school teachers and specialists from MOE headquarters. Their only responsibility was to design and write textbooks. Although they worked on flexitime arrangements, the progress of their work was monitored against the realistic work plan of each team. The team members were good teachers but had no experience in writing textbooks. They were provided with on-the-job training and were frequently updated on current pedagogical skills.

The process of development started with a steering committee made up of representatives from the Curriculum Planning Division (which was in charge of developing the syllabus) and representatives (heads of departments) from schools, specialists from the Division of Educational Technology in charge of designing nonprint materials such as audiovisual aids and tapes for TV broadcasting to support learning, and lecturers from the National Institute of Education. This team worked out a conceptual framework for how the subject could be taught at each level. The steering committee met regularly to discuss lessons designed by the project team. These lessons were pilot tested in several schools by team members and teachers.

To ensure the quality of the materials, foreign or local consultants were engaged in the development of core subjects. The consultants worked with the team to ensure content validity and effective teaching methodology. Feedback from teachers at the pilot-testing stage enabled writing teams to change and refine the materials. The National Institute of Education carried out a formative

Table 3.2 Core Textbook Packages and Supplementary Packages Prepared by CDIS

(a) **18 Core Curriculum Projects (effective May 1981)**
The core curriculum projects were selected to illustrate how CDIS responded initially to the demands of the NES.

i) The first projects in the initial years (from 1981)

At the primary school level, the projects undertaken reflected the priorities in
- English language (PEP, or Primary English Project competing with NESPE, or New English Series for Primary Education)
- Chinese language (CLIPS, or Chinese Language Instruction Materials for Primary Schools)
- Mathematics (PMP, or Primary Math Project)
- Science (PSP, or Primary Science Project)
- Correct Use of English (CUE) for upper primary school levels and subsequently at secondary levels
- Moral education (Good Citizen in mother tongue languages for primary levels and Moral Education Program, which later came to be known as Being and Becoming, in English for lower secondary levels
- SPEMS, or Special Project on English, Mathematics, and Science (a remedial program in learning English, mathematics, and science for students from a sample of academically low-achieving schools)

ii) The second group of projects

At the secondary school level, the projects included
- Lower Secondary History (LSH)
- Lower Secondary Science (LSS)
- Secondary School Geography (SSG)
- Secondary Chinese Language Teaching (SCLT), which later was renamed Chinese Language Instructional Materials, Secondary (CLIMS)

iii) The policy decision was not to introduce competing teams because of constraints of expertise, manpower, and the small market size.

Special Projects
- Japanese Language Project (under the responsibility of a visiting Japanese language consultant to provide for students taking a third language)
- Religious knowledge, such as the Hindu Studies Project (HSP), Islamic Religious Knowledge (IRK), Buddhist Studies Project (BSP), Confucian Ethics (CONTHICS)
- Computer science (CS)

This project was set up with the introduction of CS in the junior colleges to implement the GCE A-level CS certificate. CDIS managed the project and was in charge of the in-service training of the teachers.

(b) **Supplementary Curriculum Materials Projects**
These included the three projects taken over from the Education Development Division.
- Both the Supplementary English Language Program (SELP) and Supplementary Chinese Language Program (SCLP) provided students in secondary one to three with additional English or Chinese language learning materials and exercises to supplement what was already taught in the core areas. The supplementary materials were used in compensatory immersion language classes outside school hours.
- The project on Errors in Written English developed supplementary English language items and exercises for pupils from primary one to pre-university. Both remedial and compensatory materials were designed to reinforce the correct use of written English.

(c) **Monolingual (M) Course Materials Projects**
Under the NES, students of low academic ability in primary 4M to 8M were required to learn only one language—either the mother tongue or English. Hence, Chinese and English language materials were required to meet the needs of these students. Spoken Malay and spoken Tamil curriculum materials were also needed by those students who learned English as the only language. In contrast, students who registered for Chinese acquired oral fluency in spoken English.

Source: Yip and Sim 1990.
Note: CDIS = Curriculum Development Institute of Singapore; NES = New Education System.

evaluation before a summative evaluation by a foreign consultant. Then the materials were sent to printers for layout and printing. The actual process varied depending on the nature of the subject and the team's preference (see annex B).

CDIS's authors made use of education research findings and translated them into teaching materials and activities to enhance teaching and learning effectiveness. Many newly proven effective teaching approaches and strategies were infused into the textbooks. Lessons were written with cooperative learning, thinking skills, brain-compatible learning, and multiple intelligences strategies. The 4MAT learning styles approach was adopted as a basic conceptual framework for designing lessons to enhance student learning.

Even though CDIS textbooks were available, schools were free to choose textbooks published by commercial publishers in an open market. CDIS even set up competing teams to write textbooks using different pedagogical approaches in a few subjects. For example, in English language learning, both the phonic and whole-word approaches, as well as communicative and grammar-based approaches, were tried in separate packages. New teaching strategies such as the Language Experience Approach and process writing were adopted in the design of activities and provision of teaching materials.

Adopting new approaches was challenging. New approaches and strategies were often challenged by the public. Without the support of top policy makers, some projects would have been aborted. For example, a new "part-whole" model for teaching mathematics was introduced in the primary schools; it required students to go beyond number manipulation and formulae substitution to learn for understanding and thinking. The method was challenged publicly for many years. It received recognition in an international study on mathematics achievement 10 years later. (In the 1990s, many schools in America started using mathematics textbooks from Singapore.)

At that time, when there was a shortage of qualified and well-trained teachers, textbooks were an important resource for teaching. Because most teachers relied on textbooks, an efficient way to introduce more-effective teaching strategies was through the teaching materials. Most teachers tended to teach the way they were taught. Even with the new teaching materials, they tended to use the more traditional methods of teaching. The dissemination workshops conducted by the authors, who were subject specialists, showed teachers how to effectively use the textbook to meet the content requirements of the syllabus and the recommended teaching approaches and strategies.

DIVISION OF EDUCATIONAL TECHNOLOGY

Between 1965 and 1975, educational television programs were designed for broadcasting to schools. The production team was staffed by personnel trained in script writing, production, graphics, photography, cinematography, and technical support. Subject specialists formed part of a team. When CDIS was set up in June 1980, the Division of Educational Technology (DET) became part of CDIS. DET personnel worked closely with the writing teams to produce audiovisual materials as part of textbook packages. The DET produced prototypes for charts, audiotapes, slides, video cassettes, picture and word cards, worksheets, educational games, and, where appropriate, even puppets and masks. Commercial publishers mass-produced these items for schools. Once schools decided to adopt a textbook, these additional materials, together with the teachers' handbook, were given to schools without charge. Education television programs were developed and broadcast to schools to complement the textbook lessons. Teachers could record these programs and use them for teaching.

DET also loaned to all schools audiovisual materials produced overseas. A regular service delivered and collected these materials to and from schools. (To date, this service continues from Teachers' Network, a branch of the Training Division in the MOE.) The textbook was part of a multimedia package to enable teachers to teach more effectively. School-based workshops for teachers on how to used audiovisual materials effectively were conducted regularly and on request.

In 1980, DET upgraded all audiovisual hardware and software in schools in different phases. Key media teachers were given a 60-hour media course so that they were competent to train teachers in their own schools. From 1986, DET was also in charge of providing computer hardware and software to schools. Computer literacy courses, computer clubs, and computer-assisted learning were implemented in schools.

The work at DET complemented the textbook lessons. The coordinated effort enhanced teaching and learning in schools.

LEARNING POINTS FROM TEXTBOOK DEVELOPMENT, 1980–95

- Close working relationships between divisions in the MOE in charge of syllabuses, national examinations, and the National Institute of Education were necessary for the successful implementation of the new textbooks and teaching strategies.
- Continuous support from top policy makers was needed for successful implementation of new and effective teaching strategies such as the "part-whole" model for primary mathematics.
- Teachers' guides detailing strategies and activities were necessary to influence classroom practice.
- Sustained support from school principals and other MOE officials was necessary for teachers to learn and use new teaching strategies.
- New expectations in the national examination facilitated curriculum changes.

- Teachers' participation in textbook development provided insight into training needs and feedback for refinement of textbooks.
- Dissemination workshops to show teachers how to use textbooks effectively was an efficient way for teachers to learn new approaches and strategies.

CLOSING DOWN CDIS AND THE ROLE OF COMMERCIAL PUBLISHERS

In 1996, CDIS was closed down as a result of a restructuring of MOE headquarters. Commercial publishers took over the writing and printing of textbooks. Following are some of the factors that led to the closure of CDIS.

First, in 1986, the Curriculum Branch in MOE was renamed the Curriculum Planning Division. It was in charge of developing new syllabuses, continuously revising existing syllabuses to respond to the social and economic shifts, and recommending changes in teaching approaches and instructional strategies. Because of the urgency in implementing the NES, CDIS had been established to produce textbooks for the revised syllabuses to achieve the objectives of the NES.

In 1996, results showed that the NES had been successful. The attrition rate was reduced from 29 percent in 1978 to 4.5 percent in 1996 (Ministry of Education 2006). Achievement of five O-level passes by candidates in the GCE O examination in 1996 was 73.4 percent, compared with 38.4 percent in 1979. While many factors led to this, textbooks must be considered one contributory factor. Also, Singapore students attained top ranking in international studies of science and mathematics achievements (as reflected in Trends in International Mathematics and Science Study [TIMSS] and PIRLS scores).

Second, in 1996, the manpower situation had improved tremendously. The number of university graduates had increased significantly. The National Institute of Education had been training thousands of new teachers, heads of departments, and vice principals and principals. Schools were encouraged to embark on their own innovations to meet individual school needs. Schools were very well equipped with computers and audiovisual aids and had funds to buy software, train teachers, and implement innovative programs.

Third, commercial publishers were very unhappy when CDIS was set up. They wanted the monopoly held by CDIS to be lifted to allow them to write and print textbooks. But the collaboration with CDIS provided publishers the opportunity to improve their skills and capacity in publishing.

The staff of 350 in the various divisions in CDIS were sent to serve in different departments in the MOE. Most of them joined a newly formed division looking after DET and computer education. Some joined the existing Curriculum Planning Division, which took over the writing of civics, moral education, and mother tongue languages textbooks from CDIS. Some staff members joined other divisions in the MOE. Others returned to schools to be teachers, heads of departments, vice principals, and principals. This has set the trend for a regular exchange of staff between schools and the MOE headquarters.

CURRICULUM PLANNING AND DEVELOPMENT DIVISION

With the restructuring and closure of CDIS, the Curriculum Planning Division was redesignated the Curriculum Planning and Development Department (CPDD) and given charge of developing syllabuses as well as briefing publishers on specifications of textbooks. Publishers could assess textbook specification documents and appoint writers to write textbooks accordingly.

An authorization process was put in place that required commercial publishers to submit textbooks and the proposed prices for approval by the MOE. The procedure to pay for review and approval has been set by the MOE and is available on the ministry Web site. The Web site also provides the range of MOE-approved textbooks, worksheets, and activity sheets. Prices of textbooks are also listed (see tables 3.3 and 3.4).

The cost of a textbook package includes a textbook and one workbook split into Part A and Part B for two semesters. The cost of one set of textbooks per grade at the primary level is about S$10–S$15, and at the secondary level it is about S$15–$20. According to Globalis (http://globalis.gvu.unu.edu), the gross national income per capita from 1985 to 2003 increased by 300 percent, whereas textbook prices on average have increased by 70 percent.

Textbooks are still bought at school bookshops, at public bookshops, or directly from publishers. Schools are given funds from the MOE and other organizations to provide free textbooks to needy students. The commercial textbook packages

Table 3.3 Prices of Approved Textbooks for Primary Schools

Subject	Publisher	Price range per package	Grades
Arts and crafts	Commercial	S$6	P1–P6
English language	Commercial	S$12–15	P1–P6
Mathematics	Commercial	S$18–20	P1–P6
Science	Commercial	S$13	P3–P6
Mother tongue languages (Chinese, Malay, Tamil)	Curriculum Planning and Development Division (CPDD) with commercial publisher	S$6	P1–P6
Civics and moral education	CPDD and commercial publisher	S$4	P1–P6
Social studies	CPDD and commercial publisher	S$5	P1–P6

Note: In some subjects many titles are available; hence, there is a range of prices.

Table 3.4 Prices of Approved Textbooks for Secondary Schools

Subject	Publisher	Price range per package	Grades
Arts and crafts	Commercial	S$10	S1 & S2
		S$18	S3 & S4
Additional mathematics	Commercial	S$21	S3 & S4
Biology	Commercial	S$25–36	S3 & S4
Chemistry	Commercial	S$21–38	S3 & S4
English language	Commercial	S $16–20	S1–S4
Geography	Commercial	S$17–24	S1 & S2
		S$20	S3 & S4
History	Commercial	S$13–18	S1
	CPDD and commercial	S$4	S2
	Commercial	S$17–22	S3 & S4
Physics	Commercial	S$21–32	S3 & S4
Lower secondary science	Commercial	S$22	S1 & S2
Mathematics	Commercial	S$15–22	S1–S4
Social studies	CPDD and commercial	S$6	S1–S4
Mother tongue languages (Chinese, Malay, Tamil)	CPDD and commercial	S$12	S1–S4
Civics and moral education	CPDD and commercial	S$2.50–$4	S1–S4

Note: Where the textbook package applies to two grades, the price is for two grades.

often include multimedia teaching aids, charts, and a teachers' handbook. Teachers in each school decide which textbooks to use. Workshops on using textbooks effectively are conducted by publishers on request. Some textbooks are more popular than others. The open market has resulted in the discontinuance of some less popular textbook series and the development of new series through the combination of existing ones. Most textbook writers are part-timers. Some form teams and others write individually. Generally, the writers are experienced teachers or lecturers from the National Institute of Education.

Schools are now staffed by well-qualified and experienced teachers. A few schools have embarked on preparing their own teaching materials following the syllabus guidelines. Schools are encouraged to try out teaching strategies to promote more effective learning among students. The MOE facilitates professional sharing among schools. Many schools have been designated as Centers of Excellence for different teaching subjects, and they offer services to other schools.

CPDD is still in charge of the development of textbooks and other teaching materials for civics and moral education, mother tongue languages, and social studies—subjects for promoting national identity and values. The manuscripts are prepared by the division's education officers and printed by commercial publishers and then sold to schools. Hence, the prices of these books are very low.

One critical factor that ensures the relevance of textbook contents to national needs is the systematic effort by the MOE to train and equip curriculum specialists. These teachers were sent overseas by the MOE to pursue higher degrees in curricular and instructional design (languages, mathematics, humanities, and so on) and other niche areas of specializations (such as information technology in teaching, learning, reading, and literacy). This practice, started in the 1980s, continues to this day. There is a close traction between the curriculum developers and the textbook writing team (at CDIS before 1995 and at CPDD since 1996) to ensure good translation of the syllabus into learning materials. Indeed, the curriculum review cycle today involves a rigorous process that is monitored by the Instructional Material Development Committee (IMDC). Besides CPDD, IMDC involves colleagues from other relevant departments within the MOE and also university academics in the various subject areas. Education officers in the National Education Branch, for example, are consulted on the curriculum development and writing of history and social studies syllabuses and textbooks.

CONCLUSION

From 1965 to 1996, Singapore went through a cycle of using textbooks imported from many countries, to textbooks copublished by the MOE and local publishers, to textbooks published by local commercial publishers. The textbook development journey experienced by Singapore is summarized below:

- The MOE undertook all the stages in textbook publication for certain subjects from 1967 when it published the civics and mother tongue languages textbooks—developing instructional materials, elaboration of texts and illustrations, editing, printing and binding, distribution, and storage.
- From 1980, CDIS developed the instructional packages and collaborated with commercial publishers in varying degrees on a case-by-case basis. For textbook packages with small circulation, CDIS covered the full cost for publishing services in all areas. This collaboration between CDIS and the commercial publishers provided opportunities for commercial publishers to acquire skills and capacity to achieve a high standard in publishing.
- When the textbook packages were developed by CDIS, publishers sold them to schools directly. The textbook writers, who were teachers and subject specialists, were available to conduct dissemination workshops to show teachers the effective use of the textbook packages to meet the syllabus requirements. Singapore being very small, distribution costs were very low.

- Conditions from 1997 in Singapore were right for commercial publishers to take over the development and publication of school textbooks. Currently, commercial publishers can publish textbooks independently for all subjects except civics and moral education, mother tongue languages, and social studies. The MOE authorization process ensures commercially produced textbooks are of high quality and made available at affordable prices.

Imported textbooks were generally unsuitable for Singapore students as they taught to different syllabuses and values. Institutionalizing the development of textbooks to overcome the shortage of qualified and well-trained teachers arising from the rapid educational and structural changes was effective. Eventually entrusting the textbook industry to local publishers has led to the development and growth of a local educational publishing industry.

The MOE still retains for itself the development of textbooks relating to national values required for its civics, moral education, mother tongue languages, and social studies syllabuses. The MOE has put in place an authorization system for approving textbooks to maintain the quality and price of textbooks.

The cycle reflects the economic, social, manpower, and national development priorities in Singapore. Schools today have access to good and experienced teachers and to resources internationally available on the Internet. Therefore, the schools are encouraged to develop their own teaching materials to meet the needs of their students. Schools are well equipped with computers and have access to intranet and commercially produced education software. Students can access electronic learning materials even at home. Learning need not be confined to the classroom. With all these available resources, creative teachers can make learning truly meaningful and fun. The main objective is to help students to learn well enough so that they can use their knowledge and skills beyond the classroom to achieve success for themselves and Singapore.

NOTES

1. This section is contributed by Sim Wee Chee of Panpac Education Pte Ltd.
2. Mother tongues were used because students were more proficient in their native languages and could more easily learn national and cultural values at the same time.

REFERENCES

Ministry of Education. 2006.

Yip, S. K., and W. K. Sim, eds. 1990. *Evolution of Education Excellence: 25 years of Education in the Republic of Singapore.* Singapore: LongmanGlobis.

ANNEX A: PRIMARY SCIENCE PROJECT

DURATION

The Primary Science Project (PSP) team was one of the pioneer teams of the Curriculum Development Institute of Singapore (CDIS). The team, consisting of a project director and four textbook writers, started functioning on May 2, 1980. (Two more writers came on board in the next two years.) The first phase, the production of materials for P3 to P6 and P4E to P8E, ended in December 1985, when the P6 and P8E texts had been implemented for a year. Phase 2, the revision and refinement of materials, was from 1986 until the closure of CDIS.

The package for each level consisted of a textbook, two workbooks, teachers' guide, and teaching aids such as charts, cards, slides, and educational TV (ETV) programs.

The materials were first implemented in 1982 at the P3 level, with the addition of one level a year. With the closure of CDIS, the production of textbooks was taken over by commercial publishers. Thus the CDIS Primary Science series was phased out from 2001(P3) to 2004(P6).

PUBLISHER

The publisher for PSP was Pan Pacific Book Distributors (S) Pte Ltd. The team from Pan Pacific worked very closely with the project team members. In addition to typing the manuscripts, they did the graphics—photographs and sketches—and also provided an English language expert to vet and check on the language. The production of teaching aids was done by the Division of Educational Technology (DET).

The writers gave detailed information and descriptions to guide the artists, photographers, and ETV producers. Every piece of artwork was vetted and redone, if necessary—only the best was accepted. The writers also assisted in writing the ETV scripts and production of the programs. The publisher had a general editor attached to the project. Distribution of the textbooks was done by the publisher, while the teaching aids were disseminated by DET of the Ministry of Education (MOE).

PROCESS

CDIS started functioning on May 2, 1980. The PSP team was very honored to be one of the pioneers. All team members, including the project director, were primary school teachers before they joined the team. The first two years were very hectic but exciting as the team started working on the objectives and priorities, examining the syllabus set by the Curriculum Planning and Development Department (CPDD), discussing the approaches to use, distributing roles, and drawing up the schedule with highlighted deadlines to ensure production was on time.

Most of the time, PSP team members worked in pairs on a topic or subtopic. At the same time, the pairs contributed and shared resources with others on the team whenever they came across useful and relevant information or data. The team met at least once a week to review what had been written to cross-check that team members were on track and did not duplicate information or data unnecessarily.

Besides working within the PSP team, members also worked with the supporting teams from DET and the publisher. Dialogue sessions with team members from other subjects, especially the Primary English team, were also held to ensure the language used (grammar and vocabulary) was suitable for the age group. The PSP team also collaborated with other divisions of the MOE, such as the Examination and Assessment Division, CPDD, and the Primary School Branch/School Division, to ensure smooth implementation of the package.

The emphasis of PSP was on process skills. The text was written to guide the learning of concepts through the various process skills mastered at that level. Thus, the content of each textbook is activity based. Besides writing the content, each writer's responsibilities included getting accurate illustrations (photos and sketches); assignment and assessment items; as well as enrichment activities, reading materials, and relevant rhymes and games.

The team's responsibilities also included gathering feedback, observing lessons during field tests, discussing the materials with teachers, and conducting workshops for teachers to demonstrate how the lessons were to be carried out and how to write items to test process skills.

All contents were field tested in schools and feedback was also gathered from the ground (classroom teachers). The materials were then refined accordingly and retried whenever necessary.

The approaches included in the primary science package were field trips; hands-on, practical sessions; group work; self-reflection and assessment; and enhancement through ETV programs, which were broadcasted as well as videotaped.

The PSP team had a consultant from Chelsea College in the United Kingdom, Dr. Wynne Harlem. Besides vetting materials sent to her, Dr. Harlem made trips to Singapore to conduct face-to-face discussions with the team. Training sessions were also conducted for all the team members. In addition, two members had the opportunity to work with Dr. Harlem and her colleagues at Chelsea College on writing process skills assessment items.

In Singapore, professional organizations, such as the Singapore Science Centre and the Science Teachers Association of Singapore, participated actively in promoting education. These organizations conducted activities and workshops for teachers to enhance the teaching of science. Students were also provided with activities such as the Young Scientist Badge Scheme and the Science Fair to enrich their learning.

With the closure of CDIS, the MOE left the development of teaching and learning packages to the private publishers. Each publisher produces the materials according to its expertise, but the publishers are compelled to follow the guidelines and syllabuses set by CPDD of the MOE.

ANNEX B: THE BUSINESS OF TEXTBOOK PUBLICATION: THE ROLE OF PANPAC

This annex explains how Panpac Education was first established and how it evolved to what it is today. It will then explain how Panpac Education rode on its years of publishing experiences to assist developing countries to develop their textbook industry through eight case studies of different ways of collaborating in textbook publishing.

BEGINNINGS OF PANPAC EDUCATION

In the years following Singapore's independence, there was a lack of good-quality, locally published textbooks, which resulted in many schools using imported and expensive textbooks that were not very relevant to Singapore's education needs. This prompted the establishment of the Singapore Education Publishing Bureau (EPB) by the Singapore Ministry of Education (MOE) in 1967. Thus, the history of Panpac Education begins.

In the initial years of its establishment, Panpac Education, more widely known then as EPB, worked closely with the Singapore MOE to develop syllabuses for teaching civics and moral education as well as the languages of the three big ethnic races in Singapore—Chinese, Malay, and Tamil—now commonly known as mother tongue languages. The purpose then was to produce affordable textbooks with familiar contents that promoted national cohesion among the ethnic races. Today, Panpac Education continues to be the only publisher working with the Singapore MOE to publish civics and moral education content and mother tongue textbooks.

MORE THAN JUST AN EDUCATION PUBLISHING BUREAU

In the late 1970s, the Singapore government recognized that English would be the key international language of communication and promoted the importance of learning English in schools. This prompted the teaching of all subjects, except the respective mother tongue languages of the ethnic races, in English. The Curriculum Development Institute of Singapore (CDIS) was tasked to develop textbooks and multimedia instructional materials for schools. Once it achieved its objectives,

CDIS was closed, and the Curriculum Planning and Development Department (CPDD) was formed to continue the mandate of developing syllabuses and briefing publishers on specifications for textbooks, approving textbooks, and negotiating textbook prices.

Riding on the experiences accumulated since the days of EPB, Panpac Education moved into new realms of publishing when it copublished its first English language textbook series with CPDD in the mid-1980s. This series was used in Singapore by all schools for almost a decade.

It was also in the mid-1980s that Singapore saw the privatization of government-owned enterprises moving into full swing, allowing SNP Corporation—another formerly government-owned company—to acquire EPB, renaming it SNP Publishing. SNP Publishing rode on its accumulated experiences in EPB days and started publishing other subjects, including science and history. These projects were mostly tendered from CPDD.

TEXTBOOK MARKET LIBERALIZATION

In 1996, the Singapore MOE decided to open the market to competition, allowing publishers to freely bid for the publishing of core curriculum textbooks that were in accordance with the syllabuses set forth by the MOE. This was the milestone of textbook publishing in Singapore. Commercial publishers were now allowed to engage their own authors to write textbooks, and, upon approval from the MOE, publishers are allowed to print for direct sales into schools. Thus, it was during this era that commercial publishers expanded into many different subjects taught in primary schools.

Market competition prompted many mergers and acquisitions in the textbook industry. In its bid to enter into the secondary school market, SNP Publishing merged with one of the largest secondary school textbook publishers in Singapore, Pan Pacific Publications, which was strong in mathematics and geography, in 2000, to form SNP Panpac. With the combined strength of both companies and more than 60 years of publishing history, SNP Panpac became one of the two top publishers in Singapore.

In March 2006, in the ultimate merger and acquisition exercise of the Singapore textbook publishing industry, SNP Panpac was acquired by the Times Publishing Group to form the single largest education publishing group in Singapore. It is now known as Panpac Education.

BECOMING AN INTERNATIONAL EDUCATION PUBLISHER

Moving into the 21st century, SNP Panpac continued to expand its publishing capabilities through the development of numerous textbook packages in

Singapore, while retaining its status as the only publisher of civics and moral education textbooks as well as mother tongue languages textbook packages. SNP Panpac has also begun developing its international publishing capabilities with neighboring countries, starting with Brunei and Malaysia, followed by China, the United States, the Caribbean, Pakistan, Vietnam, and Thailand and Indonesia. These countries and regions are the case studies that will illustrate how Panpac Education has helped in developing the textbook industries of these countries.

Panpac Education continues to introduce its published materials and textbooks to more than 25 countries around the world. Its education publications on the English language, mathematics, and science are particularly popular in countries near and far. In the countries and regions where Panpac Education has helped to develop the local textbook publishing industries, its efforts can be broadly categorized into three types:

a. Copublishing with the Ministries of Education of the countries and/or local publishers and distributors
b. Adaptation and/or customization of existing content to suit local needs
c. Adoption of Panpac Education's existing titles coupled with teacher training workshops

Brunei. The Singapore MOE and the Brunei MOE have been working closely on exchanging educational information since bilateral relations began in the late 1960s. It was through that close working relationship that Panpac Education started its first international publishing experience with the Brunei MOE in the early 1980s.

Panpac Education was first invited to work with the Brunei MOE in a textbook tender project in science, mathematics, and history. Because Brunei lacked local publishing capability, Panpac Education was asked to publish textbooks with contents suitable for local needs. The Brunei MOE set the syllabus, and Panpac Education wrote and then published the books, which were sold by local Brunei distributors in that market. Panpac Education has been publishing for the Brunei MOE for the past 20 years.

Liaoning, one of the Northeastern Provinces of China. Panpac Education started working with the State Education Commission of Liaoning Province, which is the most developed province in northeastern China, in early 2001. Panpac Education first introduced to the State Education Commission its mathematics and science textbook packages that were all written in English and used by Singapore schools. The commission was very interested in using the contents, but their lack of proficiency in the English language was an obstacle. Panpac Education suggested creating bilingual editions for these two packages. The contents were fully translated into bilingual editions of Chinese and English and implemented throughout the province.

United States. Panpac Education first entered the U.S. market through a local distributor distributing its mathematics publications, mostly to primary and secondary schools. Subsequently, the distributor saw the potential of moving into the primary mathematics supplementary materials market and suggested customizing one of Panpac Education's best-selling publications to suit the U.S. market. The series was initially a set of four books; the customized series was published as a set of six books for each primary level. The terms used in the books were changed to ones that would be familiar to U.S. students. For example, local Singaporean names such as Fatimah or Siti were replaced with Jane or Mary, and fruit names such as durians and mangoes were changed to oranges and grapes.

Malaysia. In June 2002, the former Malaysian prime minister, Dr. Mahatir Mohammed, made a sudden announcement that mathematics and science would be taught in English starting in January 2003. This meant that all mathematics and science textbooks needed to be published by the end of October 2002 and distributed to all schools by the end of November 2002 before the school year began in 2003.

Panpac Education was shortlisted at the tender stage and subsequently won the tender to publish Mathematics Year 1 for the whole of Malaysia. The syllabus was developed by the Malaysian MOE, and Panpac Education took care of the writing, publishing, and distributing of the textbook packages in less than five months. Delivery was fulfilled by the end of November 2002 to all parts of Malaysia, including remote areas of the country as well as eastern Malaysia, via helicopter and speedboat. Panpac Education became a one-stop education service provider.

Caribbean. Panpac Education entered this market in the late 1990s through one of the largest textbook distributors in the region. The distributor managed to open the Caribbean market using Panpac Education publications to compete with international publishers that were also in this market.

In mid-2004, the distributor was awarded the tender to publish a number of core curriculum subjects of the new syllabus. The distributor relied upon Panpac Education as the publishing house to help it fulfill its publishing obligations. In the process, Panpac Education enlisted the help of locally well-known educators as reviewers of the subjects to make sure that the contents that were developed were in sync with the local context. The reviewers also helped to ensure that the contents adhered to the syllabus. Most important, these reviewers provided a strong local perspective and knowledge to the publications.

Panpac Education engaged writers to write original contents in accordance with the syllabuses developed by the local MOE. This was the first time that full textbook packages were introduced into the Caribbean—student textbooks, student workbooks, teacher's guides, teacher's editions, as well as multimedia resources. Panpac Education provided illustrations that were familiar to the Caribbean students, including details such as the skin colors of different local ethnic groups.

It was through this process of exchanging information and experiences that the distributor realized that printing and fulfillment in the Caribbean was much more expensive than in Singapore or China.

Pakistan. Panpac Education has been working with one of the largest private school education publishers and distributors in Pakistan for more than two decades, introducing its textbook packages into the large private school market throughout the country.

In the past few years, Panpac Education started adapting and customizing its existing educational contents in the English language and science for Pakistan, remaining sensitive to the kinds of subjects that could be taught in schools there. To respect the local culture and religion, sensitive topics such as "reproduction" were removed from the textbook packages, and animals such as pigs and dogs that were considered inappropriate to the Islamic religion were replaced with other animals commonly found in Pakistan. Textbook covers and many illustrations in the textbook packages were redrawn to be more familiar to the students. Panpac Education also engaged local educators to review the contents to ensure that it adhered to the local syllabus and context.

In addition, Panpac Education published and printed the textbook packages for Pakistan, making use of its networks throughout the low-cost Asian region, at a lower cost than doing it in country.

Vietnam. In every collaboration, there are always aspects that are unique. In this instance, Panpac Education managed to establish a strong working relationship with the state-owned publisher in Vietnam, who found Panpac's experiences in customization and adaptation of its contents to local conditions very appealing.

Panpac Education provided expertise in the editorial and prepress processes as well as consultation on the writing of the English language textbooks. When the textbooks were ready to be pilot tested in the country, Panpac helped them to develop teacher training materials and assisted with teacher training workshops in the country.

Thailand and Indonesia. Singapore has always maintained very close ties with Thailand and Indonesia, and it was most natural for Panpac Education to have long working partnerships with local distributors in these two countries. Many of the schools in these two countries look up to the Singapore education system and believe that one of the fastest ways to improve their own education systems is to use the Singapore-published books in their teaching and learning. Panpac Education textbooks are widely distributed in these two countries, particularly in the subjects of the English language, mathematics, and science. Schools in Thailand and Indonesia admired the Singapore comprehensive education system, which centered on using English as the key language of instruction, thus honing children's English language skills at a very young age and reinforcing it in mathematics and science instruction.

In the case of Indonesia, many schools also adopted the Chinese language textbooks used in Singapore as part of their core curriculum because a significant Chinese population in Indonesia wants their children to retain their Chinese language. However, most of the publications from China and Taiwan were not customized to suit local needs in terms of cultural affinity, style of presentation, and level of difficulty. Singapore, having gone through years of defining a curriculum suitable for learners of Chinese as a second language, thus fulfilled their needs.

Aside from introducing its published textbooks in these countries, Panpac Education believed that to enhance the experiences of both the teachers and students, it was critical to provide teacher training as part of its commitment to transfer knowledge to the country. Hence, Panpac Education conducted about three workshops a year for many teachers in these two countries in the teaching of the English language, the Chinese language, mathematics, and science.

MOVING FORWARD

Other developing countries have invited Panpac Education to help them develop their textbook industries. Iraq, under the auspices of UNESCO, has asked Panpac Education to participate in its initiative to rebuild its education system. Egypt, which will be undergoing a new syllabus cycle, has asked Panpac Education to join it in creating new educational textbooks for its schools. These parties were very interested in Panpac's flexible and modular partnership models, especially the ability to be a one-stop education services provider and their expertise in providing high-quality education contents.

Through all these experiences and partnerships, Panpac Education firmly believes that to make all these partnerships meaningful and long-lasting, it not only needs to provide high-quality, one-stop publishing, printing, and fulfillment services, but also must be committed to the transfer of knowledge.

CHAPTER 4

Making Teacher Education Responsive and Relevant

GOH Chor Boon and LEE Sing Kong

Teacher education is currently facing a number of challenges as the Singapore society and economy mature and, in the face of globalization, as its young citizens experience a multitude of cultural and technological influences. Globalization, in the new millennium, will have an impact on education from all perspectives—how we teach, what we teach, where we teach, whom we teach, and even whether we teach. New technologies not only have given teachers new tools for the classroom that have created instant and powerful connectivities between persons and ideas, across space and in real time, but also fundamentally alter our notions of what it means to teach. Within the virtual worlds of e-mail, chat rooms, virtual classrooms, and even multiplayer gaming environments, individuals from cultures and societies around the globe are interacting with a frequency that was unimaginable even a decade ago. These powerful technology-related learning environments are not culture free, but carry with them very powerful cultural content preloaded in the cyberspace curriculum and preset by transnational forces that demand sameness rather than separateness. Globalization, too, means that the transfer of technologies and expertise has brought transnational organizations into local education markets through both physical and virtual connections across space. Teachers today will have international students in the same learning space at the same time.

New technologies have not only changed the role of the teacher but, in many situations, also made the traditional teaching roles redundant for many educators.

This chapter examines how Singapore goes about developing a quality teaching force, the processes and characteristics of which have constantly been admired by many governments all over the world. After a brief historical introduction, the chapter focuses on the challenges of teacher education in the

21st century, how Singapore's Ministry of Education (MOE) builds and sustains a quality teaching service in light of these challenges, and the role of the National Institute of Education (NIE) in supporting this achievement.

TEACHER EDUCATION AND TRAINING PRIOR TO 1991

Teacher education and training in the 1960s was more of a bane than a boon. Recruitment of teaching staff was a major problem. A report of the Education Commission set up by the government in April 1962 concluded that teachers were overworked and exhausted from teaching six days a week, and "for the teachers and students, health has been affected, morale lowered" (*Straits Times*, Apr. 17, 1962). Because of the poor level of education of the workforce, it was not possible to recruit trained teachers in large numbers from any one source. To fill the gap, Singapore resorted to large-scale recruitment of teachers-in-training who, while undergoing training at the Teachers Training College (TTC), assumed partial teaching responsibility in schools. The standards of teaching in these teacher-trainees were closely monitored and supervised by the TTC lecturers and senior teachers in schools. Up to 1964, it was not possible to recruit a sufficient number of teachers-in-training with the requisite minimum qualifications. To provide an incentive, in March 1962, the government decided to give women teachers equal pay with their male colleagues.[1] Salary adjustments were gradually made and, by 1965, the lower salary scale of women teachers disappeared.

When Singapore gained its independence from Malaysia in August 1965, the education service was staffed with, in the words of Lee Kuan Yew, "teachers who are undedicated because of the nature of recruitment" (Lee 1966, 7). The then–prime minister resolved to rectify the situation because "in my experience—both as a pupil in school and in universities, and subsequently in trying to teach people large, simple political ideas—the most important person is the man who is in charge of the boy" (Lee 1966, 7). At this stage, however, the priority was to achieve universal primary education as soon as possible. The quality of teacher training was put aside as mass recruitment of teachers was needed to staff the rising number of schools. The number of pupils in Singapore increased from about 246,000 in 1957 to 520,000 in 1967, and nearly 10,000 teachers went through TTC (Department of Statistics, various years). In the process, this unprecedented expansion negatively affected the teaching profession as "crash programs had to be mounted in large numbers and often standards had to be diluted" (Lun and Chan 1983, 16). As reported in the *Straits Times* (Jan. 28, 1968), "Administrative and teaching staff are preoccupied with routine work and have little time for reflection, innovation and self-improvement; the part-time students are under heavy pressure of work—both school and college—and hardly able to do justice to either; curricular reforms are urgently awaiting; comparable standards between the different language streams need to be defined and maintained; necessary teaching materials have to be compiled."

After years of rapid educational expansion, the demand for teachers was perceived to have stabilized by 1970. Attention was shifted to improvement in the system and structure of teacher training in Singapore, especially teaching in secondary schools as the bulk of the primary school population moved into the secondary level. The rapid expansion in secondary education in the 1970s posed enormous problems in curriculum implementation in schools and at the teacher-training level; the call was made for a certain degree of specialization. New aspects of education, such as bilingualism and technical and vocational training, were also imposed on the teacher-training program. The qualitative aspect of teacher training now came to the fore, and a greater emphasis was placed on science and mathematics, technical and vocational training. At the institutional level, in early 1969, it became clear that further development of the TTC was hampered by the fact that it was administered as a government department. Promotion was stringently regulated and, as a result, there was a constant turnover of staff. This was not conducive for the attainment of good professional and academic standards. In the meantime, the teaching profession was perked up by the government's announcement of better salary scales and working conditions in 1971.

A milestone development took place in April 1973 when the TTC was revamped and became the Institute of Education (IE) and was administered as a statutory board. It was designated as the only "one-stop" teacher-training institution in Singapore for teachers at all levels in Singapore's schools, including inservice training for qualified practicing teachers. This is unlike many other countries where teacher education is carried out in a variety of institutions: teacher-training colleges for primary school teachers, and advanced colleges of education and education departments in universities for secondary school teachers. The government initially planned that the IE would have the authority to confer its own degrees, starting with the BEd and going on to postgraduate degrees in education. However, the proposed degree was shelved indefinitely, but the postgraduate programs were introduced and conferred by the University of Singapore (and later by the National University of Singapore).

The overarching mission of the IE was to improve the quality of teaching in schools. Immediate measures were taken to upgrade the faculty and facilities of the training campus. In line with the Singapore government's practice of putting the best people in positions to lead its public organizations, the IE progressed rapidly through the competent guidance of several directors from 1973 to 1991, beginning with the appointment of Dr. Ruth Wong as its first director. Under their leadership, the professional and other training programs of the IE had been subjected to reviews and changes. Many faculty members were given grants to pursue higher degrees. One significant development in these upgrading efforts was the government's appointment of Dr. William Taylor, then the director of the

University of London's Institute of Education, as the consultant to IE in upgrading professional standards.

In the 1980s, the IE made concerted efforts to establish a research culture among its academic faculty and to boost postgraduate work. Through staff development programs and recruitment drives, the number of staff with doctorates in education increased during this period of time. A center for educational research was set up. However, the roots for the growth of a research culture were slow to germinate. While the call was made for staff to conduct research and publish, the majority of the faculty were still classroom practitioners. It was difficult to alter attitudes overnight. At the MOE, the emphasis and direction was to train effective teachers strong in pedagogical methods and classroom management. Research was not a priority. Inevitably, a tension between IE and the MOE developed, and the relationship was often on a roller coaster. The gulf between the administrators and bureaucrats in the MOE and the school and academic researchers in IE seemed uncompromising. But the rift did not last long.

A landmark institutional change took place in 1991, when the present NIE was created. This signaled the beginning of an intimate working relationship between NIE and its various stakeholders, especially the MOE and schools. A high-level committee was formed to look into the next stage of development in teacher training.[2] It was also part of the government's effort in fine-tuning the tertiary sector to support its private-sector-driven economic modernization strategy, based on the development of science and technology. Good teachers were required to nurture Singaporeans with strong foundations in science and mathematics at the primary level. The outcome was the launch of degree programs for primary teacher education because, as stated by the committee, this is "in recognition of the importance and increasing complexity and demands of primary teaching in a fast-paced, technological society" (IE and CPE Development Committee 1990, i). The committee also recommended, "Many reputable teacher colleges overseas are coming or have come under the ambit of universities to enhance their standing and that of their degrees. Following this trend . . . NIE should become part of a university so as to clearly establish a tertiary status for itself and its degree programs" (IE and CPE Development Committee 1990, 6). In 1991, NIE became an autonomous institute of the Nanyang Technological University (NTU) with its own management council.

A NEW ERA IN TEACHER TRAINING

It is now universally accepted that student learning—and, hence, the quality of teacher education—are the key to 21st-century economic success. In developing and developed countries alike, political leaders and education policy makers constantly have education and the challenge of preparing high-quality teachers at the top of their agenda. Singapore is no exception. The success of what Singapore hopes to achieve in education hinges on the quality of its teachers.[3] They form the most vital component of the country's organizational capacity. Teachers must be dedicated to the vision and mission of education, understand the rationale behind education policies, and be committed to their own professional development. In turn, they will be well trained and equipped to nurture, challenge, and inspire their charges in schools. These precepts guided the recruitment and training of teachers in the 1990s and beyond. Up to the mid-1990s, however, the MOE had difficulties in getting teachers and was able to achieve only about 55 to 70 percent of its annual targets (*Straits Times*, Mar. 21, 1996).

Singapore's education service is more vibrant today as a result of past efforts to improve its appeal to potential teachers through more competitive remuneration, faster promotions, and strong emphasis on continual upgrading and professional development. In 1996, the Singapore government implemented wide-sweeping changes in the salaries and promotion prospects in the education service, estimated to cost about S$420 million a year (Department of Statistics, various years). The incentives were also applicable to trainee teachers who now received a teacher's salary, including service benefits, instead of a bursary. In 2001, a move was initiated to look into the promotion tracks and performance incentives for teachers and, after a few years of preparation, a new system of assessing teacher performance was introduced in all schools.

The overall objective of the government was to attract and retain good people to preserve and further enhance the quality of Singapore's education system. Further improvements and monetary incentives have been introduced in the past few years, including greater autonomy given to school leaders, a performance bonus system, and a performance management system to reward good performance and help retain teachers. Today, the Singapore teacher enjoys competitive starting salaries, as shown in tables 4.1 and 4.2.

Table 4.1 Starting Salary for Graduate Teachers (in S$)

BEFORE NIE AND DURING NIE TRAINING		
	Gross starting salary	
Qualifications	Without NS	With NS
Pass degree	$2,472	$2,822
Honors	$2,647 to $2,822	$2,997 to $3,172
AFTER NIE TRAINING		
	Gross starting salary	
Qualifications	Without NS	With NS
Pass degree	$2,585	$2,939
Honors	$2,762 to $2,939	$3,115 to $3,292

Source: http://www.moe.gov.sg/teach/SalaryBenefits.htm
Note: NIE = National Institute of Education; NS = National Service (for males).

Table 4.2 Starting Salaries for Nongraduate Teachers (in S$)

BEFORE AND DURING NIE TRAINING		
	Gross starting salary	
Qualifications	Without NS	With NS
Polytechnic diploma* (technical)		
Year 1	$1,779	$1,978
Year 2	$1,879	$2,077
Polytechnic diploma* (nontechnical)		
Year 1	$1,586	$1,779
Year 2	$1,663	$1,879
A-level		
Year 1	$1,431	$1,586
Year 2	$1,509	$1,663
O-level		
Year 1 and 2	$800	$800
Year 3	$1,431	$1,586
Year 4	$1,509	$1,663

AFTER NIE TRAINING		
	Gross starting salary	
Qualifications	Without NS	With NS
Polytechnic diploma* (technical)	$2,028	$2,226
Polytechnic diploma* (nontechnical)	$1,829	$2,028
A-Level	$1,630	$1,829
O-Level	$1,630	$1,829

Source: http://www.moe.gov.sg/teach/SalaryBenefits.htm
Note: NIE = National Institute of Education; NS = National Service (for males); A-Level = Advanced Level General Certificate in Education; O-Level = Ordinary Level General Certificate in Education.

Teachers are now promoted through three "fields of excellence": the teaching track, the leadership track, and the senior specialist track.[4] Besides remunerations that are compatible with (or even better than) beginning lawyers, engineers, and even medical doctors in the government service, each teacher is entitled to 100 hours of fully subsidized professional training per year. A Connect Plan provides monetary reward for teachers who stay in service more than a certain number of years. Finally, in the spirit of lifelong education, school leaders and teachers are encouraged to take sabbatical leave to pick up new knowledge and skills—and not necessarily in an education institution, but in other sectors as well, such as the hospitality industry.[5]

The MOE has also been raising the public profile of the teaching service by actively marketing its teaching scholarships and awards, publicly recognizing exemplary teachers, and highlighting good stories to the media. Other initiatives have been launched to further improve the staffing situation in schools. A part-time scheme for teachers was introduced. In addition, schools were given greater flexibility in deciding how best to organize and deploy their teaching resources according to their needs. The MOE has also created more administrative and support posts (e.g., full-time counselors) while streamlining work procedures.

Beginning teachers are being inducted into the profession through a series of talks and enrichment courses prior to leaving school for full-time teaching positions. At the school level, they continue to receive mentoring sessions from experienced teachers. This hand-holding during the first year or so helps to prevent the early exit of freshly trained teachers who are now facing the full realities of teaching in schools.[6] All said, Singapore is perhaps one of the few countries in the world to provide a generous employment package to retain teachers and maintain a high-quality teaching force. The country wants to produce a world-class teacher education so its citizens can lead the country into the next lap of development in the new century. The success of Singapore's attempt at attracting and sustaining the teaching population and providing a quality learning environment is reflected in tables 4.3 and 4.4.

There is no question that Singapore's teachers are accorded professional status and enjoy public recognition. However, teaching in the small city-state is a very demanding job. Besides the need to consistently upgrade professional knowledge

Table 4.3 Total Number of Teaching Staff, 2001–05

	2001	2002	2003	2004	2005
All schools	23,507	24,685	24,914	25,716	26,382
Primary	12,065	12,423	12,925	12,209	12,343
Secondary	9,552	10,246	10,830	11,240	11,495
Pre-university	1,890	2,016	2,059	2,267	2,544

Source: Ministry of Education 2006.

Table 4.4 Ratio of Students to Teaching Staff

	2001	2002	2003	2004	2005
Primary	25.1	24.4	24.9	24.3	23.5
Secondary	19.6	18.9	19.1	19.0	18.5

Source: Ministry of Education 2006.

and skills and nurture young Singaporeans in character development and core values, the teacher today also has to develop a high level of technological literacy. The teacher must be prepared to teach in the classroom and school of the future. The MOE is establishing a new primary school in 2008 to serve as a model for how students can be prepared for a future dominated by technology and information. It will be one of the 15 "schools of the future" the government envisioned in its 2015 Intelligent Nation plan to exploit the latest information and communication technology to transform various sectors. As the country is well on its way to transform into a fully "wired" and "virtual" life and work environment in the near future, the teacher has to incorporate best-of-class technology solutions in nearly every area of the learning environment, including curriculum delivery, school–home–community collaboration, content creation, and assessment.

EXCELLENCE IN TEACHER EDUCATION: THE ROLE OF NIE

NIE is well positioned to support Singapore's education vision of the new millennium. Established in 1991 and positioned as one of NTU's schools and institutes, NIE has more than 50 years of progressive institutional history to fall back on. But it was in the 1990s that NIE finally took off on a trajectory of sustained growth. Its move to the new 17-hectare, S$400-million, purpose-built campus, situated within NTU, enabled it to expand its range of preservice and in-service training programs. Table 4.5 shows the intake figures of trainee teachers since 2000. Note that about 30 percent of the entrants are male. Many developing countries have difficulties recruiting male teachers. In the case of Singapore, concerted efforts, both past and present, at improving the professional status (including compensation packages) of teachers has produced a steady inflow of male teachers. NIE now has set out to achieve two broad targets. First, helmed by its vision of "Towards an Institute of Distinction," it constantly invents and reinvents itself to achieve excellence in teacher training. Second, NIE works toward establishing a strong tripartite relationship with the MOE and the schools.

In response to the nation's need for quality teachers, NIE conducted a comprehensive review of the teacher training curriculum in 2003. It adopted a series of measures or approaches to develop a comprehensive teacher education framework:

- An expert consensus-building approach. This relies on experts in teacher education to reach a consensus on high-quality indicators and to use them to judge the quality of particular teaching preparation programs. One of the key tasks of the review was to articulate what attributes were required of the beginning teachers across the three preservice programs in NIE.[7]
- A research-based approach. The task is to obtain research evidence to arrive at a set of evidence-based postulates or determinants regarding teacher education.

Table 4.5 Intake of Teacher Trainees, 2000–07 (as of August 2007)

Academic year intake	Intakes (in July and January)	Male		Female		Total	
		No.	%	No.	%	No.	%
2007/2008	July 2007	555	29	1,343	71	1,898	100
2006/2007	July 2006 January 2007	686	31	1,504	69	2,190	100
2005/2006	July 2005 January 2006	791	32	1,690	68	2,481	100
2004/2005	July 2004 January 2005	621	34	1,218	66	1,839	100
2003/2004	July 2003 January 2004	599	32	1,303	68	1,902	100
2002/2003	July 2002 January 2003	783	29	1,901	71	2,684	100
2001/2002	July 2001 January 2002	678	28	1,730	72	2,408	100
2000/2001	July 2000	570	28	1,454	72	2,024	100
1999/2000	July 1999 January 2000	616	28	1,617	72	2,233	100
1998/1999	July 1998 January 1999	671	29	1,609	71	2,280	100

Source: National Institute of Education 2006.

An in-depth review of the recent literature on research in teacher education to learn how and why other countries go about preparing their teachers was conducted. This process was useful for decision makers to discover the latest trends, issues, and concerns in teacher education, such as subject knowledge, foundational educational knowledge, teaching practice models, quality control, and assessments.

- A professional-consensus approach. This draws upon the wisdom and best practices of experienced school leaders and teachers in the education system. Major stakeholders (principals, the MOE, faculty, students) were asked about NIE graduates who have gone on to teach in schools to gauge how effective their preparation has been, what further attributes principals and the MOE would like to see in new teachers, and best practices that were promoted in schools.

The overall framework articulates in broad areas the skills and knowledge components that are desired in a beginning teacher, with the underlying core values as the basis of the curriculum. To ensure standards, NIE has an international advisory panel to review holistically NIE's role and functions as well as its strategic thrusts; included in these is the quality of its teacher preparation programs.

External examiners/assessors look at each of the programs. At the academic subject and curriculum studies level, external examiners/assessors have been appointed for each academic discipline. To strengthen NIE's international presence and networking, deans of eight world-class teaching training institutions recently convened at NIE and signed a document that marked the birth of an international alliance.[8]

Apart from preparing new teachers for the schools in Singapore, NIE has an equally important role of keeping the country's 28,000 teachers in the schools and the MOE abreast of the latest changes in classroom teaching and school administration. In today's context, teachers do not just teach within the four walls of the classroom. The teacher is the key to everything we do in education. Teachers must be equipped and supported to carry out their roles and responsibilities effectively in the classroom and beyond. This requires a shift in the teacher's perception of his or her professional role. A teacher must be able to create a learning environment in which experimentation is not stifled, where creative thinking and intellectual inquiry thrive, where change is perceived as a challenge toward a better education. Above all, teachers need to not only prepare their charges to develop and excel academically, but equip them with life skills, values, and attitudes. Singapore's MOE and NIE recognize that teaching is a multifaceted and demanding profession; hence, beginning teachers must be trained to meet the basic level of competency needed for them to function effectively in schools. In addition, there is a need to promote a culture of continuous learning among the serving teachers. Responding to the 100 hours of annual professional development time, which every teacher is entitled to, NIE has developed a comprehensive framework to provide different pathways for teachers to upgrade themselves. In 2004, the Professional Development Continuum Model (PDCM) was introduced. Under the PDCM, professional development for teachers is considered as a continuation of the preservice program. It is based on the philosophy that teachers must pursue learning on a lifelong basis so that they can be relevant to the students.

The PDCM framework provides different pathways for teachers to participate in a whole range of professional development modules. At the end of each module, teachers can choose to be assessed and, in the process, are able to accumulate academic credits. Through a building-block approach, the cumulative number of academic units can permit the teachers to obtain formal certifications such as advanced diplomas, advanced postgraduate diplomas, and master's degrees. The different pathways under the PDCM framework are illustrated in figure 4.1.

NIE's curriculum is effectively translated by close to 400 faculty members and supported by about the same number of administrative support staff. One outstanding feature of the institute's academic staff composition is the presence of academic content colleagues (in the humanities and sciences) among

Figure 4.1 PDCM Framework

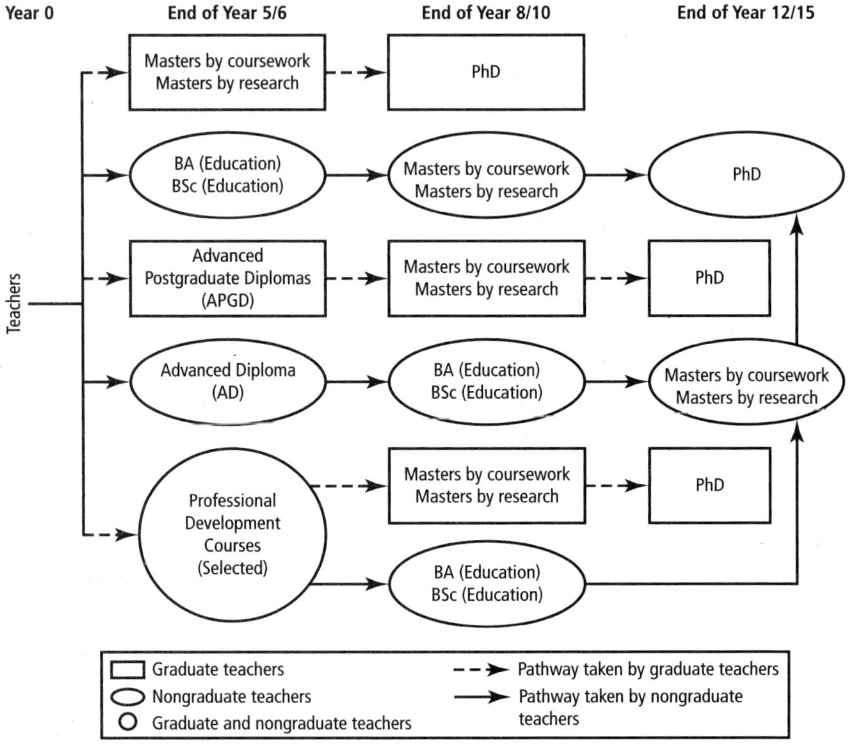

the pedagogues. Over the years (since 1991), this combination of "content" and "pedagogy" staff under one roof has been inextricably synergized into an integrated, all-in-one model of teacher training, in which the student-teacher is able to upgrade his or her content knowledge and link the content with the latest pedagogy approaches. This unique feature is seen by many international observers as a success formula for NIE's remarkable rise as one of the premier teacher-training institutions in the world. To streamline the organizational structure and promote efficiency, NIE in 2000 embarked on a bold move to discard the traditional schools model (such as School of Arts, Science, and so forth) and, in its place, a program-driven matrix structure was adopted. Content and pedagogy staff alike are not compartmentalized and segregated into schools; instead, collectively, they contribute to one or two of the program offices: the Foundation Programs Office and the Graduate Programs and Research Office.

As part of the NTU's set-up, NIE has to focus on academic research as one of its key performance indicators of excellence. Although research in teacher education began in the 1980s, the research culture was not well grounded when NIE began its institutional history in 1991. It took more than a decade of persistent effort to cultivate a research environment. Action-based research in schools was also actively promoted and, in this respect, the support from the MOE was invaluable. Teachers were encouraged to participate in research that has direct impact on the quality of teaching in the classroom. One effective way is to increase the enrollment of teachers in postgraduate programs. NIE ensured that its higher degree programs stayed relevant to the needs of the MOE and schools. Admittedly, it took several years of internationally recognized research by the NIE faculty to convince the MOE in 2002 to approve an unprecedented funding of S$48 million to develop the Centre of Research in Pedagogy and Practice in NIE. Groundbreaking research findings on pedagogical issues in the Singapore classroom are now meticulously scrutinized by the MOE, and, if necessary, new policies or changes will be introduced. Many governments in the developed world would think twice about investing heavily in research and development in education, but for Singapore, it is yet another clear signal of the importance the government places on the provision of quality education to young Singaporeans.

However, despite the significant impetus given to research and the need for NIE academic staff to be prolific in their academic publishing, there is a need to address the issue of a category of staff who are essentially "true-blue" teacher trainers—staff who had years of teaching experience in the school system before becoming academic staff of NIE, but whose strengths are in delivering quality teaching, not academic research. One strategic approach NIE is reviewing is to develop a "teaching track" performance management framework that enables the practitioners to be promoted to full professors. Another issue of concern is the theory-practice linkage within the teacher-training curriculum. While the practicum component of the preservice training requires student teachers to be attached to schools for a period of about 12 weeks, NIE is still mindful of feedback provided by schools that more could be done to customize education theories, such as in classroom management and learning motivation, to the real world of the classroom and school. To ensure that the desired outcomes of teacher training are achieved and that the curriculum stays relevant and responsive to the needs of the schools, longitudinal studies that track the performance of cohorts of beginning teachers are conducted by NIE.

NEW ECONOMY, NEW CHALLENGES FOR NIE

Singapore has successfully made its transition from the Third World to the First. The city-state is seen by the international community as one of the most competitive and open economies. The government actively promoted a brain-gain policy by welcoming talents from all over the world. At the same time, Singaporeans are urged to move out of their comfort zones and market their talents and expertise to the world. The rise of the new economy requires young Singaporeans to see that survival in the 21st century means the acquisition of 21st-century skills. Workplace competencies are now more complex, requiring workers to possess complex problem-solving skills, communication skills, inductive and deductive reasoning skills, creative thinking, and an innovative mind-set. The worker in the new millennium has to be intelligent, technologically savvy, and able to pick out pertinent and relevant knowledge from abundant sources of information. Access to telecommunications and technology has caused shifts in power from nation-states to multinational corporations, public and private economic entities, sociocultural groups, and even individuals. Indeed, informed citizens worldwide are beginning to articulate wider principles, policies, and politics of "global awareness." Central to these efforts is the belief that trade, investment, and technology are not ends in themselves; they are tools for promoting the ideals of equality, democracy, good jobs, a clean environment, and healthy communities.

Increasingly, young Singaporeans, as digital natives in this Digital Age, need the knowledge and capabilities to interact with peoples of various ethnicities and cultural background. They need to be sensitive to the role that culture plays in the behaviors, beliefs, and values of themselves and others. The advent of new communications technology only makes this sensitivity more imperative. Within the virtual worlds of e-mail, chat rooms, virtual classrooms, and even multiplayer gaming environments, individuals from cultures and societies around the globe are interacting with a frequency that was unimaginable even a decade ago. Increasingly also, Singapore's classrooms will have more young foreign students sharing their knowledge and experiences.

These are the new challenges facing education in Singapore, and the leaders in various capacities are proactively responding to these challenges. At NIE, a Learning Sciences Laboratory unit was set up in 2005 to harness advanced technologies into the teaching and learning process. Plans are already in place to carry out research and development (R&D) in interactive digital media (IDM), which has great potential for teaching, learning, and inculcating values in a fun and engaging manner. These R&D activities are aimed at developing useful IDM-based pedagogies, tools, and content to foster students' deep learning. Within the formal curriculum, there are modules and enrichment programs that the student-teachers could enroll in to promote multicultural literacy and global awareness.[9] To work cooperatively with individuals from vastly different backgrounds, student-teachers must appreciate and understand the beliefs and values that drive them. Being culturally literate would enable our young to see the dangers of stereotyping and other biases and remain aware of and sensitive to issues of racism and prejudice.

At the instructional and curriculum level, NIE made provisions for teaching the relatively new skills and understandings that would enhance the student-teachers' capacities to handle the impact of globalization. They would then be able to transfer these skills to their students in schools at certain appropriate points of the school curriculum. Gardner (2004, 253–255) has suggested that these skills and understandings include the following:

- *Understanding of the global system.* The trends of globalization need to be understood by the young people because they are operating in a global community. As digital natives, they are totally comfortable with technology, and yet could be all alone while communicating in a crowded superhighway.
- *Capacity to think analytically and creatively within and outside disciplines.* The Academic Studies modules of the initial training programs in NIE are taught for in-depth disciplinary understanding, focusing on the analysis of principal ideas and approaching them from different perspectives, including pertinent references to other disciplines.
- *Knowledge and ability to deal with people from different cultural backgrounds.* NIE recently launched the Group Endeavors Service Learning initiative, which provides opportunities for student-teachers to participate in local and international projects, especially in developing countries in Asia. This component of the teacher-training curriculum enhances cultural understanding, fosters a sense of tolerance for others, and establishes a closer link between the various ethnic groups in Singapore and between Singaporeans and people in the region.

Finally, NIE places strong emphasis on the training of school leaders—heads of departments, vice principals, principals, and superintendents. This is one area of teacher education and training that tends to elude the attention of policy makers in developing countries. NIE customizes its leadership program to match the changing demands on school leaders. The departmental heads program, known as the New Diploma in Departmental Management, provides an intensive experience that prepares these middle-level management leaders for the new and challenging context of leadership. The 17-week program gears them toward leading change in dynamic and innovative ways. It introduces participants to some important concepts of direct relevance to their jobs: team learning, curriculum innovation, and dynamic learning systems. The participants learn through a diversity of experiences (such as from their peers and from visits to schools to see models of good practice) designed to generate new knowledge. They also have the opportunity to tailor their own training program by selecting modules (by themselves or with their principal's input) that are of direct use to them.

The task of the school principal has shifted from one who manages to one who innovates. He or she leads through innovative actions and decisions in entrepreneurial leadership, knowledge management, global leadership, ethical leadership, and social responsibility. NIE's state-of-the-art school leadership program, known as the Leaders in Education program, is designed for selected principals-to-be, and it prepares them for leadership in schools. The six-month program is future oriented, with an emphasis on leadership capability in a dynamic and complex context. Through a process of learning in diverse contexts, including the authentic workplace of the school and international locations, the learning platform addresses a range of issues that are seen as critical to the success of future leadership. They include designing and managing learning school organizations that can sustain a competitive advantage in a fast-changing and turbulent environment, strategic choice and marketing, innovative communication and information technology, designing an integrative and innovative curriculum to achieve excellence in teaching and learning, and building human and intellectual capital.

SOME LESSONS FROM THE SINGAPORE EXPERIENCE

In the 1960s and 1970s, Singapore leaders, too, grappled with the task of creating a teacher education system that could solve the more serious educational issues during this period, such as high educational wastage, unequal educational performance by the races within Singapore society, and the concern regarding some minority ethnic groups being marginalized in the rapidly developing country. As elaborated in other chapters of this book, the Singapore government assumed full control of steering the directions of education change by implementing a slew of policies, some deemed to be unpopular and draconic. The curriculum, including textbook writing and publication, with its emphasis on English literacy and bilingualism, was standardized and strictly under the purview of the MOE. Centralized control in all aspects of education at this time was crucial, however, because it allowed the government to introduce changes quickly and monitor outcomes effectively.

Unlike the situation in many developing countries, Singapore put strong emphasis on teacher education based on the premise that if teacher salaries were high enough and working conditions good enough, the education system would have less trouble finding enough teachers of high quality. The MOE recognizes that teaching is a multifaceted and demanding profession, particularly for the beginning or novice teacher. One major lead-in measure to induct new teachers is off-loading one-fifth of the normal responsibility load in their first year in schools. This policy came into effect in January 2000. The released time is then spent on classroom observations of experienced teachers and on-the-job training to enable them to settle in. Continual upgrading of serving teachers is also a key priority. Every teacher is expected to undergo at least 100 hours of professional training, the expenses of which are fully covered by government funding. Teachers are also given approved study leave (with either half- or full-monthly pay, depending on the years of service) to gain new knowledge and skills through academic pursuits. In short, the MOE continues to look into ways to enhance the status and image of the teaching profession. These include giving more public recognition to outstanding teachers and holding official presentation ceremonies for recipients of teaching scholarships and awards.

Training of teachers was also centralized under one institution, and this framework ensured some uniformity of standards at the preservice and inservice levels (at least, in terms of content knowledge and pedagogical skill mastery) in all novice and experienced teachers. In this respect, another critical factor for Singapore's success in the provision of quality teacher education is the creation of a well-planned, well-staffed teacher-training institute, as in the case of NIE. The institute itself is still evolving and continuously building on its institutional strengths to provide the country with its articulate, knowledgeable, and creative teachers.

How does one explain the seemingly "seamless" flow of decisions and actions among NIE, the MOE, and the schools? Unlike some developing countries, where bureaucratic red tape and overly protective jurisdictions imposed by government departments work against each other, NIE, the MOE, and the schools gradually metamorphosed into an organic operational network, with the primary, overarching objective of planning, teaching, and nurturing the future leaders of Singapore. This network operates on a formal and informal platform of professional sharing of knowledge, problems, and issues; policies; resources; and needs. Cloning of such an institutional working relationship in other cultural and political contexts may not result in the same effectiveness and positive outcome as happened in Singapore's case.[10] Besides the key organizations (such as the MOE and NIE), there is an entire government machinery helping in myriads of ways.

In the final analysis, the key lesson to be learned from an understanding of Singapore's planning and development of its teacher education and training system is that education and teacher education must change in tandem whenever the need arises. But many education ministries and teacher education institutions in developing countries may not be up to the task, mostly because of their resistance to change. For Singapore, the major stakeholders—the MOE, NIE, and the schools—perceived that the key issue of globalization versus diversity, the need for high-quality preservice programs, and well-managed and supported integration of new teachers into the teaching force and ongoing professional development for that workforce will lead to two major factors that will impinge on the teaching profession in the future: the need for the teacher to become a consistent, reflective practitioner and the need to use rapidly developing technologies, both information and communication technology and other learning technologies, in an increasingly effective manner to promote high-quality learning for all students.

Understandably, educational systems, especially those that have existed for many decades in developing countries, are inherently conservative institutions, and change is often resisted. But globalization will create inevitable changes. For teacher education and training in Singapore, remaining unchanged will lead to degeneration. NIE will continue to work closely with the MOE to meet its demand for quality teacher training, to refine existing practices, and to adopt best practices and models that can meet different needs arising from the changes in the national and global landscape. The strategy is to keep what is useful from the past, integrate it with the newness of the present, and be ready for the future. And the whole cycle repeats.

NOTES

1. In the final year of training, male teachers were paid S$168 plus a variable allowance of S$42–S$210 per month, and female teachers were paid S$160 plus a variable allowance of S$40–$200 per month.

2. The Institute of Education (IE) and the College of Physical Education (CPE) Development Committee was formed in August 1989 to examine two key issues in teacher training in the 1990s: the need to merge the IE and the CPE, and the upgrading of primary teacher education. Its report was titled *Teacher Training in the 1990s: Issues and Strategies.*

3. The age profile of teachers is changing rapidly as senior teachers (recruited during the 1960s and 1970s) retire from the service and young teachers join the service. By 2010, about 25 percent of the present teaching workforce will have retired or reached retirement age. The median age of teachers has declined from 43 years in 1996 to 38 years in 2000 and 33 years in 2005. Thus, training is integral to the development of a quality teaching service. To ensure a smooth transition from the older to a younger generation of teachers, we need to facilitate the imparting of wisdom, values, and experiences. Several measures were introduced to safeguard against this loss of desirable values and accumulated experience of the senior teachers when they retire. Besides inviting retired teachers to continue as "relief teachers," the MOE introduced an innovative scheme known as the Adjunct Teacher Programme in 2000. Adjunct teachers can be appointed either on contract or on more flexible working arrangements, to ensure that they still have time to pursue numerous other activities. There are currently more than 500 adjunct teachers engaged by schools, and about 60 percent of them are retirees.

4. A groundbreaking system of assessing the quality of Singapore's teachers was introduced in 2005. Known as the Enhanced Performance Management System, it is a competency-based model that encapsulates the knowledge, skills, and professional characteristics appropriate for each of the three fields of excellence. The system involves regular coaching and feedback between teachers and their reporting officers.

5. Teachers in aided or mission schools in Singapore also receive the same working benefits and promotion prospects as do their counterparts in the mainstream government schools. They are either MOE employees or "aided staff," that is, employees of the aided or mission school. Apart from their religious affinities, aided schools operate under the same governance framework as the government schools.

6. Attrition rate of teachers is a serious problem in many developing countries and even in industrial nations like the United States. In the United States, for example, it could be argued that much of this attrition is due to novice teachers being given the most difficult classes and left very much on their own to teach and manage the unruly students. See Kelly (2004) and Riggs and Sandlin (2007).

7. The three different preservice programs offered by NIE are the one-year postgraduate diploma in education, the two-year diploma in education, and the four-year BA/BSc (education).

8. The event took place on August 21, 2007. The international colleges involved are University of Aarhus, Denmark; Beijing Normal University, People's Republic of China; University of London, United Kingdom; University of Melbourne, Australia; Seoul National University, Korea; University of Toronto, Canada; University of Wisconsin, United States; and National Institute of Education, Singapore. The alliance aims to hold constant dialogues on teacher education and exchanges of educational research information.

9. Defined simply, multicultural literacy is the ability to understand and appreciate the similarities and differences between the customs, values, and beliefs of one's own culture and the cultures of others.

10. The tripartism model has its roots in the 1960s, when then–Prime Minister Lee Kuan Yew had to struggle against a militant left to establish industrial peace so that foreign investment would flow in and jobs be created. Hence, the critical link between the government and the unions was established. Cabinet ministers were appointed to head the unions, while unionists were invited to sit on statutory boards so they could learn to understand and appreciate the problems the government faced.

REFERENCES

Department of Statistics. Various years. *Yearbook of Statistics.* Singapore: Department of Statistics.

Gardner, Howard. 2004. "How Education Changes." In *Globalization: Culture and Education in the New Millennium,* ed. Marcelo M. Suarez-Orozco and Desiree Baolian Qin-Hilliard. Berkeley: University of California Press.

IE (Institute of Education) and CPE (College of Physical Education) Development Committee. 1990. *Teacher Training in the 1990s: Issues and Strategies.* Singapore: IE and CPE Development Committee.

Kelly, L. M. 2004. "Why Induction Matters." *Journal of Teacher Education* 55: 438–448.

Lee, Kuan Yew. 1966. *New Bearings in our Education System.* Singapore: Government Printing Office.

Lun, C. Y., and W. C. Chan. 1983. "A Brief Survey of Teacher Education in Singapore." In *Experience: The First Ten Years,* ed. C. Y. Lun. Singapore: Institute of Education.

Ministry of Education. 2006. *Education Statistics Digest.* Singapore: Ministry of Education.

National Institute of Education. 2006. *Enrolment Statistics 1997–2005.* Unpublished sources.

Riggs, Iris, and Ruth Sandlin. 2007. "Workplace Contexts of New Teachers: An American Tradition of Paying One's Dues." In *Handbook of Teacher Education,* ed. T. Townsend and R. Bates, 317–330. Netherlands: Springer.

Straits Times. April 17, 1962.

Straits Times. January 28, 1968.

Straits Times. March 21, 1996.

CHAPTER 5

Vocational Technical Education and Economic Development—The Singapore Experience

LAW Song Seng

INTRODUCTION

Policy makers, administrators, and educators in vocational technical education (VTE) all agree that VTE plays a crucial role in the social and economic development of a nation. In Singapore, VTE refers to a vocationally oriented technical education aimed at equipping graduates with the necessary occupational skills and standards for the industry and economy. The focus is to train technicians and skilled personnel. It is not the basic vocational education normally offered in schools. The target student groups are more diverse. The image, standards, and values remain elusive. Often viewed negatively by society, VTE is the weakest link in the total education system in many countries. Parents today continue to cherish the hope and aspiration that their children will make it to university. This intense desire to pursue a university degree generates unrealistic expectations among parents and adds pressure in schools. The consequence is a prejudice against and less-than-positive image of VTE as well as all its negative associations with those who are less academically inclined. Yet, the greatest gaps in human resource development are in vocational education and technical skills.

Shaped by the needs of the changing economy and local community, the challenges and opportunities of VTE are unique. What, for example, makes an effective and responsive VTE system? What options are available to accommodate the needs of different social, economic, and cultural conditions? Is the VTE system responding to the appropriate level of and demand for skilled manpower in the economy? How is it positioned within the national education and training system? Is it meeting the training needs of school leavers and working adults? How well is VTE accepted by school leavers, parents, industry, and society? What is its public image? What are the policy, funding, and educational issues? How can the goals and objectives be translated into reality? How do we measure the results?

These are some of the basic questions we ask as we search for the best VTE system to serve our economy, society, and the community. The fact is that there is no one "ideal" education and training system that will suit the needs of all countries. The so-called "best" system is often one shaped by the history, social motivation, and economic needs of the local community. There should be a clear mission and vision in articulating the role of VTE within the national education and training system. The greatest challenge for VTE today is remaining true to its mission in staying focused in the area of vocational and technical skills. The real tests of success of VTE are the employability of the graduates, personal development, opportunities for further education and career development, public acceptance, and image. Ultimately, the effectiveness and responsiveness of a VTE system will be measured by its impact on the social and economic development of the nation.

In this respect, the Singapore government believes in and has invested heavily in education and training, not only in the universities and polytechnics, but also in vocational and technical education under the Institute of Technical Education (ITE). The Singapore experience will be presented in two parts. Part I traces the different phases of Singapore's economic development and corresponding VTE strategies since independence in 1965. Part II describes the modern history of the ITE since its establishment in 1992—what it is today and its unique mission, features, and transformation as a world-class educational institution focusing on vocational technical education.

OVERVIEW OF SINGAPORE

But first, an overview of Singapore. Founded as a British colony in 1819 and centrally located in Southeast Asia, as shown in figure 5.1, Singapore achieved independence as a nation in 1965. A multiracial society of 4.35 million people living on a small island of 700 square kilometers, Singapore today is a modern city-state and global center for industry, business, finance, and communications. Major industries are petrochemicals, pharmaceuticals, high-end manufacturing, tourism, and services. Key trading partners include Malaysia, the United States, China, the European Union, Hong Kong (China), and Japan. Per capita gross national income was US$26,700 in 2005. As a young nation with limited natural resources, one of Singapore's highest priorities has been education, training, and human capital development.

Figure 5.1 Location of Singapore

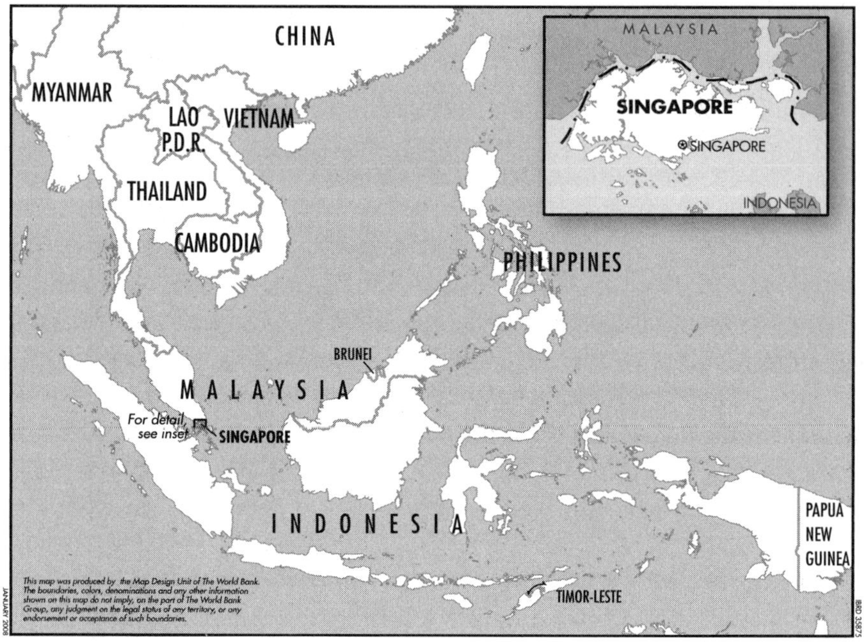

Source: World Bank.

PART I: ECONOMIC DEVELOPMENT AND VTE STRATEGIES

PHASES OF SINGAPORE'S ECONOMIC DEVELOPMENT

In the early years of independence, it became clear that the traditional trading, commerce, and service sectors alone could not provide sufficient jobs for the number of school leavers in a growing population. The overall strategic plan of the Singapore government then was to diversify and accelerate economic growth through industrialization. During this early phase of economic development, from the 1960s to 1970s, the educational priority was to provide and expand primary and secondary education, including technical education and training, to lay the necessary foundation for the acquisition of basic vocational and technical skills. It was only from the 1980s onward that an increasing emphasis was placed on improving the level of skills and quality of the education and training system, including the schools, universities, polytechnics, and VTE.

The economic development of Singapore may be characterized in three phases, as shown in figure 5.2. A factor-driven economy in the 1960s and 1970s, involving intensive labor, progressed to a capital-intensive investment-driven economy in the 1980s and 1990s, and then to the innovation-driven economy of the 2000s, powered by the needs of knowledge-intensive industries. Through these three phases, Singapore also evolved from an early industrialization economy to

Figure 5.2 Phases of Singapore's Development

a newly industrialized economy and to the globalized and diversified economy it is today. In tandem with the changing economic landscape, the VTE system evolved in response to the changing manpower needs. The education and training system ensured that graduates from the various educational institutions had the necessary knowledge and skills for the many new jobs that were created in a rapidly growing economy.

Labor-Intensive Economy (1960s–1970s). In the early days of industrialization after Singapore's independence, the main challenge was to create enough jobs. The high unemployment situation was compounded by the sudden decision of the British government to pull out its naval bases in Singapore. The economic strategy then shifted in 1968 from one of import substitution to one of rapid industrialization by attracting foreign investment for export-oriented and labor-intensive manufacturing. From the education and training perspective, the immediate task was to ensure that the workforce had the basic vocational and technical skills to support the labor-intensive manufacturing activities such as ship repair, turning and fitting, sheetmetal working, plumbing, and radio and TV maintenance and repair.

The priority in the 1960s was to expand the educational system, especially primary and secondary education. The first vocational institute, the Singapore Vocational Institute (SVI), was established within the school system in 1964. With the increasing pace of industrialization, there was growing concern about how best to expedite and expand VTE to meet the technical and skilled manpower needs of new emerging industries. The mainstream of education remained largely academic. In 1968, 84 percent of students in schools were enrolled in the academic stream, with only 8 percent in the technical stream, 7 percent in the vocational stream, and 1 percent in the commercial stream (Law 1984).

As a result, the Technical Education Department (TED) was established within the Ministry of Education in 1968 to oversee the development of technical secondary education, industrial training, and technical teacher training. The secondary vocational schools were phased out in favor of vocational institutes. The apprenticeship schemes were transferred from the Ministry of Labor to the TED in 1969. By 1972, there were nine vocational institutes, and the number of graduates increased 10-fold from 324 in 1968 to more than 4,000 (Law 1984).

By 1973, the TED had developed a training infrastructure of sufficient strength for the next major phase of its development. Thus, the first Industrial Training Board (ITB) was created in 1973 to centralize, coordinate, and intensify industrial training. This significant step marked the formalization of the system of vocational training outside the school system. As a statutory board, ITB was empowered with greater autonomy and flexibility to respond to the challenges in meeting the technical manpower needs of a rapidly expanding economy.

Even at this early phase of development, it was abundantly clear that to remain market-relevant and responsive, there must be strong links and collaboration between the VTE system and industry. There were three important aspects. The first was in the area of curriculum development. Delivery of theory and knowledge in VTE in the classroom was not sufficient. To equip graduates with the required competencies for the job markets, the skills standards for the various occupations needed to be developed in partnership with employers and industry. This was done by establishing an extensive system of training advisory committees with industrywide participation and supported by a rigorous curriculum development process. The second aspect was tapping into the wealth of technology and capabilities of major players in industry to supplement training that was otherwise too costly or impractical to replicate in vocational institutions for areas such as printing, ship repairing, and aircraft maintenance. Consequently, various industry-based training schemes were developed and administered by ITB so that companies were able to support apprenticeships and on-the-job training that directly responded to their manpower needs. The third aspect of industry partnership was the exchange of technology and sharing of learning resources through the signing of memoranda of understanding (MOUs). These MOUs—with partners such as Mitsubishi Electric Asia, Robert Bosch (SEA), Siemens, IBM, Cisco System, and Sun Microsystems—helped teaching staff to keep abreast of technological developments in industry and equipped students with up-to-date knowledge and skills. Today, this tradition of a strong culture of collaboration with industry partners continues to be an integral part of the ITE system.

In line with the changing needs of the economy, a new system of skills certification, the National Trade Certificate (NTC), was introduced to meet the different levels of skills and standards required by industry, starting with the NTC-3 semiskilled level of certification. A wide range of courses was introduced in areas such as electrical, electronics, metal working, mechanical engineering, and heavy-duty diesel and motor vehicle mechanics. The unique feature of this system is that the same competency standards were used for the full-time vocational training courses and the public trade testing system for working adults. In the early 1970s, another government agency, the Economic Development Board (EDB), whose mission was to promote foreign investment in Singapore, also played a significant role in strengthening the industrial training system. By partnering with multinational corporations (MNCs) such as Tata of India, Rollei of Germany, and Philips of Holland, the EDB established joint government training centers that helped to enlarge the pool of trained technical manpower. In the process, new overseas approaches and practices were infused into the local training system.

Capital-Intensive Economy (1980s–1990s). In 1979, the government embarked on a major restructuring of the economy toward higher-value-added, high-technology, and more capital-intensive industries. The restructuring was driven by a decline in the domestic labor supply, increasing competition from resource-abundant neighboring countries, and rising trade protectionism from the industrial countries. The new focus was the development of new industries such as petrochemicals; biotechnology; and information technology as well as manufacturing services in testing, financing, warehousing, and purchasing. To stay competitive through higher productivity, mechanization, automation, and computerization of the industries were promoted. Once again, the education and training system was called upon to respond to the manpower needs of more capital-intensive industries.

In the area of VTE, a new stage was set for the establishment of the Vocational and Industrial Training Board (VITB) by amalgamating ITB and another existing board, the Adult Education Board (AEB), in 1979. AEB was established in 1960 to meet the educational needs of working adults, including general education and some basic vocational training. With increasing educational and training opportunities, it became apparent that the domains of AEB and ITB were complementary components of the same system of training for school leavers and working adults. With the formation of VITB, efforts were directed toward expanding the training system, developing new programs, and improving the quality of vocational training. In particular, the higher NTC-2 skilled level of certification was extended to include electrical, electronics, precision engineering, and automotive technology. A new Certificate in Business Studies (CBS) was introduced in 1981. For the first time, a Centre of Vocational Training was set up within VITB to develop professional capability in areas such as curriculum development, training of trainers, and instructional media development. These were important areas of functional expertise necessary to develop and support a quality vocational training system.

Economic restructuring had a direct impact on the capability of the existing workforce. What was expected of the workforce in terms of knowledge, education, and skills before was no longer adequate. National efforts were therefore directed toward developing a comprehensive Continuing Education and Training (CET) system to facilitate upgrading and reskilling of the workforce, especially those with lower education and skills. So, between 1983 and 1987, three national CET programs were launched: the Basic Education for Skills Training (BEST), Work

Improvement through Secondary Education (WISE), and Modular Skills Training (MOST). Focusing on English language and mathematics, BEST and WISE had benefited a quarter million working adults by helping them to acquire a primary (BEST) or secondary (WISE) education. For ease of access, the classes were conducted through an extensive network of vocational institutes, schools, companies, union centers, and Ministry of Defence centers. MOST, on the other hand, provided a system of training for working adults to upgrade and acquire technical skills qualification on a modular basis. In 1990, the industrial training system was further strengthened with the introduction of a New Apprentice System, patterned after the well-known Dual System of Apprenticeship in Germany.

In 1991, the government published a new economic plan, charting the next phase of Singapore's development. The goal was to turn Singapore into a first-league developed nation within the next 30 to 40 years. The new direction was focused on building the manufacturing and service sectors as the twin engines of economic growth. Companies were encouraged to diversify, upgrade, and develop into strong export-oriented companies and to invest in the regional economies. From the educational perspective, the stage was set for a critical review of the postsecondary education system, including the universities, polytechnics, and VITB, to ensure the availability of well-trained and qualified manpower in the high-technology, knowledge-intensive, and service industry sectors.

So, in the same year, a review of school education and vocational training resulted in a crucial decision by the Ministry of Education to adopt a new policy of a minimum of 10 years of basic general education for all pupils in the school system. It became clear that to meet the skilled manpower needs of Singapore's future economic development, a primary school education was no longer sufficient for those who wished to pursue VTE. Employers needed vocational graduates who have had a secondary education and higher-level NTC-2 skills to respond and adapt to the dynamic changes in the global economy. As the chairman of VITB and ITE from 1981 to 1993, Dr. Tay Eng Soon played a pivotal role in the transformation of Singapore's technical education and the massive expansion of the ITE. The review was a turning point for the establishment of the ITE as a postsecondary educational institution in 1992. (The education system in Singapore is based on a 6-4-2 structure, that is, six years of primary, four years of secondary, and two years of pre-university education. A postsecondary education in ITE actually means the last two years of a high school or upper-secondary education in many other countries.) ITE replaced the former VITB. It was an example of the forces driving change in the schools and the rising expectations of industry and society. For ITE, it meant new opportunities for making a major impact in transforming and building a world-class postsecondary education in VTE.

Among the postsecondary educational institutions in Singapore are the polytechnics. Patterned after the earlier British model, they are better known for their career- and practice-oriented education in preparing graduates for middle-level professions and management. But, unlike some countries that have phased out or upgraded their polytechnics into universities, the Singapore government chose to retain the polytechnics as valuable institutions playing a critical role in the economy and educational system. In fact, the number of polytechnics more than doubled from two in 1990 to five in 2002.

Knowledge-Intensive Economy (2000s). Moving forward into the 2000s, Singapore saw the increasing need to develop into a globalized, entrepreneurial, and diversified economy. While Singapore continued to strengthen the higher-end manufacturing activities, there was a clearer recognition of the importance of the service sector as an engine of economic growth. Concerted plans were formulated to attract and nurture new growth sectors such as the biomedical sciences, information and communication technology, integrated resorts, and high-value engineering. The response in the educational sphere has been to position Singapore as an education hub by attracting good foreign students and internationally renowned institutions to Singapore. Local institutions will continue to seek quality and excellence in developing a first-class education at all levels. This will also indirectly help to enlarge the talent pool to sustain Singapore's continuing growth and development.

Meanwhile, the ITE in Singapore was well on its journey in transforming itself into a world-class educational institution by 2005. Its mission focus and consistent use of five-year strategic plans has created a unique brand of an ITE college education for a quarter of the school cohort in Singapore. Two such plans were successfully completed over a 10-year period from 1995 to 2005. The first, *ITE 2000 Plan* (1995–1999), was aimed at positioning ITE as an established postsecondary education institution. The vision of the second plan, the *ITE Breakthrough* (2000–2004), was to build ITE into a world-class technical education institution. Under the third and current five-year plan, the *ITE Advantage* (2005–2009), the vision is to be a global leader in technical education (Law 2005).

ITE has developed a unique and highly successful system of VTE that is attractive to 25 percent of the school cohort today. However, given the natural aspiration for a university education and ever-increasing emphasis on higher-knowledge-based industries, what are the prospects of ITE maintaining its unique attractiveness and leading position in VTE? The response depends on economic, social, and political factors. It is true that the types, proportions, and levels of manpower needs will vary according to the changing economy. Parents and school leavers will always aspire to the prestige of a university degree. This is not new. However, education systems are also shaped by the tough political decisions that have to be made in ensuring sufficient educational opportunities for all, but also maintaining quality and standards at all levels of education.

Surprisingly, the lower 25 percent of a cohort of students who are less academically inclined and who need and can benefit from VTE has not changed significantly over the years. The VTE system itself has to change and respond to changing economic manpower needs, as was the experience in the restructuring of the former VITB to the present-day ITE. But, the current educational system has matured over the years, with about 90 percent of students already achieving a post-secondary education in ITE (25 percent), polytechnic (40 percent), and university (25 percent). In the context of the Singapore educational system, progression paths already exist for graduates who have the potential to upgrade from the ITE to the polytechnic and university. Many polytechnic graduates upgrade to a degree in overseas universities. All economies, including the developing and developed, will always need people with vocational technical skills. To simply respond politically with more places at the polytechnic or university without due consideration for the quality of students and standards of education would only damage the value and credibility of the educational system. At the lower end of the education system, there will always be a place for an ITE college education. The important thing is not so much the proportion, which I believe will not vary significantly in the future, but that all school leavers have the opportunities to develop their potential to the highest level, including those who need and can benefit from VTE.

PART II: THE JOURNEY OF TRANSFORMATION

What I have presented so far represents the earlier years of evolution in VTE in parallel with Singapore's economic development. Part II represents the modern history of VTE: the transformation of ITE into a world-class postsecondary educational institution since its establishment in 1992. The first educational institution to win the prestigious Singapore Quality Award (SQA) in 2005, ITE has achieved organizational excellence in an academic environment. The SQA, modeled after the American Malcolm Baldrige and the European and Australian Quality Awards, is the national benchmark for "World-Class Business Excellence" for both public and private sector organizations in Singapore. Organizations are assessed in seven areas: leadership, people, planning, information, processes, customers, and results. Many innovative and pioneering initiatives have been implemented in the journey of transformation. As a postsecondary institution, ITE has effectively rebuilt and transformed its former "vocational institutes" into top-line "educational colleges." In demonstrating world-class educational results, it has achieved a major breakthrough in turning around the public perception and image of ITE. Today, its unique brand of an ITE college education is recognized locally and internationally for its relevance, quality, and values in a global economy.

So, what is ITE and what is so unique about its mission and challenges? ITE is a government-funded postsecondary institution focusing on vocational technical education. It is not a university or a polytechnic. Focusing on career-based VTE, its goal is to train technicians and skilled personnel for jobs and careers in the major sectors of the economy. Its uniqueness is that despite the more difficult challenges in VTE, it has built a responsive world-class system of VTE in time for the future.

ITE today is well positioned among the postsecondary educational institutions in Singapore, as shown in figure 5.3. An integral part of the total national education system, its mission is "to create opportunities for school leavers and adult learners to acquire skills, knowledge and values for lifelong learning." There are clear demarcations with respect to the missions of the university, polytechnic, and ITE. ITE's mandate is to provide an attractive pathway for those who do not progress to the junior colleges or polytechnics. As a matter of policy, all students receive at least 10 years of general education in schools, consisting of 6 years of primary education and 4 or 5 years of secondary education.

Only the first six years of primary education are compulsory by law. Starting at primary four, students are streamed according to their academic abilities, based on examinations in the English language, a second language, and mathematics.

Figure 5.3 ITE as a Postsecondary Institution

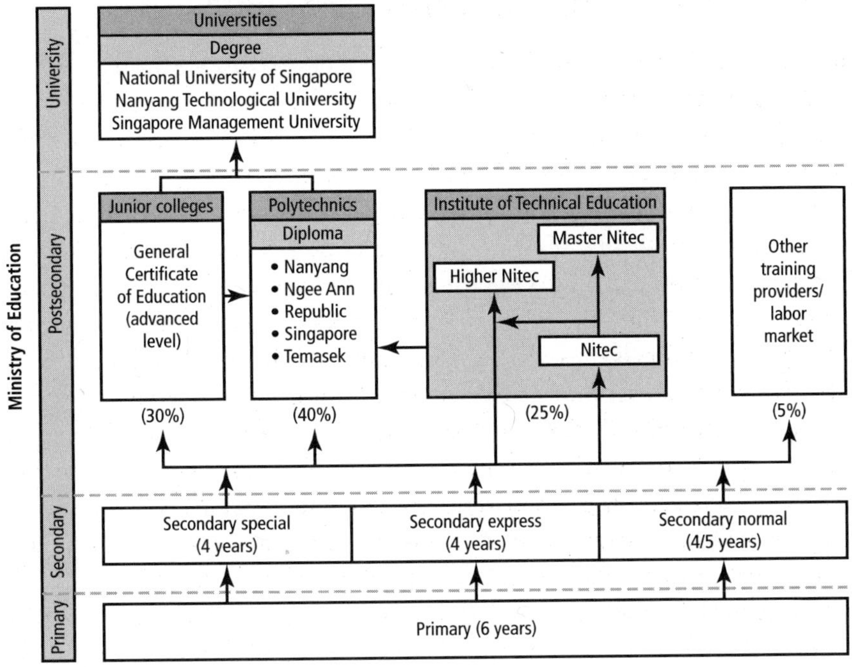

Source: Institute of Technical Education.

The objective is to allow for a differentiated curriculum and pace so that students can better cope with their studies. At the secondary level, students are streamed into the Special, Express, and Normal courses. The Normal (technical) course caters to students who are more technically inclined, while the Normal (academic) course offers an academic-based curriculum for students who need five years to complete the O-level curriculum. Depending largely on their academic achievements, about 95 percent of a secondary student cohort would progress to the junior colleges, polytechnics, or colleges of ITE. Today, about 30 percent of each cohort enters the junior colleges, which provide an academic high school education in preparation for a university education. The next 40 percent of school leavers enter the polytechnics for a wide range of practice-oriented three-year diploma courses in preparation for middle-level professions and management. Essentially, the difference between the ITE and polytechnic courses is in the extent of practical skills. ITE courses are more hands-on, with a 60–70 percent competency-based curriculum. Polytechnics courses are on average 50 percent practical. In terms of jobs, ITE graduates would be recruited at the technician level and for their competencies in producing, installing, or maintaining operating equipment and systems. Polytechnic graduates, on the other hand, will be given higher responsibility and supervisory roles in industry.

The 25 percent of a school cohort with the lower academic abilities are oriented toward VTE in ITE colleges. With the differentiated curriculum, these students take fewer academic subjects such as English language and mathematics in school. On the other hand, they all take computer applications and are offered other vocationally oriented electives such as elements of office administration, art and design, and technical studies. For these students, ITE provides an alternative pathway for a postsecondary education with good opportunities for employment and progression to higher levels of education. While it is true that school leavers who are eligible for the junior colleges or polytechnics will normally apply to these institutions, it cannot be taken for granted that those who do not will automatically take up training in ITE. It is an opportunity they have to consider against enrolling in a private school or seeking direct employment with a secondary education.

ITE's courses are mainly full-time, institutional based, and conducted under the "One ITE, Three Colleges" system of governance. With a range of 40 different courses, full-time student enrollment was about 25,000 in 2007. About 30,000 working adults take part-time CET courses in ITE every year. There are two basic levels of qualifications under the National ITE Certificate (Nitec) system of certification. Depending on their academic achievements in schools, students may enroll at the Nitec or Higher Nitec mainly two-year courses in engineering, business and services, information communication technology, and applied and health sciences. As a total national education system, there is formal articulation for progression from ITE to the polytechnic and from the polytechnic to the university based on merit performance. As the natural aspiration of school leavers and their parents is a university degree, the challenge is in managing expectations and maintaining high standards at all levels while responding to the diverse interests, aptitudes, and needs of school leavers.

UNIQUE FEATURES OF ITE

What are the unique features of ITE's system of vocational technical education? One unique feature, as shown in figure 5.4, is the "One ITE, Three Colleges" system of governance. Under this initiative to build a more responsive VTE system, the overall plan was to regroup existing smaller campuses into three megaregional campuses, renamed "ITE colleges." Under this system, the ITE headquarters continues to oversee the policy formulation and common functional areas of interest such as curriculum development, student intake, examinations, quality assurance, and consistency of standards throughout the colleges. The economy of scale has helped to achieve synergy and resource savings through greater collaborations, and yet promotes competition among the colleges. At the same time, each college, built for a full-time student enrollment of 7,200 and headed by a principal, has more autonomy to grow and specialize in niche areas, thus adding choices and diversity to the programs. The first regional campus, the ITE College East, was built

Figure 5.4 "One ITE, Three Colleges" System

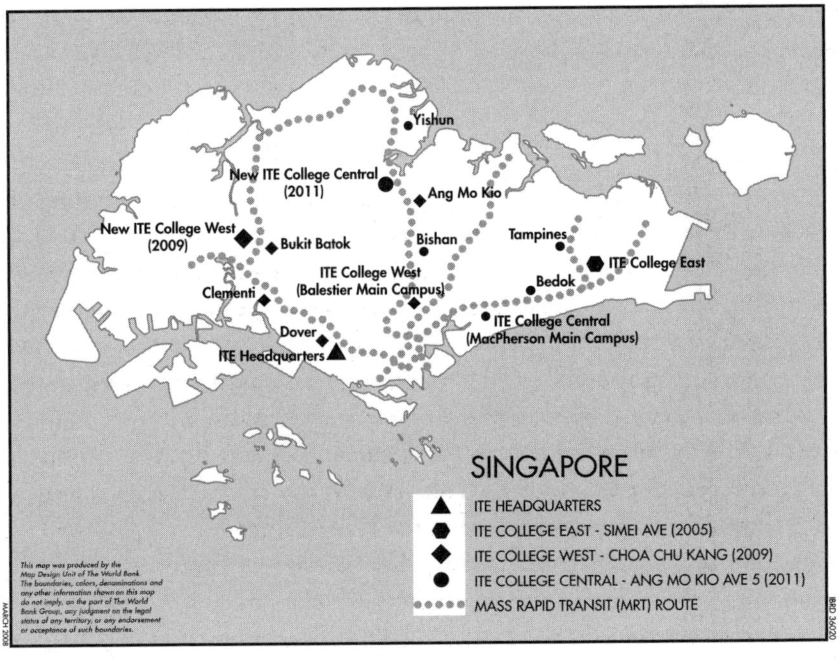

Source: Institute of Technical Education and World Bank.

Figure 5.5 "Hands-on, Minds-on and Hearts-on" Education

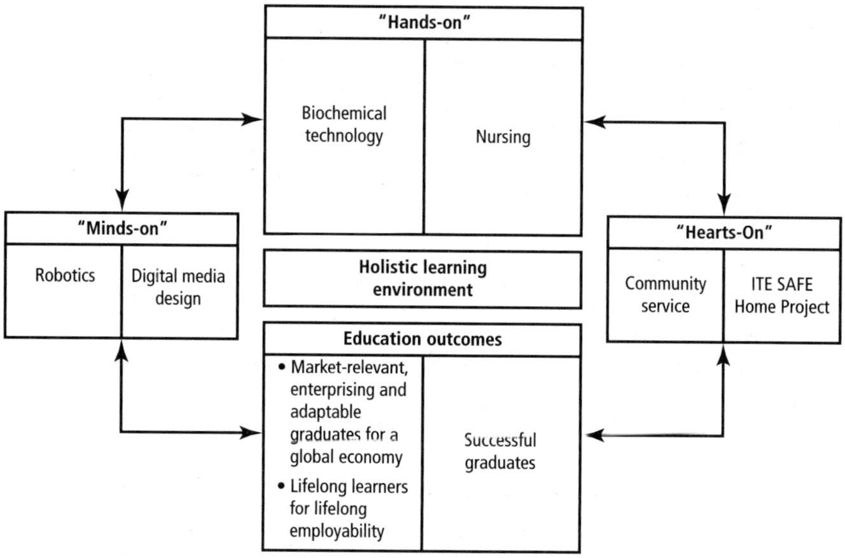

Source: Institute of Technical Education.

in 2005. The remaining two, ITE College West and ITE College Central, will be completed by 2009 and 2011, respectively.

Another feature is the unique brand of an ITE college education called "Hands-on, Minds-on and Hearts-on," illustrated in figure 5.5. This is a holistic college education that has provided motivation, assisted student learning, and nurtured well-rounded graduates who are ready to take on the challenges of the global economy. The "Hands-on" training ensures that the students acquire a strong foundation in technical skills. "Minds-on" learning develops independent thinking and flexible practitioners who are able to cope with changes. And "Hearts-on" learning develops the complete person, with passion for what they do and confidence and care for the community and society. These attributes underpin a comprehensive education in which students integrate theory with practice through coursework, projects, industry partnerships, community service, and global education. The intent is to produce graduates who are market relevant, enterprising, and adaptable as lifelong learners in a global economy.

Two key elements define the relevance and quality of ITE's programs and, hence, the quality of its graduates. The first is the curriculum model representing the contents—the "what" to be delivered—as shown in figure 5.6. ITE's courses are built on skills competencies and standards. As hands-on courses, typically, 70 percent of curriculum time is practical and 30 percent theory. To ensure a strong foundation in technical skills and high employability, 80 percent of the

Figure 5.6 Practice-Oriented Curriculum Model

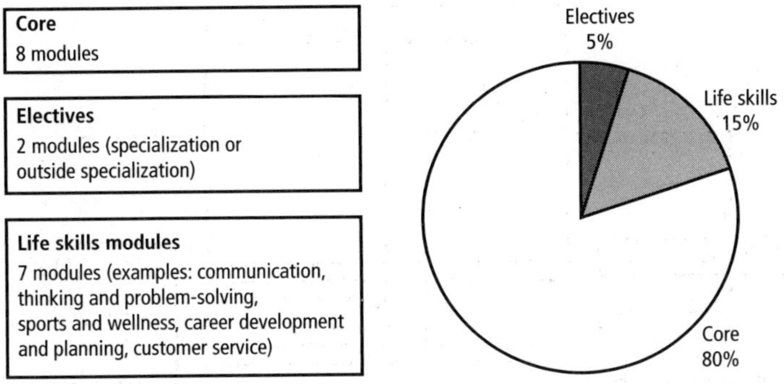

The curriculum of a typical course comprises 70% practical training and 30% theoretical lessons

Source: Institute of Technical Education.

curriculum time is devoted to core modules, which define the occupational areas in which the graduates will seek employment. In view of its importance, the life skills module is compulsory for all students. Taking up 15 percent of the total curriculum time, the life skills module ensures that students also acquire the skills of communications, teamwork, thinking and problem solving, sports and wellness, career development and planning, and customer service. In this way, students will be better equipped as lifelong learners and remain adaptable in the global job market.

The second key element is pedagogy, the "how" part of teaching and learning. The underlying objective in ITE's pedagogic model, as shown in figure 5.7, is to develop "thinking doers," graduates who can apply what they have learned into

Figure 5.7 Process-Oriented Pedagogic Model

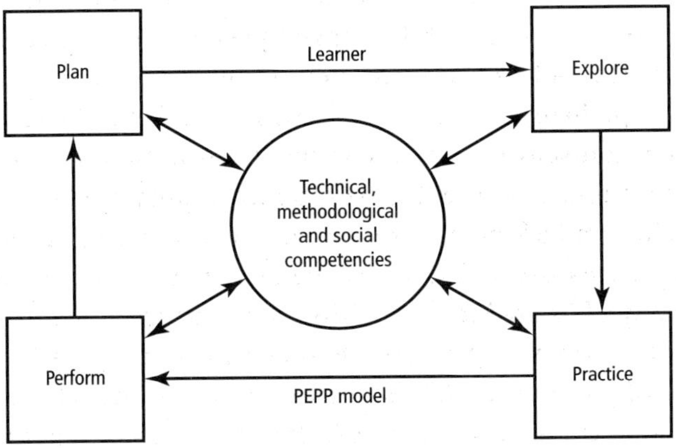

Source: Institute of Technical Education.

practice. Called the Plan, Explore, Practice and Perform (PEPP) Model, the approach is interactive and process based. Under the guidance of a teacher, the student plans the work to be done; explores the information required; practices what he has learned; and finally performs with the competence, knowledge, skills, and values he has mastered. Through this approach, the student acquires three key competencies: technical, methodological, and social.

Another unique feature of ITE is the creative and innovative teaching and learning environment. With the pervasive use of information technology (IT) in society and the knowledge economy, it is important that students learn in a rich, IT-based environment that better prepares them for the real working world. The eTutor and eStudent were pioneering systems when launched in 2002. Leveraged on the advances in IT and e-learning technologies, the Web-based eTutor system has transformed ITE into a community of connected, online learning campuses. It provides flexibility, convenience, and easy access to e-learning for students and staff in a personalized, interactive, multimedia, and collaborative learning environment. As ITE's courses are heavily practice oriented, e-learning is presently focused on the knowledge and theoretical component of the curriculum. Even so, this e-learning system has enabled ITE to deliver 20 percent of its total curriculum time on a Web-based platform.

The eStudent system is a Web-based, fully integrated student services administration system. The first of its kind in the region when it was developed, this system has changed the way ITE students manage their academic and student-related services, from enrollment to financial transactions, choice of elective modules, and academic advising—anytime, anywhere. In the process, they take responsibility for planning their studies and initiatives, in doing things independently. This seamless one-stop center on the Web replaces the many otherwise manual and unproductive systems of student enrollment and administration. eStudent has helped ITE to redefine its academic structure, streamline processes, and improve student services. Significantly, the eTutor and eStudent systems have created a new way of teaching, learning, and living on ITE campuses. They provide an important bridge in preparing our graduates to better face challenges in the 21st century.

Last but not least is a feature resulting from the continuous efforts devoted toward building a positive image of VTE: the integrated system of communications, marketing, and rebranding of ITE. Once an excellent and unique ITE education was developed, the question then was to whom and how to cultivate support and recognition for VTE in the schools, industry, and community (Law 2006). There are two aspects to this. The first is communications and marketing. Over the years, ITE has put in place a comprehensive marketing program, focusing on reaching out to students, teachers, parents, and the community. Annually, promotional talks are conducted for potential ITE students in secondary schools. Those in secondary two and three also spend two days in an innovative *Experience ITE Programme* on ITE campuses, discovering the relevance of an ITE college education to themselves, the economy, and society. The highlight of this experience is the exposure to a range of hands-on manufacturing, office, and service skills required in the real world through an integrated simulated learning system. Other regular marketing activities include open houses, road shows, and media publicity. This comprehensive approach reaches out to some 50,000 individuals and receives 300 to 400 positive media mentions every year.

The second important aspect of image building is creative rebranding. The community and public need to be able to identify with ITE and its role in education, industry, society, and values. Since 1998, ITE has launched three branding campaigns with creative themes such as "ITE Makes Things Happen"(1998–2000), "ITE—A Force Behind the Knowledge-Based Economy" (2001–03) and "Thinking Hands Create Success" (2004–06). Professionally commissioned and executed through advertising media such as newspapers, posters, buses, and trains, the underlying messages have helped the public to associate the success of ITE students with the dynamic transformation of ITE as a world-class education institution. A brand-equity tracking model has shown that the image and public perception of ITE have improved by 76 percent from 1997 to 2006.

LESSONS FROM SINGAPORE'S EXPERIENCE

Singapore's system of VTE may be a world-class model today, but the transformation had its share of obstacles and challenges. The political, social, and economic conditions in the early years following independence were difficult and vulnerable.[1] Politically, the birth of Singapore as an independent nation in 1965 through separation from Malaysia was sudden and traumatic. For this tiny island left on its own without natural resources or a hinterland, the problems of survival as a young nation seemed insurmountable. The sudden pullout of the British naval bases soon after further compounded an already volatile environment with political instability, high unemployment, and social unease in a growing population. Many, in fact, believed at the time that Singapore would not make it. Indeed, the nation's survival was at stake.

However, through the sheer political will of the people, hard work, and a strong and effective government, Singapore eventually succeeded in transforming itself from a "third world" nation to the "first world." These difficult conditions prompted the parallel development of a relevant and responsive VTE system that would address the skilled manpower needs of the expanding economy. In this respect, it took a government that not only believed in but had invested heavily in education at all levels to make a difference. In particular, special attention was paid to the lower 25 percent of a school cohort who needed and could benefit from vocational technical education.

So, in Singapore's experience, what are some of the key lessons learned in the development of VTE? How did it respond to the dynamic forces driving change in the school system, the skilled manpower demand of a rapidly changing economy, and the expectations and aspirations of the people? How did it promote the importance of technical skills and gradually change the image and public perception of VTE? What were some of the obstacles and difficulties? How may this experience be extended to the international community?

POLICY SHIFT TOWARD VTE AND ECONOMIC DEVELOPMENT

There was very little VTE prior to Singapore's independence. The limited primary and educational places available were geared toward preparing white-collar workers for the clerical and administrative jobs in the colonial civil service. This posed a major obstacle when the priority shifted toward the process of industrialization. There was limited education and training infrastructure, a dearth of trained manpower, and a workforce without the relevant skills. It was, therefore, a farsighted government that began to pursue a policy of relentless and systematic development of education and training in keeping with each phase of economic development. The role of the Singapore polytechnic and vocational schools in the education system was realigned with the manpower needs of industrialization. It was a painful and slow process in the beginning. With limited resources, the expansion of the technical education system had to make do with basic school buildings, shared centralized workshop facilities, and even crash programs for training technical teachers. Then came the urgency in establishing the first ITB in 1973. This was a clear policy shift to expand VTE and to do it through the formalization of a system of preemployment VTE for young school leavers outside the school system. This then became the model of VTE in Singapore, a system subject to constant review and restructuring as it responded to changing economic, social, and manpower needs. Another milestone policy decision was the repositioning of VTE from a postprimary to a postsecondary system with the formation of ITE in 1992.

CHANGING PUBLIC PERCEPTION AND IMAGE

As a former British colony, Singapore started industrialization without the benefit of tradition or experience in production and manufacturing. Culturally, there was a steep preference for an academic education. Parents want their children to attend university. The desire for a university degree is pervasive in society. The respect for the "scholar" and disdain for the "mechanic" and all the negative associations with those who do poorly in school and perform manual labor only helped to perpetuate the poor image of VTE. To overcome this barrier and change people's mind-set, public campaigns on "using the hands" were organized; basic workshop subjects such as metal work, woodwork, technical drawing, and basic electricity were made compulsory for all secondary students. Top of the Trade television competitions and Apprenticeship of the Year awards were used to create interest and promote the importance of technical skills among the young. Eventually, as the economy grew and VTE graduates were recognized with high employability and successful careers, the acceptance of VTE and its image gradually improved. Extensive efforts in communications, marketing, and branding continue even today toward building a positive image of VTE in Singapore. Modern and conducive teaching and learning campuses, strong support of political leaders, and success of graduates have all helped to achieve a significant turnaround in the public perception and image of ITE.

LEVERAGING ON INDUSTRY PARTNERS

The main approach in VTE in Singapore is a full-time system of institutional training for school leavers with 10 years of general education. The availability of technical manpower was an important strategic tool used by the EDB in promoting foreign direct investment in Singapore. However, this system alone was not enough to ensure the sufficiency and range of skills required by industry. To do so, it was necessary, especially in the early days of industrialization, to leverage on the experience, skills, and technology that resided in the private sector companies. Many of these were foreign MNCs that needed specialized skills and had in-house training capability not available or too costly to develop in the formal VTE system. To meet the skills gaps, several major MNCs (Tata, Rollei-Werke, and Phillips) were offered total investment packages by the EDB, including incentives for the establishment of government training centers, in the late 1960s. This strategic promotional tool for the government to ensure the availability of specialized technical manpower was later extended to the establishment of government-to-government technical institutes with Japan, Germany, and France in the 1970s. These joint technical institutes and training centers were eventually absorbed into the Nanyang Polytechnic and ITE. This experience demonstrated an important phase of economic development when it was necessary to leverage on foreign government assistance and private sector industry partners in complementing the formal VTE system.

TRANSFORMATION OF ITE: IT CAN BE DONE

ITE is not a university or a polytechnic. It is government-funded postsecondary institution focusing on vocational technical education. Today, it is widely recognized for its transformation into a world-class institution. The first educational institution to win the Singapore Quality Award in 2005, it has created a unique brand of an ITE college education for the lower quarter of every school cohort and many working adults in Singapore. It has achieved a breakthrough in enhancing its public image. So, what are the important lessons? In ITE, there is constancy of purpose in pursuing its mission, vision, and goals. The consistent use of five-year strategic plans has helped to provide a clear focus and successful platform for implementing many of the initiatives and programs. It has built a strong team of leaders and staff who are professionally qualified and dedicated to the cause of VTE. Their commitment and enthusiasm to achieve the mission and goals are reflected in the "ITE Care" culture, especially the care and concerns of the staff for the students. Embedded in this culture is also the relentless pursuit of organizational excellence and a proactive approach in always asking how they can better serve, add value, and meet the needs of students. There is an open willingness to learn from and adopt the best relevant practices from other educational systems in building the ITE system—in using the pedagogic concept of key competencies from Germany, the Developing a Curriculum (DACUM) methodology from the United States, and on-the-job-training practices from Japan. The goals and concerns in VTE may be the same, but the systems are unique and often shaped by the schools, industry, and needs of the local community. And so with a new vision and strategic plan, the journey of the transformation of ITE continues.

CONCLUSION

In conclusion, VTE systems are dynamic. The challenges and opportunities are unique. The key issue today is how to build a responsive VTE system in time for the future. However, from the international perspective, no one ideal system will suit the needs or aspirations of all countries. The systems are often shaped by the economic, social, and cultural conditions of the local community. VTE provides an important pathway in the total education system. A fundamental question is whether sufficient attention has been paid to those who need and can benefit from VTE. There are policy decisions and choices to be made.

Each VTE system is unique in its history and development. In the case of Singapore, VTE has evolved in response to the various phases of economic development since independence in 1965. As the economy restructured and moved from labor intensive to capital intensive, and then to knowledge intensive, the VTE system responded to ensure that the workforce had the relevant knowledge, skills, and values. The educational and training systems were reviewed, upgraded, and remodeled to stay relevant and responsive to the needs of school leavers, industry, and community. In particular, the experience of Singapore has shown how the ITE has successfully transformed into a world-class postsecondary educational institution focusing on VTE. Its success can be seen in the doubling of full-time student enrollment from 1995 to 2005. It has maintained a remarkably high satisfaction rate of more than 90 percent from employers and graduates since 1999. The graduate employment rate over a five-month job search period has also been consistently high and was at 90 percent in 2005. The student success rate in completing their courses of studies significantly improved from a low of 61 percent in 1994 to 77 percent in 2005. Students have given ITE lecturers and the college environment a very high satisfaction rate of 94 percent. In short, ITE has created a unique brand of VTE college education that is widely recognized locally and internationally for its relevance, quality, and values in a global economy.

NOTE

1. ITE is recognized as a world-class institution focusing on vocational technical education. Leveraging on its experience of more than 40 years, it has shared and extended its knowledge, experience, and services overseas through ITE Education Services Pte Ltd (ITEES), a wholly owned subsidiary of ITE. ITEES has three broad areas of business: licensing of ITE courses; consultancy services; and professional training covering a wide range of core capabilities in the development of VTE systems and centers, curriculum design, standards setting, pedagogy, and management systems. So far, ITE has licensed its courses to 10 private schools in Singapore and 4 schools overseas in China and Vietnam. Professional and customized training courses have been conducted for principals and teachers from China, India, Indonesia, Laos, Myanmar, and Cambodia.

An example of a major consultancy project undertaken on behalf of the Singapore government is the establishment of the Vietnam-Singapore Technical Training Center (VSTTC) in Ho Chi Minh City, Vietnam, in 1998. The objective was to provide quality technical training for high school leavers to support the skilled manpower needs of the Vietnam-Singapore Industrial Park as part of Vietnam's industrialization program. Carried out over eight years, this project included the design and development of five VTE courses, setting up the facilities, and training 30 Vietnamese instructors and administrators. A team of one director and seven department heads was also deployed over different periods in Vietnam to spearhead the management and operations of the center before its transfer to the Vietnam management staff in 2006. Today, the VSTTC, with a modern campus environment, up-to-date training facilities, professionally trained staff, and close links with industry, is held up as a model for quality technical training in Vietnam.

REFERENCES

Law, S. S. 1984. *Trend of Vocational Training in Singapore.* VITB Paper No. 1. Singapore: Vocational and Industrial Training Board.

_______. 2005. "Dynamics and Challenges in Vocational Education and Training—The Singapore Experience." 21st Century Education Symposium, Western China's Vocational Education and Socio-Economic Development, Liuzhou, China.

_______. 2006. "Winning the Singapore Quality Award—A Journey Towards Organizational Excellence." International Conference on Vocational and Technical Education, International Perspectives, Singapore, Institute of Technical Education.

CHAPTER 6

Polytechnic Education

CHAN Lee Mun

INTRODUCTION

In Singapore, children start formal education at the age of six. They typically spend six years in primary school followed by another four or five years in secondary school. At the end of their secondary school education, they sit for the national General Certificate of Education (GCE) Ordinary level (O-level) examinations. They would, by then, be about 17 or 18 years old. After receiving their O-level examination results, these secondary school leavers have three different educational pathways open to them (figure 6.1).

About 25 percent of each age cohort gains admission to the Institute of Technical Education (ITE). Close to 30 percent of them go to junior colleges that prepare them for the GCE Advanced level (A-level) examinations. About 40 percent enroll in one of the five polytechnics in Singapore.

At ITE, students spend two years working toward the National ITE Certificate (Nitec) or Higher Nitec qualification in various fields of study. The focus of ITE training is on developing highly skilled technicians for industry. Those students going to the polytechnics take three-year diploma-level programs to be trained as technologists and middle-level professionals in their respective fields.

The number of students admitted each year to ITE, polytechnics, and universities closely match the broad targets set by the National Manpower Council (NMC). Chaired by the minister for manpower, the NMC sets the direction for Singapore's manpower planning and development strategies. The targets are based on the plans and projections provided by the various economic development agencies and ministries on the number, type, and level of manpower required by Singapore's industries.

The NMC targets take into consideration the upgrading mobility of graduates across the various educational pathways. For example, graduates from ITE and school leavers with A levels can enroll in a course of study at a polytechnic.

Figure 6.1 Singapore Education: A System of "Bridges and Ladders"

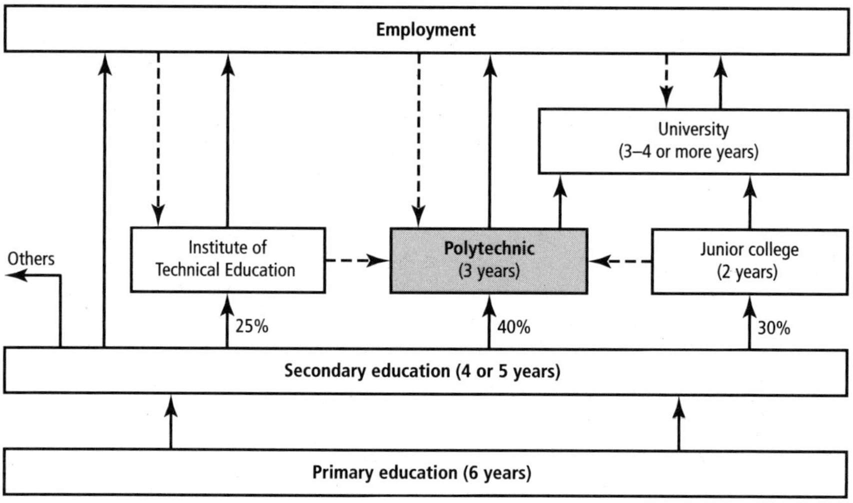

A majority of polytechnic graduates enter the workforce after graduation, but about 4 in 10 continue their education and obtain a university degree within five years of graduation from the polytechnic.

This system of "bridges and ladders" allows Singaporeans opportunities to go as far as their interests and abilities can take them. Technical and polytechnic education in Singapore is seen by many students and their parents not just as a terminal, industry-ready exit qualification, but also as a viable alternative to a junior college education for progression to the university. Some choose to enroll in a polytechnic because they prefer a practice-oriented education to an academic one at a junior college. Others opt for polytechnic education because of the wide range of programs and courses that lead directly to employment opportunities. These include programs in exciting new fields such as design, interactive and digital media, biomedical and life sciences, and hospitality and tourism management. Today, more than 30 percent of the students admitted to the polytechnics also qualify for admission to a junior college. Among them are some of the brightest secondary school leavers who can gain admission to any of the top junior colleges.

POLYTECHNICS IN SINGAPORE

THE FIVE POLYTECHNICS

Polytechnic education began in Singapore in the 1950s. Singapore Polytechnic, established in 1954, was the first polytechnic institution. The second, Ngee Ann Polytechnic, has roots that go back to 1963. In the early 1990s and under the guidance of Dr. Tay Eng Soon, then the minister in charge of the polytechnics, two

Figure 6.2 Singapore's Industrial Development Phases

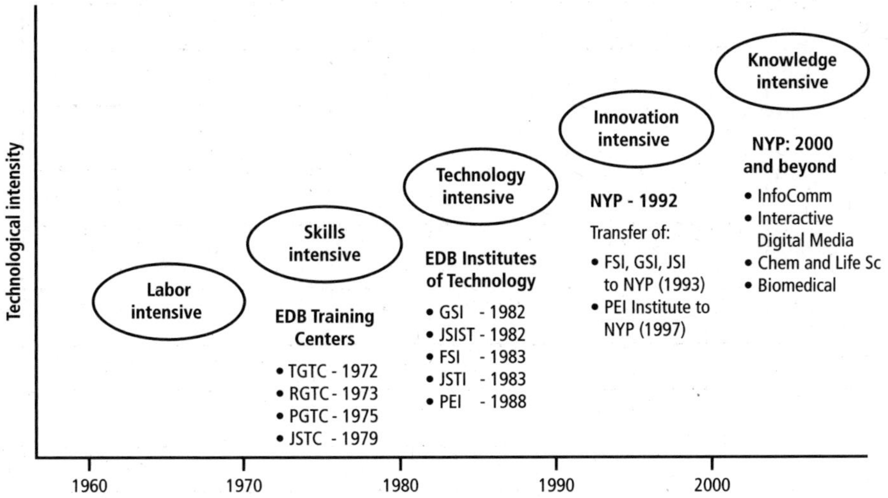

other polytechnics were set up in quick succession: Temasek Polytechnic in 1990 and Nanyang Polytechnic in 1992. In 2003, Republic Polytechnic was established (see figure 6.2).

Student Intake and Enrollment. Polytechnic education in Singapore has grown, gradually in the initial years but much more rapidly over the past 25 years. According to statistics from the Ministry of Education, the percentage of cohort gaining admission to a polytechnic to pursue full-time diploma programs rose from 5 percent in 1980 to nearly 40 percent in 2006. The five polytechnics took in a total of about 22,200 freshmen and had a combined student enrollment of more than 60,000 in 2006.

Budgets and Staffing. The annual operating budget of each polytechnic is about S$180 million, with variations depending on the actual student enrollment. A separate development budget is provided for capital expenditures on buildings, information technology (IT) infrastructure, furniture, and equipment. Each polytechnic has between 1,200 and 1,400 staff, of which about 800 are academic staff.

Fields of Study. Polytechnic education today offers a diverse range of courses targeted at meeting the manpower needs of industry. All of the polytechnics are well equipped to provide training in cutting-edge technologies. In academic year 2006/07, the five polytechnics offered a total of 146 full-time preemployment diploma courses in disciplines such as the built environment, business, chemical and life sciences, engineering, IT, maritime studies, media and design, and the health sciences. While all five polytechnics offer courses in engineering and IT, only selected polytechnics offer courses in fields like maritime studies and health sciences.

Degrees. The polytechnics offer courses leading to the award of the diploma, the specialist diploma, and the advanced diploma. Full-time diploma courses form the bulk of the courses offered by the polytechnics and are targeted primarily at O-level school leavers undergoing preemployment training (PET). Specialist and advanced diploma courses are designed for working adults seeking continuing education and training (CET) opportunities. The polytechnics also offer a whole host of certificate-level and other short courses.

ROLE OF POLYTECHNICS IN SINGAPORE'S ECONOMIC DEVELOPMENT

In the 40 years since independence, Singapore has seen its economy undergo tremendous change and transformation. From a country dependent on entrepot trade during its preindependence days, Singapore made a swift change to an export-oriented and investment-driven economy. This prompted a very rapid program of industrialization designed to move up the value chain from low-skilled, labor-intensive production to higher-value-added, capital-intensive manufacturing and services.

Polytechnic education has been the backbone of Singapore's industrialization program. From the beginning of this economic evolution, the role of polytechnic education has been to produce suitably trained manpower to support the growth of new industries in Singapore. Throughout the various phases of Singapore's industrialization program, the polytechnics (and the Singapore Economic Development Board [EDB] institutes of technology, which later became part of Nanyang Polytechnic) were instrumental in training the increasing numbers of technologists and middle-level professionals needed for the emerging and growing industries.

It was, and continues to be, a matter of national and economic priority for Singapore to train manpower with the right type of knowledge and skills and to retrain the existing workforce to sustain growth and fuel the twin engines of the economy—manufacturing and services. The polytechnics do this by working very closely with industry as well as the country's economic planners and development agencies. In doing so, the polytechnics are alerted to changes on the horizon and receive timely information on national manpower and industry development plans of the various agencies.

Throughout, the polytechnics have worked at staying relevant to the market and industry that they serve by being nimble and responsive to the challenges of a changing economic landscape. Such rapid changes not only demand a higher level of technological expertise and know-how, but also call for integrated multidisciplinary knowledge and skills. The polytechnics respond by regularly rolling out new courses and constantly reviewing and updating existing ones to keep pace with—oftentimes ahead of—the changes in industry and commerce.

FEATURES OF POLYTECHNIC EDUCATION

The polytechnics' core mission is to train and produce technologists and middle-level professionals to support the technological, economic, and social development of Singapore. Reflecting the wide range of abilities, aptitudes, and interests of their students, the polytechnics seek to equip students with relevant and specific skills for the workplace to give Singapore a competitive edge as it moves into a knowledge- and innovation-intensive economy. As a result, polytechnic graduates today are highly valued as practice-oriented technologists and knowledgeable middle-level professionals, much sought after by industry.

Industry Focus. The polytechnics have a very clear mission: to prepare their students for the workplace. Graduates leave the polytechnics equipped with relevant knowledge and skills to enable them to secure gainful employment. While polytechnic graduates are also more than adequately prepared to pursue further education at the university degree level (and many of them do), their training prepares them to be productive in the jobs that they have been trained for. This clear focus is perhaps the underlying success factor of polytechnic education in Singapore.

Application and Development-Oriented Training. Polytechnic students are trained not only to know what to do, but also to know how to do. Apart from understanding the theoretical principles behind what they learn, polytechnic students are trained to apply their knowledge and skills to creatively and innovatively solve practical problems from industry.

Practice-Oriented Training. Particularly in the later stages of their studies, students are required to work in teams, together with their mentors, on projects. The projects they do are not academic paper exercises, but real-life challenges that exist in industry and in the business world. These could be as real and as authentic as building a diagnostic device for a biomedical engineering company, developing software applications for a bank, or conducting market research for a commercial firm.

Balance between Broad-Based Foundation and Specializations. The polytechnics provide a balanced, broad-based training to ensure that students are equipped with fundamental knowledge and core skill sets, including communication and other soft skills. In a typical three-year polytechnic diploma program, the broad-based foundation is laid in the first two years. Electives and specializations are offered in the final year to provide students with a focus on industry-relevant specialist areas. Final-year projects also provide valuable opportunities for students to integrate and apply their knowledge and skills creatively to design and develop solutions to problems.

Industrial Attachment Program for Students. As an integral part of their course of study, polytechnic students are attached to industry to gain experience in a real-life work environment. The students' progress is monitored to ensure that their attachments are meaningful and useful for them. With the strong support of both multinational companies and small and medium enterprises, polytechnic students are able to gain practical work experience and to appreciate industry expectations even before they graduate.

To inculcate a global mind-set in polytechnic students, much emphasis has been placed in recent years on creating more opportunities for them to participate in industrial attachments with companies and organizations in foreign countries. Through these programs, students get to work outside Singapore, learn about other cultures, and appreciate diverse business and industry practices, as well as experience different economic and social situations.

Close to Industry. The polytechnics work very closely with industry. For a start, their governing boards have many members from industry who bring with them knowledge of and experience from industry. They provide advice on what industry needs and where it is heading.

Advisory committees, made up of industry practitioners in relevant fields, provide valuable input on a wide range of training-related matters such as new course proposals, curriculum development, and program reviews. These committees also advise the polytechnics on student attachment, graduate employment, and staff development. And, through their contacts, they help the polytechnics widen their network and connections with other players in industry.

The polytechnics build strong links and work in close partnership with industry. They collaborate with technology partners to jointly set up specialist centers and laboratories. These are excellent platforms for training students and developing staff capabilities in key and emerging technologies. The polytechnics also actively engage in joint projects with industry. Such collaborations help the polytechnics to keep up with the latest developments in industry practices and advances in technology.

A CASE STUDY OF THE GROWTH AND DEVELOPMENT OF POLYTECHNIC EDUCATION IN SINGAPORE: NANYANG POLYTECHNIC

This section takes a closer look at Nanyang Polytechnic as an example of a modern polytechnic in Singapore.

ROOTS

Nanyang Polytechnic (NYP) was the fourth polytechnic in Singapore, set up to augment the training capacity of the three earlier polytechnics and to help meet the growing demand for polytechnic education. Although it was officially established in 1992, NYP's history goes back to the EDB's company-based training centers in the 1970s and the institutes of technology in the 1980s.

As the Singapore industrialization program entered its skills-intensive phase, EDB embarked on its own program of setting up training centers in collaboration with large industrial companies (figure 6.2). Between 1972 and 1975, EDB set up the Tata-Government Training Center (TGTC), the Rollei-Government Training Center (RGTC), and the Philips-Government Training Center (PGTC). These training centers churned out highly skilled technicians to support the precision engineering, optics, and electrical appliances industries of that era.

Toward the end of the 1970s and early 1980s, EDB started to work with foreign governments to set up institutes of technology at the same time as Singapore underwent economic restructuring to focus on higher-value-added and technology-intensive industries. EDB adopted the strategy of learning from the best in the world. It adopted and adapted the best international practices in technology education and training for Singapore. It worked with foreign experts and forged close links with foreign partners. EDB embraced a transnational approach to technology transfer and embarked on an aggressive staff development program to develop the capabilities of its people to run the institutes of technology.

The German-Singapore Institute (GSI) was set up to train technologists for the manufacturing industry, while the French-Singapore Institute (FSI) produced technologists for the electronics industry. Two institutes—the Japan-Singapore Institute of Software Technology (JSIST) and Japan-Singapore Technical Institute (JSTI, later upgraded to Japan-Singapore Institute, JSI)—were set up with technical assistance from the Japanese government. These two institutes focused on IT and mechatronics training, respectively. In 1988, the Precision Engineering Institute (PEI) was set up.

With their close ties with industry and great flexibility, these EDB institutes of technology were uniquely able to respond quickly to changing industry trends and needs. Programs, courses, and curricula could be updated and modified rapidly while new areas of training could be introduced quickly—unlike those of other institutions that operated within a formal education structure.

In 1993, soon after the establishment of Nanyang Polytechnic, the FSI, GSI, JSI, and PEI were transferred to NYP to form part of its School of Engineering.

From this perspective, NYP has a unique experience that was tightly interwoven with the history of Singapore's industrialization program. This experience has been valuable to NYP and has been instrumental in shaping its philosophy and approach to technologist education and training. The innovative "teaching factory" concept was developed during the era of the institutes of technology and has now evolved as the hallmark of NYP's teaching and learning pedagogy.

SCHOOLS

In 1992, NYP started off with the School of Business Management and School of Health Sciences. The School of Engineering and School of Information Technology were added in the following year. These four schools offered courses much needed by industry and commerce in the early 1990s. As Singapore moved toward a more knowledge-based and value-creating economy, the School of Design and School of Chemical and Life Sciences were established in 2000. With interactive and digital media being identified as one of three key research areas to help drive Singapore's economy into the next decade, NYP set up the School of Interactive and Digital Media in October 2006.

Through these seven schools, NYP offers courses that cover most of the major sectors of industry supporting Singapore's manufacturing and service industries.

MISSION

NYP's mission has three main objectives: To provide quality preemployment training to school leavers, to provide relevant continuing education and training to working adults, and to provide value-added industry services to companies and businesses.

Preemployment Training. PET is the bread-and-butter of NYP's core business. It involves the provision of full-time diploma-level training of school leavers, preparing them for the job market.

Since its inception in 1992, NYP has been introducing many new courses in response to—sometimes ahead of—industry needs. In the early 1990s, the types of courses offered addressed the immediate needs of the health care, business, engineering, and IT industries. Toward the latter half of that decade, more hybrid courses were introduced when convergence of different technologies became more common. These included courses like business informatics and multimedia and information communication technology. Introduced in 1996, the digital media design course was ahead of its time. In the early 2000s, there were more courses in the fields of biotechnology, biomedical engineering, and digital entertainment.

In 2006, NYP had some 15,000 full-time diploma students enrolled in 26 courses. In April 2007, NYP offered six new courses, bringing the total course offerings to 32.

Continuing Education and Training. NYP's mission also focuses on providing CET for working adults. To understand what industry wants for its workers, NYP works closely with economic and development agencies, the unions, and industry.

NYP offers CET courses in many fields. It taps the vast capabilities, expertise, and resources residing in its seven schools and corporate departments. Although

Table 6.1 Full-Time Diploma Courses Offered in Academic Year 2007/08

School of Engineering	School of Interactive and Digital Media
• Electronics, Computer and Comms Eng	• Digital Media Design
• Manufacturing Engineering	• Digital Entertainment Technology
• Mechatronics Engineering	• Motion Graphics and Broadcast Design
• Biomedical Engineering	School of Business Management
School of Information Technology	• Business Management
• Information Technology	• Banking and Financial Services
• Multimedia and InfoComm Technology	• Accountancy and Finance
• Business Informatics	• Marketing
• Engineering Informatics	• Sport and Wellness Management
• Business Enterprise IT	• Media Studies and Management
School of Design	• Hospitality and Resort Management
• Industrial Design	School of Health Sciences
• Space and Interior Design	• Nursing
• Visual Communication	• Dental Hygiene and Therapy
School of Chemical and Life Sciences	• Physiotherapy
• Molecular Biotechnology	• Occupational Therapy
• Chemical and Pharmaceutical Technology	• Diagnostic Radiography
• Food Science	• Radiation Therapy
• Pharmaceutical Sciences	

a few of the courses are standard offerings for the public to choose from, most of NYP's CET programs are customized to the needs of a company or organization. For example, if the local telecommunications company requires a training course in a specialist technology area for its technical staff, NYP would tailor-make the special program for that company. In effect, NYP becomes an extension of the company's own training department.

The CET courses offered are very diverse. Some are pitched at very basic levels, while others are targeted at the specialist and professional levels. Depending on the needs, some CET courses provide basic training or upgrading opportunities for adults; some are specifically designed to reskill workers with new skill sets or convert them from one career to another.

To accommodate the work schedule of the adult learners, these courses can be offered on either a full-time or a part-time basis, and they can range from short courses lasting a few days to full-fledged, four-year part-time diploma programs.

Industry Services. NYP supports industry through various programs and initiatives with companies and economic agencies. These include partnerships on joint research and development (R&D) work, collaborations on industry projects, and provision of professional and technical services.

Table 6.2 Working with Agencies and Industry

- Economic Development Board (EDB)
- InfoComm Development Authority (iDA)
- Ministry of Health (MOH) and Hospitals
- Ministry of Manpower (MOM)
- Workforce Development Agencies (WDA)
- International Enterprise (IE) Singapore
- National Trade Union Congress (NTUC)
- Business associations
- Companies and organizations

Table 6.3 Examples of Continuing Education and Training Courses (Formal Awards)

Diploma	Specialist Diploma	Advanced Diploma
Engineering • Electronics, Computer and Comms Engineering • Precision Engineering IT & InfoComm • Multimedia and InfoComm Technology • Information Technology • Engineering Informatics Business • Correctional Administration • Business Management Health Sciences • Nursing (Accelerated Program) • Diag Radiography (Accelerated Program)	IT & InfoComm • InfoComm Technology • IT Security • e-Commerce (Business / IT Focus) Business • Strategic Brand Management • Supply Chain Management • Insurance Studies • Workplace Health Promotion Health Sciences • Nursing (Diabetes Nurse Edu) • Counseling	Business • Management (International Business) • Strategic Management of Human Resources • Strategic Marketing Management Health Sciences • Sonography • Case Management • Palliative Care • Nursing (various specializations)

Partnerships with Industry. Leveraging on its strong links with industry, NYP collaborates with leading industry players to jointly establish specialist centers and laboratories that provide excellent platforms for training students and developing staff in key and emerging technologies. Besides developing capabilities in specialist areas, these centers also undertake industry projects to develop systems, solutions, or services for local and multinational companies in the various industry sectors. These real-life industrial projects are critical to the technology and capability development of the polytechnic, as staff working on these projects can keep abreast of the latest developments in the industry as well as rapidly changing technologies.

Table 6.4 Examples of Partnerships with Industry Leaders

- NYP-IBM RFID Integration Zone (RIZ)
- NYP-Microsoft Windows Mobile Solution Center
- NYP-DSO Innovation Center for Application Specific Integrated Circuit
- NYP-Cisco Internet Protocol (IP) Convergence Laboratory
- NYP-RosettaNet Architecture Center of Excellence
- NYP-Oracle Grid Innovation Center
- NYP-SiTF SOA (Service-Oriented Architecture) Center

The NYP-IBM RFID Integration Zone (RIZ) was set up to promote the adoption of radio frequency identification (RFID) technology through industrial projects, collaborations with the business community, and RFID training. This center also trains students on the business and technical aspects of the new technology.

The NYP-Microsoft Windows Mobile Solution Center is an upgrade of an existing partnership with Microsoft to deliver capabilities in embedded and mobility applications and to focus on delivering secure, real-time enterprise solutions for key industries such as health care, biomedical engineering, and defense.

NYP has also collaborated with DSO National Laboratories to set up the NYP-DSO Innovation Center for Application Specific Integrated Circuit to spearhead research efforts in developing technologies in advanced integrated circuit innovations, and provide scientific and engineering solutions for both government and industry in advanced integrated circuit solutions.

Hosting Industry Communities. In collaboration with EDB and other partners, NYP is host to several industry "communities."

The Community is an ecosystem of key partners from the integrated circuit (IC) design industry set up to support local technopreneurs and start-up companies engaged in fabless IC design. These start-up companies can tap into the capabilities and services of the partners in the entire value chain—from design and software support, IP management, and access to manufacturing and markets, to incubator support and venture capital funding. Other similar communities hosted in NYP include the Wireless Technology Community, the Embedded Systems Community, and the Games Creation Community.

In October 2005, the Medtech Concept Lab was set up and hosted in NYP. This community is an ecosystem of collaborative partners, including EDB, NYP, and established medical technology companies. Its objective is to support local clinicians and researchers seeking "proof-of-concept" validation of the feasibility of their innovative ideas and concepts for new biomedical devices and products. Through the Medtech Concept ecosystem, they can tap into EDB's proof-of-concept funding, the industry partners' mentorship, and NYP's biomedical and engineering capabilities to develop functioning prototypes of their devices.

The most recent addition to the family of communities is the Security Technology Community, begun in 2006. This community brings together private and public sector players and public institutes to stimulate the development of market-driven products and solutions in the physical security and infocomm security industries.

INDUSTRY MANPOWER AND SKILLS DEVELOPMENT

The polytechnic is also involved in supporting national manpower and skills development initiatives.

In late 2000, NYP signed a memorandum of understanding (MOU) with EDB, taking on the task of developing and managing the Chemical Process Technology Center (CPTC) located on Jurong Island.[1] CPTC trains personnel from industry as well as students from the ITE, polytechnics, and universities to produce skilled manpower for Singapore's chemical and pharmaceutical industries. CPTC began operations in January 2003.

Under another MOU signed in April 2005 with the Singapore Workforce Development Agency (WDA), NYP took on the role of managing the Center for Employability Skills (CES). Located in Bukit Merah, CES is a national center for the assessment and training of workers under the Employability Skills System. It also coordinates training schemes aimed at equipping workers with job-specific competencies and skills under the Workplace Skills Qualification (WSQ) framework.

In January 2006, NYP signed another MOU with the WDA to develop and manage the Singapore Institute of Retail Studies (SIRS). SIRS's primary mission is to provide CET training for the retail workforce in Singapore leading to the award of a certificate, advanced certificate, and diploma under the WSQ system, as well as providing executive education.

INDUSTRY PROJECTS

An important and integral component of the "teaching factory" concept is the use of industry project work as a platform to provide NYP's students with industry-like experience on campus. Students and staff work closely in teams to solve industry problems under real-life conditions of having to meet the demands of cost, quality, reliability, and deadlines.

Industry projects are an ideal platform on which to network and connect with key industry players and support them in their applied R&D and product development. The added benefit of doing projects for industry is that it provides capability development opportunities for NYP staff to keep abreast of developments in industry and advances in technology.

INTERNATIONAL PROGRAMS

Apart from providing preemployment and CET programs, NYP also conducts various programs for international participants. In doing so, NYP is able to extend its network and connections with partners in the regional countries and to enhance the international and global orientation of the polytechnic.

Three of NYP's major international programs are highlighted here.

- *World Bank–China Vocational Education Reform Project.* In 1997, the World Bank and the Chinese Ministry of Education requested, through the Singapore Ministry of Foreign Affairs (MFA), that NYP provide training and consultancy to help reform the technical and vocational education system in China. Eighty-two key schools from the provinces of Jiangsu, Guangdong, Liaoning, and Shandong and the capital city of Beijing were selected to participate in this World Bank–China Vocational Education Reform Project.

  Under the project, 75 principals and 82 key specialist teachers of the selected schools underwent specialized training at NYP. The objective was for the schools to learn about the management practices and pedagogical concepts of NYP. The schools would then serve as models for other schools in China to emulate. A series of four follow-up consultancy trips to China, led by senior staff members of NYP, were also made. The three-year project was successfully completed in December 2000.
- *Suzhou Industrial Park Institute of Vocational Training.* In May 1997, after a visit by the then-prime minister of Singapore, Goh Chok Tong, to the Suzhou Industrial Park in China, a decision was made to set up the Suzhou Industrial Park Institute of Vocational Technology. Subsequently, the Software Project Office and EDB requested NYP to provide assistance in developing and establishing the institute.

  Following three on-site consultancy visits to Suzhou in 1997 and early 1998, NYP helped to draw up the concept plan for the institute, conducted training programs for 14 senior management staff, and shared with them the management practices and pedagogical concepts of NYP. Eight training courses were also conducted for 35 key specialist teachers between 1998 and 2002.
- *Initiative for ASEAN Integration (Train-the-Trainers in IT).* The Initiative for ASEAN Integration was launched at the 4th Association of Southeast Asian Nations (ASEAN) informal summit held in Singapore in November 2000. The aim was to provide a framework for regional cooperation by enabling the newer members to integrate into and enhance the competitiveness of the ASEAN region.

  Shortly thereafter, NYP was invited by Singapore MFA to draw up a five-year training program to assist Cambodia, Lao People's Democratic Republic, Myanmar, and Vietnam to develop a pool of IT talent that would facilitate their integration into ASEAN.

WHAT'S NEXT IN POLYTECHNIC EDUCATION

In August 2004, a Polytechnic Sector Review Committee, headed by the Singapore Ministry of Education (MOE), was set up to review the broad directions, strategies, and mandates of the polytechnics in light of future challenges, and recommend strategies, directions, and policies to guide the polytechnic sector over the next 10 years.

It was recognized that an increasing number of polytechnic graduates choose to pursue degree studies after graduation. Many see polytechnic education no longer as a terminal, industry-ready, exit qualification, but rather as a viable, alternative route to university education. Data show that, within five years of graduation, about 4 in 10 of all polytechnic graduates have obtained or are in the process of obtaining a university degree. This is an attractive route for many polytechnic graduates. Their diploma qualification is well recognized by both the local and foreign universities as more than meeting their entry requirements. If polytechnic graduates apply for a university program related to their field of study at the polytechnic, they will receive various exemptions, credit transfers, or advance standing amounting to between one and two years of study. Many polytechnic graduates are, hence, able to obtain a bachelor's degree at a top British or Australian University in two years. Their counterparts who take the junior college route would normally require three to four years to complete a bachelor's degree.

Given such trends and to help promote diversity in university education in Singapore, the Polytechnic Sector Review Committee recommended that polytechnics be allowed to collaborate with foreign specialized institutions to offer degree programs in the name of the foreign institutions in science and technology disciplines with an applied, practice-oriented focus, and in services and creative disciplines.

This—and other MOE initiatives planned for the next few years—will change the higher education landscape in Singapore. Polytechnic education is poised to enter a new phase of development.

NOTE

1. Jurong Island resulted from an innovative vision of the government in the mid-1990s to reclaim and amalgamate seven small islands off the southwestern coast of Singapore into a single 3,200-hectare island, which laid the foundation for this country to be a global hub for petrochemicals and specialty chemicals.

CHAPTER 7

The Development of University Education in Singapore

GOH Chor Boon and Leo TAN Wee Hin

This chapter traces the growth and development of higher education in Singapore since 1965. Emphasis is placed on how universities in the city-state have responded to changing national agendas, especially in meeting economic and manpower needs. Beginning in the 1990s, as the "old" economy gave way to the new knowledge-based economy of the new millennium, the Singapore government attempted to equip the people with creative and critical-thinking and entrepreneurial skills. This was to create a change-adaptive workforce capable of meeting the new economic and manpower demands. This ideology continues to permeate the education system. At the higher-education level, the universities have implemented reforms that empowered them to take the lead in making the country more competitive in global and regional markets.

HIGHER EDUCATION IN COLONIAL SINGAPORE

Because Singapore was a colony of the British Empire, the development of education was very much influenced by the colonial administration's laissez faire policy. The British also believed that imperial subjects must not be too educated because this would pose a threat to the colonial administration. To the ruling British, higher education—and English education in general—possessed an aura of power and rarity; only a minority and privileged few could enjoy it. It is not an exaggeration to state that, in Singapore, there were only two noteworthy developments in tertiary education during the 150-odd years of colonial rule. In spite of this, it is Singapore's "good fortune that under the British, Singapore had been the regional centre for education" (Lee 2000, 158).

The first noteworthy development was the decision to set up a college for higher education, to be known as Raffles College of Arts and Sciences, to mark

Singapore's centenary in 1919. It was eventually established in 1928. Aside from an unsuccessful attempt in 1938 to introduce an engineering department and to upgrade the college to university status, Raffles College was largely left on its own, with little direction and support from the government.

The second bright spot was the progress made by the Straits Settlements and Federated Malay States Government Medical School. Formed in 1905 as a result of concerted pressure by the Straits Chinese and their generous donations, the school's name was changed to King Edward VII Medical School in 1912; the school was further upgraded to become King Edward Medical College with a full-time teaching faculty in 1921. Through the years, the college built up its reputation, supported by the fact that its medical degree was recognized by the British Medical Council in 1916. This is perhaps one of the more significant colonial legacies as it laid a strong foundation for medical teaching and research. Today, Singapore is recognized as a leader in medical advances in this part of the world. In 1949, the union of King Edward College of Medicine and Raffles College led to the founding of the University of Malaya.

Besides setting up Singapore Polytechnic in 1954, the Nanyang University in 1955, and the University of Singapore in 1962, there were hardly any significant developments in tertiary education until the late 1970s. Nanyang University, or Nantah, the first Chinese-language university in Southeast Asia, was started with donations from people of all walks of life, from Singapore and elsewhere in the region. However, Nanyang University became a center of turbulence during the 1950s and 1960s. Established by the Chinese community, Nanyang University became a hotbed of trouble for communist student activity. The student extremists wanted to establish a socialist independent state and destroy capitalism and colonialism. In 1962, the University of Singapore was established. This followed the decision of the governments of Singapore and the Federation of Malaya that the Singapore Division and the Kuala Lumpur Division of the University of Malaya should become separate national universities in their respective countries.

MERGING THE UNIVERSITIES: THE DAINTON REPORT 1979

By the end of the 1970s, the Singapore economy had consistently achieved high growth and was considered a "newly industrializing economy." To sustain this high-growth trajectory, the government felt it was crucial to review the development of university education at this juncture. It was imperative for the economy to be supported by highly qualified people. The government wasted no time in sourcing for international experts to study and produce an unbiased report. Then–Prime Minister Lee Kuan Yew initiated the search himself and met four British academics in London in June 1979 to discuss how university education in Singapore could best be organized. Sir Frederick Dainton, then chancellor of

Sheffield University, was invited by the Singapore government to lead the study (Dainton 1979, i).

The *Dainton Report,* as it became known, was submitted to the government in December 1979, and the conclusion was, "The arguments for maintaining two universities [University of Singapore and Nanyang University] whether on two campuses or one (an absurd proposition) are extremely weak whilst those in favour of a single, strong university at Kent Ridge are compelling and I recommend accordingly" (Dainton 1979, i). Taking into consideration Singapore's demographic changes and manpower needs, the report recommended that "a total student population in the range of 12–14,000 students by the year 2000 is likely to be adequate" and that "the mix of undergraduate study should be roughly half science based and half arts and social sciences, but no dispositions should be made which ossify this distribution for all time" (Dainton 1979, 1). The report also pointed out that more could be done to enhance the quality of research.

On August 8, 1980, the National University of Singapore (NUS) was formed through a merger of the University of Singapore and Nanyang University. The latter made way for the establishment of Nanyang Technological Institute (NTI) in 1981, and it would eventually become a full-fledged university in 1991.[1] It was a milestone development that, in retrospect, paved the way for the rise of a world-class university education system.

While the merger of the University of Singapore and Nanyang University was generally accepted as the right decision, there was also a sense of tension and uncertainty at the ground level. As observed by Dainton, the expectation of a quick takeoff could also create a lot of strains, arising not so much from the amalgamation as from the sheer rate of expansion (*Straits Times,* May 11, 1981). The new university would need to rely on expatriate staff because it would be some time before the university could generate from within itself the people to staff the system. Because of the strong emphasis on science, medicine, and engineering—which attracted brighter entrants and prepared students for better-paying jobs upon graduation—academics in the arts and social sciences, especially the Chinese-educated ones, were uncomfortable about their prospects in the new university.

NUS faculty staff were actively recruited. By 1984, its staff doubled from 600 in 1980 to 1,200. During the same period, student enrollment increased from a pioneer cohort of 8,600 to 13,000 (as compared with about 2,000 for NTI), and S$212 million was spent on developing its infrastructure and physical facilities at the Kent Ridge campus (*Straits Times,* July 3, 1984). These were impressive achievements, and many observers pointed to three reasons for the university's rapid growth: intellectual quality of its staff, community's support of higher education, and the government's recognition of the university's role in national progress. As for NTI, the early years of its institutional history were not totally devoid of achievement. Engineering education here leaned more toward a practical-oriented approach (as opposed to a more research-oriented engineering curriculum in NUS). As a result, NTI's engineering graduates were seen by prospective employers as more hands-on and ready for the job. In an employment survey of new graduates conducted in late 1987, NTI graduates fared better than did their NUS counterparts—98 percent of NTI graduates were employed, compared with 82 percent of the NUS graduates (*Straits Times,* Aug. 27, 1988). NTI was also singled out as one of the best engineering institutions in the world by the Commonwealth Engineering Council in November 1986 (*Straits Times,* Nov. 30, 1986). This accolade was earned because NTI's engineering faculty possessed relevant industrial experience that provided a strong, practical training of skills necessary to support Singapore's industries.

CHANGE SINCE 1990

By the late 1980s, higher education in Singapore was well poised to meet the challenges of the 1990s. Coming out of a mid-1980s recession, the Singapore economy grew robustly. Upon recommendations by a high-level economic committee, Singapore's economic growth trajectory in the 1990s and beyond shifted toward a high-technology policy, with the following goals (Ministry of Trade and Industry 1986):

- To encourage all industries to exploit and apply new advances in technology as widely as possible;
- To develop competence in selected new technologies where Singapore has a comparative advantage; and
- To move into high-technology industries as an area for growth.

The advanced technologies that were considered to have a big impact during this time were information technology, biotechnology, robotics and artificial intelligence, microelectronics, laser technology and optics, and communication technology. A bigger pool of graduates was needed to drive the economy forward into the 1990s. It was time for higher education to take another big leap—and what better way to start than the formation of Singapore's second full-fledged university.

In 1991, the Nanyang Technological Institute, together with the National Institute of Education (which was an amalgamation of the Institute of Education and the College of Physical Education), became the Nanyang Technological University (NTU). The formation of NTU in itself is a useful case study for many developing countries where, more often than not, tertiary institutions were opened for business in double-quick time.[2] The Singapore planners took close to a decade to refine and nurture a strong foundation for the country's second university. Sir Frederick Dainton was once again invited to review university education, and he concluded, "By 2000, Singapore should aim to have two strong university-level institutions, one at Kent Ridge and the other at Jurong, with many subjects being offered on both campuses. This would introduce a healthy element of friendly competition for students, for current and capital resources and for research grants and contracts and links with industry and commerce" (*Straits Times,* Feb. 14, 1990). Singapore's success in the provision of primary, secondary, and junior college (or pre-university) education had resulted in larger proportions of 18-year-old age groups performing well at national examinations and eager to seek university education. In terms of enrollments in higher education in Singapore, in 1965, 3 percent and 2 percent of the relevant age cohort gained admission to local universities and polytechnics, respectively. By 1989, 14 percent of the primary one cohort would eventually enroll in local universities, while 17 percent would receive polytechnic education (Ministry of Education 2006).

The 1990s saw the consolidation of the government's effort in fine-tuning the tertiary education sector to support its private sector–driven economic modernization strategy. The objective was to create a diversified, flexible tertiary education system capable of producing a highly qualified human resource base. Polytechnics were geared toward providing cutting-edge mid-level technical, management, and service skills, while the universities were tasked with training in high-level skills for both the public and private sectors. Polytechnics graduates who performed well academically were also given the opportunity to progress into NUS and NTU.[3]

Singapore's drive toward a high-technology economy required tertiary institutions to embark on research and development (R&D) activities and to establish close university–industry links.[4] The universities responded by accelerating their research and postgraduate training to foster a more stimulating research environment and meet the growing demand for qualified research scientists and engineers. The recruitment of talented staff was pursued both locally and internationally and supported by a stringent tenure policy, rewards for good teaching and research performance, favorable staff–student ratios, well-equipped teaching and research facilities, and staff training opportunities to upgrade skills and performance. The vision set by the government for NUS and NTU was to have both institutions among the best in the world by the beginning of the new millennium.

Taking the cue, NUS and NTU embarked on ambitious expansion programs in the 1990s and, in the process, laid the foundation for their rise as world-class universities in the 21st century (*Straits Times,* Feb. 16, 1990). The universities adopted the following strategies:

- Expand undergraduate and graduate education by attracting students from the region and beyond. Research was boosted with the establishment of new research institutes at Kent Ridge and Jurong. These research institutes provided strong links between university and industry. At NUS, an Industry and Technology Relations Office was set up in 1992 to enhance cooperation in R&D between the university and industry.

- Review the undergraduate curricula in NUS and NTU to update them and to place more emphasis on creativity and thinking skills. At NUS, for example, three new areas of study in mass communications, European studies, and materials science were developed. A key priority for both universities was revamping the engineering curriculum to meet job and industry demands.
- Upgrade physical facilities to standards comparable to renowned universities like Oxford and Cambridge. A multi-million-dollar plan was adopted.
- Encourage all students to take optional enrichment courses offered by other faculties to broaden their academic horizons.
- Upgrade social and recreational facilities, including a state-of-the-art concert hall, a museum, and a visual arts center, to give university students a rich cultural and social life on campus.

By the mid-1990s, NUS had made the strategic shift from a basically traditional British model of a public university focusing primarily on teaching, to a more comprehensive research-intensive university, emphasizing entrepreneurship, R&D, and university-industry links. Together with NTU, the university sector provided the largest pool of trained research manpower in Singapore and was best placed to contribute to the country's effort in making R&D a key factor in Singapore's economic development.

The performance of the university sector was evaluated by a panel of eminent academics from the United States, Japan, and Europe in August 1997. The panel endorsed the directions the two universities had taken in their bid to become world-class institutions (*Straits Times,* Aug. 10, 1997). The panel also suggested that the establishment of a third university would meet the demand for tertiary education among Singaporeans and attract international students to meet the manpower needs of Singapore. Within three years after the idea was mooted and meticulously assessed, the Singapore Management University (SMU) received its first class of business students in 2000. The university is partnered with one of the United States' best business schools, the Wharton School of the University of Pennsylvania. This inspired collaboration aims to build a world-class university for creative entrepreneurs and visionary business leaders. SMU signed a five-year joint agreement with Wharton in 1999 to create a unique learning and research environment. Diverse and challenging programs have equipped, enriched, and honed the skills, knowledge, and experience of the men and women now capable of leading in a rapidly changing and dynamic world.

RESOURCE ALLOCATION AND GOVERNANCE

One key issue facing many developing countries is the allocation of resources to the tertiary education sector when faced with growing resource constraints. In this respect, they could learn much from the Singapore experience.

Table 7.1 University Enrollment and Output in Singapore

Year	Enrollment	Output
2000	36,121	9,244
2001	37,983	9,586
2002	39,156	9,923
2003	40,095	10,010
2004	41,628	10,165
2005	43,663	10,031

Source: Ministry of Education 2006.
Note: The figures represent the whole (full-time) student population in the education institutions for a particular year.

Admission into universities is highly competitive to avoid high dropout rates, a waste of scarce resources, and the lowering of degree standards. The size of student enrollment and course offerings are based on labor market needs, rather than a supply-driven higher education system. Despite restricted admissions, the growth in student numbers has been dramatic. Enrollment increased from 3,502 in 1960 to 36,121 in 2000, a ten-fold increase in four decades (Ministry of Education 2006). Table 7.1 shows the university enrollment and number of graduates since 2000, when SMU opened its doors.

Enrollments were stimulated by:

- The expansion of primary and secondary education with a high quality of output.
- Subsidies to higher education.
- Rising family incomes.

Since the mid-1990s, about 60 percent of secondary school graduates have enrolled in the universities and polytechnics sectors—comparable to the enrollment rates of 40–60 percent in developed countries. Recurrent expenditure on universities increased two-fold, from S$520,289,000 to S$1,012,860,000 between 1995 and 2005. As for polytechnics, it was also a two-fold increase, from S$338,960,000 to S$622,933,000, during the same period (Ministry of Education 2006).

When Singapore gained its independence in 1965, the government was quick to recognize that long-term economic development is dependent on a critical mass of an educated and skilled workforce. For the past 30-odd years, university enrollment and manpower planning have been closely intertwined. Projected manpower requirements based on forecasts of economic growth determine or guide the trends in university intakes, such as the number of places allocated to each cluster of disciplines. Applicants then compete for the available places in the courses of their choice. How are these decisions made? The universities depend on market signals from employers who hire their graduates, students and their parents who choose (and pay for) degree programs, and the demand for and supply of academic manpower in various specializations. The market responsiveness ensures flexibility and efficiency in resource allocation. During the period of the dot.com and information and computer technology boom (especially the early 1990s), university intakes for computer science and computer engineering students increased to feed the expected expansion in the information technology industry with the skilled manpower. Similarly, in the late 1990s, the government had anticipated the rise of the biotechnology sector and planned for the training of polytechnic and university graduates in this field. The underlying assumption is that there would be no misallocation of human resources.

Hitherto, Singapore's manpower planning model and its link to university enrollments worked well because the nation was catching up to developed-country levels of industrialization by enticing multinational corporations to base their mass-manufacturing operations in Singapore. In the new millennium, changing technology and skills requirements make it difficult for planners to determine the directions of manpower needs. It is also obvious to many employers in the private sector that, while manpower planning could result in a marked increase in the number of trained computer or scientific engineers, anecdotal evidence suggests that many of these graduates will switch to nonscience careers, such as banking, finance, and business, within a few years. This is not surprising because pragmatic Singaporeans would deploy their analytical skills honed during their engineering training years and put them into effective use in occupations that are perceived to provide higher rewards and status in the long run.

As reiterated throughout this book, the provision of affordable and accessible education, from preschool to university education, is a top national priority. Consequently, the state's annual budget allocation ensures that education receives a large portion of the country's public expenditure. Up to 1995, universities received an increasing proportion of the total education budget; their share rose from 10.5 percent in 1975, to 14.3 percent in 1990, and to 15.1 percent in 1995 (see table 2.2). Higher education expenditure increases were kept in line with increases in student numbers. The government understands that high-quality education costs money, and student subsidies are essential to improve equality of opportunity as well as to attract talent into higher education, particularly into economically critical fields of study. The eventual objective was to lower the student subsidy to around 75 percent of tuition costs, to reduce the overdependence of public tertiary institutions on government funding, and to introduce an activity-based funding mechanism.

In response, tertiary institutions have adopted policies to diversify their revenue sources. Student tuition fees have increased gradually since 1986 and substantially since 1989. Since 1992, tuition fees have increased between 5 and 7 percent annually to keep pace with wage and other cost increases. In addition, institutions have established endowment funds to tap nongovernment sources. The two universities, with government support, launched a S$500 million Universities Endowment Fund. The objective is for higher education to move toward becoming more self-supporting and less dependent on the government. Giving the public a direct stake by soliciting contributions from individual and corporate citizens—rather than indirectly through government grants—can help build up multiple links between the universities and the community at large. The government has also committed to contribute another S$500 million to the fund if each university is able to raise at least S$250 million (that is, a dollar-to-dollar matching grant). The income generated from this fund is to be used for a range of activities, such as special and innovative projects, as well as to develop programs that will nurture intellectual development and research. When tuition fees were increased in 1989, a Tuition Loan Scheme was instituted to ensure that no deserving student was deprived of a tertiary education. All full-time university undergraduates, regardless of parental income, could borrow up to 65 percent of their tuition fees, while polytechnic students can borrow up to 50 percent of their tuition fees.[5]

By the late 1990s, as Singapore's higher education was gaining a reputation for its academic rigor and research quality, and because of Singapore's need to respond to global competition, the issue of autonomy and governance of the universities became more significant. During the early decades, the guiding hand of the government was extended even to the direct appointment of vice chancellors to the universities and forbidding the formation of a trade union of academics. Critics argued that this close involvement of the government marked the transformation of a university modeled along classical principles of autonomy and academic freedom into one in which government influence and control had become the norm.

However, the governance and interventionist style began to change, especially as the government realized that its model was increasingly inappropriate in the globalization context. Hence, since the late 1980s, the Singapore government has started a process of decentralization and carried out various comprehensive reviews of its higher education system (such as the *Dainton Report* in 1989 and the July 2005 report of an international advisory panel suggesting the public universities be given more autonomy). Different reform strategies to strengthen and make higher education competitive have been tried. The guiding principle is that tertiary institutions have a strategic role in the creation and application of knowledge to provide a better Singapore to live in. Curriculum is constantly reviewed and emphasis is now placed on a broad-based, cross-disciplinary university education. More innovative pedagogy and assessment have been introduced, with a focus on creative and critical thinking. Universities' role in the advancement of knowledge has been strengthened through postgraduate and research education. At the same time, a comprehensive quality assurance and management system has been put in place to enhance each institution as a center for quality education.

While the government has basically controlled the provision of higher education because tertiary institutions are primarily state funded, it has always been prepared to make changes—as happened in 2000 with the establishment of SMU. Unlike NUS and NTU, which operated like statutory boards until 2006, SMU was set up as a private limited company and governed by the Companies Act.[6] A different governance framework could be tried at SMU, and best practices could then be applied in all three institutions. To encourage competition, avoid wasteful duplication, and enjoy greater autonomy, the three universities—NUS, NTU, and SMU—were urged to develop their own unique characteristics and niches.

Finally, to make Singapore's universities more innovative and entrepreneurial to meet the demands of the knowledge-based economy, the Ministry of Education decided to allow NUS and NTU to be corporatized in 2006.[7] This is a distinctive milestone in Singapore's history of tertiary education. Corporatization would provide the universities with the flexibility to recruit world-class talent; manage their budgets; and build a stronger sense of loyalty and ownership among students, staff, and alumni. NUS and NTU are expected to reach high international standards in both teaching and research and even become models for other regional universities to emulate. An underlying objective is to broaden the coverage of various disciplines and to foster the emergence of cross-disciplinary teaching and research.

With the corporatization process completed, the Singapore government would remain the major source of funding. However, all three universities have their own endowment fund programs and actively seek partnerships with alumni, industry, and the local community as alternative sources of funding. The next target is for Singapore's higher education to attain and sustain world-class status and continue as one of the engines to create wealth for the city-state.

RESPONDING TO THE CHALLENGES OF THE NEW ECONOMY

Higher education in Singapore is now challenged to make the fullest use of the autonomy granted by the government. Producing academic excellence and technological innovation now rests squarely on the university itself. In most developing countries, the government provides the bulk of the funding for universities and, hence, has a strong say in the governance and goals. Universities in Singapore, in the new millennium, decide what undergraduate programs to offer; enrollment targets and criteria for admission; tuition fees; terms and conditions of faculty recruitment; and how faculty, students, and the university as an institution are evaluated and benchmarked. Central to this approach is the introduction of competition between education institutions and of rigorous institutional reviews, both of which are meant to ensure the quality, efficiency, and effectiveness of higher education.

The knowledge-based economy requires graduates to possess higher-order thinking and communication and information technology skills. Employers value professionals with the capacity to learn, unlearn, and relearn. They also seek a diverse workforce in terms of training, outlook, and subject knowledge. In industrial economies, the trend is for undergraduates to gain a basic knowledge of disciplines and breadth of coursework (rather than narrow specializations) because highly specific skills and knowledge can quickly become outdated. As stated by Gardner (2004, 250), "Trends in our increasingly globalized society have brought interdisciplinary concerns to the fore. Issues like poverty reduction, antiterrorism, privacy, prevention of disease, energy conservation, ecological balance—the list could be expanded at will—all require input and syntheses of various forms of disciplinary knowledge and methods."[8] Responding to the changing landscape, university education in Singapore, too, is shifting gradually but surely toward a more interdisciplinary approach. Teaching pedagogy in Singapore's tertiary institutions is now galvanized toward developing in young adult Singaporeans

- The capacity to think analytically and creatively within and beyond disciplines.
- The ability to tackle problems and issues that do not respect disciplinary boundaries.
- An understanding of the global system.

The concept of an "enterprising university" was assiduously supported by NUS, NTU, and SMU. Since 2003, the Singapore economy has rebounded strongly from a recession at the start of the new century. The role of higher education in a knowledge-driven economy has never been more crucial as innovation and human capital are seen as keys to future economic growth. Several initiatives are being introduced by the universities to position Singapore's tertiary education in the new century:

- The establishment of global campuses (and external campuses in countries like India and China and in the Silicon Valley) using state-of-the-art multimedia technologies to plug into the worldwide revolution in information and communications, and facilitate cross-boundary learning.
- Quality teaching programs, with emphasis on multidisciplinary learning and cross-faculty modules, to produce highly qualified graduates who have broad intellectual horizons and are steeped in a culture of lifelong learning.
- A thriving culture of research enhanced by state-of-the-art research institutions.
- A vigorous external relations program with strong links to industry collaborators and international academic partners.

In the New Economy, the ticket to faster and broader income growth is innovation. The New Economy puts a premium on what Nobel Laureate economist Douglas North (2005) calls "adaptive efficiency," which refers to the ability of institutions to innovate, continuously learn, and productively change. As markets fragment, technology accelerates, and competition comes from unexpected places, learning, creativity, and adaptation have become the principal sources of competitive advantage in many industries. As in the industrial economies, university administrators and government leaders alike in Singapore have wanted to make the research university more relevant to business and the economy. Advocates of a greater economic role believe that the university's most important contributions are the transfer of research to industry, the production of commercial inventions and patents, and the creation and spinoff of start-up companies. To meet this challenge, the research university must change its mission from the static categories of research, teaching, and service to the more dynamic ones of discovery, learning, and engagement. For example, some university courses could be conducted through the "learning by doing" approach (instead of in the classroom)—working in a research laboratory, helping create a start-up company, participating in a theater or arts group, or working at a nonprofit community organization. Universities must change how they grant promotion and tenure for faculty members and grade and evaluate students in ways that encourage such engaged activity throughout the institutions.

NUS is the more "mature" university in terms of having had a head start in research, and R&D indicators affirm the rapid infusion of a research and entrepreneurial culture in that institution. The number of invention disclosures and patents filed by and granted to NUS increased from 169 in 1998 to 298 in 2004. During the same period, the number of NUS spinoffs and start-ups increased from 1 to 13.[9] Research staff increased from 843 (59 percent of total teaching staff) in 1996 to 1,087 (62 percent of total teaching staff) in 2004 (National University of Singapore 2005). Economists, including Joseph Schumpeter and Robert Solow, have demonstrated the central role that technology plays in economic growth, and, undoubtedly, university technology—as measured by patent applications, disclosures of inventions, licensing income, and business start-ups—is closely associated with the level of technological change and innovation in the country. Singapore's higher education sector demonstrates the fact that the successful commercialization of university R&D requires a systematic approach, starting with the championing by top leadership to make intellectual property creation and commercialization an integral part of the institutional mission. Filtering downward are policy changes and incentives, including availability of research funding, that support and motivate a mind-set change of faculty. Although new knowledge is created in universities and research institutes, actually absorbing and applying those ideas by industry is a different story altogether. The latter, including local small and medium technological companies, must be consistently looking at the universities for new processes and products and have the absorptive capacity to use them to generate wealth.[10]

While Singapore's higher education sector is nurturing a pro-enterprise and research climate, university leaders and policy makers recognize that there is still room to carefully explore the economic and social effects of the university's role in contributing to the development of talent and tolerance. These are significant benchmarks of the growth and development of a creative economy—a concept that the city-state of Singapore is propagating, not just in the areas of science and technology, but also in entertainment, performing arts, architecture, building construction, and so forth. For the university to become a truly creative hub, it has a crucial role in producing and attracting talented students and renowned faculty members who, in turn, would draw companies, venture capitalists, laboratories, and research institutes to locate nearby to take advantage of the institution's talent and infrastructure. The higher education sector is also attempting to establish an open and tolerant social climate between the community of learners within the campuses and between the university and its surrounding social community. Societies throughout history have tended to flourish when they are open to new people and ideas, while stagnating during periods of insularity and orthodoxy. Talented and creative people favor diversity and a wide variety of social and cultural options.[11] Openness to ideas is crucial in both attracting talent and succeeding economically. Talented and creative people "vote with their feet," and they tend to move away from communities where their ideas and identities are not accepted.

The creation of a "university hub" is also a mechanism to reduce brain-drain and to achieve brain-gain of talented university graduates and faculty members. Its development will have all sorts of positive outcomes, such as employment, population, and income growth; a vital high-tech industry; and regional innovation.[12] Indeed, the target would be a seamless connection between communities and universities so that it is hard to tell where one begins and the other ends.

LEARNING FROM THE SINGAPORE EXPERIENCE

For many developing countries, such as the African nations, Singapore's case illustrates the paramount role of the state at all levels of society. The adoption of a developmental state model in which the state was a key economic player succeeded brilliantly. As examined in the chapter on the evolution and management of education in Singapore since 1965, the Singapore government has skillfully used a state-control model in regulating education changes to match manpower planning and, in the process, to make education a valued social institution. The establishment of tertiary institutions was carefully planned.

Singapore's success story has several best-practice implications for higher education policy makers in developing nations as well as for higher education experts working in donor agencies:

- Maintain a sustained and consistent policy over the long term.
- Ensure strong links among education, the labor market, and economic development.
- Develop mechanisms to matriculate high-quality students, including a merit-based admissions policy, and to recruit quality staff, accompanied by stringent tenure and reward systems.
- Develop a prioritized, development-oriented research strategy backed by an excellent infrastructure, support facilities, and incentive schemes with an aim to achieve excellence; to develop management strategies to maintain cost effectiveness in program offerings and research.
- Implement a concerted policy effort to diversify resources to complement the high government subsidies without jeopardizing quality. This policy is justifiable and feasible in areas with relatively high household incomes.

The primary function of Singapore's higher education sector is to educate and train skilled professionals to meet the manpower needs of the economy. High standards at the universities and competition for places allow only the top 25 percent of the cohort to gain admission. However, the impact of globalization has motivated many universities in industrial countries to provide lifelong learning experiences to the entire population. In Singapore, the establishment of the Singapore Institute of Management University (UniSIM) in 2005 aimed at adult students is a major step in addressing this issue. No one can predict all the likely developments associated with a major reconfiguration of the learning process, fueled by rapid technological change. Polytechnics and universities in Singapore, however, are expected to respond to some of the possible scenarios:

- Multiple learning opportunities offered by diverse sources will replace the past monopoly of formal academic institutions.
- Learners will demand and find greater flexibility and fluidity in the learning process and the accrediting of learning.
- Technology not only will open up access to more learning, but will conquer barriers of time, distance, and convenience that previously have been prohibitive.
- Greater collaboration will be necessary among institutions to share resources and between institutions and client groups, such as employers and government agencies, to achieve mutually sought learning goals.

The Singapore government is now looking at ways to expand the university sector. However, whether to increase the number of universities will be guided by economic considerations, that is, alignment with the needs and development of the Singapore economy. This approach will "avoid falling into the error which some countries have done of simply producing more university graduates to satisfy a social demand, many of them in disciplines which do not enable them to find jobs and be productive members of the workforce".[13] Three steps would be taken to expand the university sector:

- Working out a plan to make available an additional 800 to 1,000 places by 2008.
- Developing a conceptual plan to expand the university sector in the long term, including deciding on the number and type of universities Singapore needs.
- Implementing and executing the conceptual plan once it is approved by the government.

The current forecast is that as the Singapore economy grows and the population increases from the present 4.6 million to more than 6 million in 2015, three medium- to large-size universities (NUS, NTU, and SMU) and three smaller specialist institutions would be appropriate for Singapore, based on a rough ratio of one university per million population.

CONCLUSION

As a source for the country's future as a knowledge-based economy, Singapore's higher education system has received great attention. The universities have undergone dramatic changes in recent years, especially in the area of governance and involvement in advanced research.

In spite of its success, Singapore's education system faces a number of emerging problems. The ability of a highly controlled system to respond independently and quickly to the growing education, training, and research needs of a rapidly expanding, highly competitive, and technology-driven private sector is limited. The future affordability of higher education for lower-income students will be difficult to maintain with sharp increases in tuition fees and costs of living. Although not a systemic or policy outcome, female students are underrepresented in professional fields such as medicine, engineering, and law. The government's policy of maintaining quotas for undergraduate admission into some critical fields of study (such as law and medicine) may encourage many talented students to pursue their choice of university study overseas. These issues are recognized by the authorities and are being addressed.

In the new millennium, the higher education sector in Singapore will continue to see exciting and transformational changes in response to the country's economic planning. The universities are now creating the measures—and infrastructure—to become effective contributors to regional creativity and economic growth. In the process, they hope to become the "Harvard and MIT of Asia" and the "Boston of the East." The pathway is toward an integrated universities–communities ecosystem that allows for the free flow of ideas, technology, creativity, and social activities. The old model of a university pumping out research results and educating students, or even commercializing innovations and creating start-up companies, is no longer sufficient for the era of creative-knowledge-based capitalism. Universities and their communities have taken the technology agenda seriously; now they must do the same with talent and openness. By drawing upon the collective creative energy of thousands of people, new ideas are generated, and new talent is created on campuses and potentially in their communities as well. Higher education in Singapore will realize considerable advantage in generating innovations, attracting and retaining talent, and creating sustained prosperity.

NOTES

1. The decision to close down Nanyang University and set up Nanyang Technological Institute, as argued by critics, was both an economic and a political one. In terms of efficient resource allocation, Singapore was deemed too small to require more than one university, and with the declining enrollment of Chinese stream students, the demise of Nanyang University would be a matter of time. Those who argued against the move felt that the pace of closure was forced, with Nanyang University graduates finding themselves being discriminated against in the job market because of their low level of proficiency in English.

2. One common strategy adopted by governments to meet public demand for access to university education is to convert polytechnics into universities. In Singapore, educational planners recognized the importance of striking the right balance in postsecondary education between subdegree and degree-level work to avoid wastage of valuable resources. Universities and polytechnics in Singapore preserve their distinctive roles, and each understands and respects the difference. The overall driving factor is to meet the manpower needs of the economy.

3. The government paid close attention to polytechnic education to build a wide base of skilled technical workers. Because of the government's consistent marketing of the high value of polytechnic education, more and more students, many of whom had academic results that could allow them to enter universities, opted for polytechnic education instead of going down the old path to a general academic education. Good performance in their polytechnic studies would enable them to gain entry into the second or third year of university education. Hence, by 2004, 19,147 students (9,104 of whom were females) enrolled in the five polytechnics, while 12,194 opted for university education.

4. R&D is critical to Singapore's economy, and the government formulates its R&D policies according to the country's long-term economic development needs. R&D strategies concentrate on incremental technology and focus on the attainment of realistic goals. The National Technology Plan 1991 aimed to achieve a total national expenditure on R&D of 2 percent of gross domestic product by 1995, with the private sector contributing a minimum of 50 percent. The ratio of scientists and engineers engaged in R&D will be raised to 40 per 1,000 labor force participants.

5. The maximum amount that can be borrowed has since been increased to 90 percent.

6. SMU, which follows the Wharton business school model and was meant to be a research university, has made excellence in research a crucial agenda for its academic faculty.

7. In Singapore's context, "corporatization" refers to the transition of a statutory board to a "privately run" corporation.

8. Gardner added, "While standards are in place for judging the quality of work in the traditional disciplines, there has not been time—perhaps there has not been the motivation—to set up analogous kinds of indices for quality work in various interdisciplinary amalgams."

9. Spinoffs refer to new companies formed by NUS faculty members/researchers to commercialize NUS intellectual property (IP), while start-ups refer to companies formed by NUS faculty/researchers that do not involve IP owned by NUS. Between 1980 and 2004, a total of 82 spinoffs and start-ups were formed.

10. Although many observers have suggested that the role of higher education in a knowledge-driven economy has never been more crucial because it stimulates innovation and develops human capital, in reality, it is not easy to measure the exact contributions of universities (and other tertiary institutions, such as the polytechnics) to economic growth in the region or country. A joint project by the Massachusetts Institute of Technology and the University of Cambridge found that universities are most successful in influencing economic growth when they are attuned to the economic structure of their local economies. The nature of the industrial transformation in the local economy in large part defines what the best role is for the university to contribute to change. See Richard H. Mattoon (2006).

11. That is why regions with large numbers of high-tech engineers and entrepreneurs also tend to be havens for artists, musicians, and culturally creative people. Austin, Boston, and Seattle are cases in point.

12. It reflects a virtuous cycle whereby high levels of talent lead to more technology generation, innovation, and entrepreneurship, which then lead over time to higher rates of economic growth and more job generation, which in turn lead to higher rates of talent production, retention, and attraction.

13. From a speech by Dr. Tony Tan on ways to expand the university sector, published in the *Sunday Times,* September 2, 2007.

REFERENCES

Dainton, Frederick. 1979. *Report on University Education in Singapore.* Singapore.

Gardner, Howard. 2004. "How Education Changes: Considerations of History, Science, and Values." In *Globalization: Culture and Education in the New Millennium,* ed. M. Suarez-Orozco and D. B. Qin-Hilliard. Berkeley: University of California Press.

Lee, Kuan Yew. 2000. *From Third World to First: The Singapore Story: 1965–2000.* Singapore: The Straits Times Press.

Mattoon, Richard H. 2006. "Can Higher Education Foster Economic Growth?" *Chicago Fed Letter,* no. 229, August.

Ministry of Education. 2006. *Annual Report.* Singapore: Ministry of Education.

Ministry of Trade and Industry. 1986. *Economic Committee Report of 1986.* Singapore: Ministry of Trade and Industry.

National University of Singapore. 2005. *Annual Report.* Singapore: National University of Singapore.

North, Douglas C. 2005. *Understanding the Process of Economic Change.* Princeton, NJ: Princeton University Press.
Straits Times, May 11, 1981.
Straits Times, July 3, 1984.
Straits Times, November 30, 1986.
Straits Times, August 27, 1988.
Straits Times, February 14, 1990.
Straits Times, February 16, 1990.
Straits Times, August 10, 1997.

CHAPTER 8

Digital Skills and Education: Singapore's ICT Master Planning for the School Sector

KOH Thiam Seng and LEE Sai Choo

INTRODUCTION

The global landscape is driven by interrelated forces of a knowledge-based and innovation-driven economy, globalization, and rapid advances in science and technology. These trends are accelerating the pace of competition among countries across the world. This competition is taking place in an increasingly uncertain operating environment where there are constant disruptive threats from terrorism and natural calamities. In this evolving competitive and uncertain economic landscape, human capital is Singapore's key competitive differentiator (Chang 2003; Economic Review Committee 2002).

Singapore saw the potential of information and communication technologies (ICT) as a key enabler in accelerating its economic development as early as the late 1970s (Chia and Lim 2003; Wong 2001). Since the 1980s, Singapore has formulated and implemented national ICT master plans that have resulted in ICT manpower development, increased ICT awareness, and literacy of the populace and businesses.

In terms of global economic competitiveness, Singapore was ranked number one in Asia and fifth in the world in the *Global Competitiveness Report 2006–2007*.[1] The report ranked Singapore at the top for its high-quality infrastructure, flexible and efficient markets, healthy and well-educated workforces, and high levels of technological readiness and innovative capacity.

One of the key contributors to Singapore's economic success has been the alignment of the deployment of ICT with the needs of the economy and society, as well as the coordinated efforts arising from the national ICT plans. Each master plan built on the foundation and achievements of the previous plans and complemented national plans in other related sectors.

This chapter is divided into three parts. In the first part, we briefly describe Singapore's journey in national ICT master planning to illustrate that the ICT master plan for education was developed in the larger context of these national ICT plans. In the second part, we share the salient features of the two ICT master plans for education to illustrate the thinking and process of ICT master planning for education.[2] We limit the discussion to the ICT master plans for the school sector (year 1 to year 12) only. In the last part, we summarize some of the key lessons learned from Singapore's implementation of the two ICT master plans, which may be of interest to policy makers in other countries.

ICT MASTER PLANS

In the course of Singapore's history, six national ICT master plans have been implemented.[3] The concept of ICT as a key enabler to drive limitless possibilities in the economy and society underpins all these plans.

FROM 1980s TO 1992

The first three national ICT master plans were the National Computerization Plan (NCP), National IT Plan (NITP), and IT 2000: The Intelligent Island. The aims of the first master plan, NCP, were (a) to initiate the computerization of major functions in all the government ministries to deliver better and efficient services to the public, (b) to facilitate the development and growth of local ICT industry, and (c) to develop a pool of ICT professionals to meet the needs of the ICT industry (Committee on National Computerisation 1981). The second master plan, NITP, opened up the computerized government systems to the private sector to enable electronic data interchange across government departments, industry, and the public (National IT Plan Working Committee 1985). The aim of the third master plan, IT2000, was to develop a national information infrastructure to transform Singapore into an "intelligent island" where ICT is available everywhere—in the home, offices, schools, and factories (Cordeiro and Al-Hawamdeh 2001; National Computer Board 1992).

FROM 2000 TO 2006

The next three plans were the Infocomm 21, Connected Singapore, and iN2015. With the ICT infrastructure generally in place, the fourth master plan, Infocomm 21, was targeted at nurturing an environment to develop a sufficient pool of high-caliber ICT manpower and Net-savvy users to sustain the growth of the economy as well as to deliver as many integrated public sector services online as possible to increase public access to e-government services (Infocomm Development Authority 2000). The fifth master plan, Connected Singapore, extended the broadband capabilities to provide an infrastructure that supported wireless and wired networks and value-added mobile services (Infocomm Development Authority 2003). The latest plan, iN2015, aims to develop Singapore into a global ICT capital, e-economy, and e-society.[4] To achieve the latter, an ultra-high-speed network on the order of one gigabit per second will be developed to link every home and office. This will include a wireless broadband network throughout the island to further improve the ability of all Singaporeans to stay connected at all times. In particular, Singapore will be building peaks of excellence in schools in their use of ICT to enhance learning to position Singapore as a center for innovation in the use of ICT in the education and learning sector.

In addition, two massive government initiatives cut across all six ICT national master plans:

- *Two ICT Master Plans for Education:* First Master Plan (1997–2002) and Second Master Plan (2003–2008)

The first ICT master plan for education (mp1) focused on setting up the basic infrastructure for schools and training teachers to use ICT for teaching and learning (Cheah and Koh 2001). It was implemented in three phases, starting with 22 schools in phase 1 and extended to all schools by 2002. The second ICT master plan for education (mp2) focuses on the pervasive and effective integration of ICT into the curriculum for engaged learning. Both master plans adopt the strategy of equipping students with ICT skills through integration of ICT into the curriculum.

- *Three e-Government Plans:* eGaPI (2000–2003), eGaPII (2003–2006), and iGov2010 (2006–2010)

eGaPI focused on delivering integrated public sector services online, while eGaPII focused on making these government services user friendly through streamlining the processes for integrated e-services. The latest master plan, iGov2010, aims to make government e-services even more user friendly.

Table 8.1 gives an overview of Singapore's ICT journey over the last 25 years.

USE OF ICT IN SINGAPORE SCHOOLS: A HISTORICAL PERSPECTIVE

CREATING COMPUTER AWARENESS AND LITERACY IN SCHOOLS

In the 1980s, the Ministry of Education (MOE) initiated projects such as the School Link Project to bring ICT into schools through the provision of computers for administration and for teachers' use. Computer Appreciation Clubs were also

Table 8.1 Singapore's ICT Journey

Year	National ICT Plans	Government ICT Plans	Use of ICT in Education
1980	The National Computerization Plan	Civil Service Computerization Program	
1981			Computer science as A-level Subject* Computer Appreciation Clubs* School Link Project*
1982			
1983			
1984			
1985			
1986	The National IT Plan		
1987			
1988			
1989			
1990			
1991			Professional Computing Support Program*
1992	IT2000: The Intelligent Island		
1993			
1994			Computer Applications*
1995			
1996			Elements of Office Administration*
1997			First Master Plan for ICT in Education
1998			
1999			
2000	Infocomm 21	e-Government Action Plan I	
2001			
2002			
2003			Second Master Plan for ICT in Education
2004	Connected Singapore	e-Government Action Plan II	
2005			
2006			
2007		iGov2010	
2008			
2009			
2010			

Note: * = the year in which the subject, project, or activity was introduced into the schools.

started in secondary schools as extracurricular activities, and computer science was introduced as an A-level subject in junior colleges (JCs).

In the 1990s, the Professional Computing Support Program was started to ensure that all teachers became proficient in software packages useful to their work. By 1994, computer applications (CPA), a skills-based subject, was included as part of the new Normal (technical) stream in secondary schools.[5] In 1996, the elements of office administration (EOA) subject was launched in secondary schools to train upper secondary students in the Normal (academic) and Normal (technical) streams in office administration. A significant part of the EOA curriculum focused on the development of ICT knowledge and skills for office administration that would be relevant to the needs of industry. The secondary schools had to be equipped with computer laboratories to facilitate the CPA and EOA courses.

PILOTING THE USE OF ICT FOR TEACHING AND LEARNING

In the mid-1990s, pilot studies were conducted to explore the use of ICT for teaching and learning. Three separate pilot studies were initiated at primary, secondary, and JC levels as the teaching and learning requirements were expected to be different at these three levels.

- *Accelerating the Use of ICT in Primary Schools Program (AITP)*. The MOE initiated the AITP at the primary school level to introduce the use of multimedia learning in key subjects. The AITP was implemented in six pilot schools in mid-1995. Students in pilot schools spent about 10 percent of the curriculum time using ICT media such as CD-ROM educational packages for learning. The program was found to be helpful to most students in their learning. Academically inclined students using ICT became more independent learners, while others, encouraged by hands-on lessons, showed greater interest in their studies and motivation to achieve the curriculum objectives.
- *Student's and Teacher's Workbench (STW)*. In the STW project, a fully ICT-enabled secondary one science curriculum was implemented in six pilot secondary schools in 1996. It provided a central repository of digital educational resources and lesson packages for teachers. Several good practices of the STW were incorporated in the implementation of mp1. These good practices included, for example, developing digital media repositories (DMRs) of educational resources for use by teachers anywhere, anytime within the schools and involving private sector content providers in the development of the DMRs.
- *JCNet*. The JCNet was initiated because of the increased interest in the use of the Internet for education. The JCNet, structured as a research and development (R&D) project, was implemented in two JCs in 1997. The project explored the benefits of using the Internet for learning at the JC level, specifically to support the learning of General Paper, physics, and chemistry. The MOE worked with the two JCs to experiment and model new approaches in the use of ICT in JC education. These included studying the infrastructure required as well as the

strategies for curriculum integration and for enhancing teaching and learning. The lessons learned from the JCNet project guided other JCs and schools in their use of the Internet for teaching and learning.

FIRST MASTER PLAN FOR ICT IN EDUCATION (1997–2002)

Mp1 was launched by then–Minister of Education Chee-Hean Teo in 1997 (Teo 1997). It provided a blueprint for the integration of ICT into the curriculum as a strategy for equipping students with the necessary ICT skills to meet the challenges of globalization and rapid technological changes. The Educational Technology Division (ETD) was set up within the MOE to spearhead this integration of ICT into the school curriculum. The good practices and key lessons gained from the implementation of AITP, STW, and JCNet projects guided the formulation of the concept plan for mp1.

ALIGNING GOALS AND OBJECTIVES WITH THE MOE'S VISION

The underlying philosophy of mp1 was that education should constantly anticipate the future needs of the society and work toward fulfilling those needs. Four overarching goals govern the implementation of mp1. These goals were based on the MOE's vision of Thinking Schools, Learning Nation (MOE 1998), where the emphasis was on the acquisition of thinking, communication, and lifelong learning skills. The four goals were as follows:

- *Enhance links between the school and the world around it to expand and enrich the learning environment.* With ICT, teachers and students were able to access the wide range of educational resources outside the school and collaborate with other educational institutions—local and foreign—and the community at large. These new connections would help students develop appropriate perspectives on working and living in an increasingly borderless world.
- *Encourage creative thinking, lifelong learning, and social responsibility.* Students, through the appropriate use of ICT for learning, would be able to develop critical competencies in accessing, analyzing, and applying information for independent learning, to develop the ability to think creatively, to cooperate with one another, and to make sound value judgments.
- *Generate innovations in education.* The process of integrating ICT effectively into the curriculum would require experimentation and exploration on the part of teachers and educators. The experimentation and exploration would include the possibilities of new curricula and assessment modes as well as new school designs to take into consideration the new needs that would arise from the introduction of ICT into the curriculum.

- *Promote administrative and management excellence in the education system.* The use of ICT would enable greater and more efficient communication within the school, among schools, and between the MOE and schools. It would also provide schools ready access to online data and information to support effective decision making at all levels. The School Cockpit, a Web-based administration portal, was developed for use by school teachers to carry out their administrative tasks. This portal provided a single point of access to all students' data and resources for management, planning, and decision making within schools and school clusters.

KEY DIMENSIONS OF mp1

In the implementation of the ICT master plan, the four main goals were translated into four key dimensions: (a) curriculum and assessment, (b) physical and technological infrastructure, (c) content and learning resources, and (d) human resources development.

Curriculum and Assessment. With the advent of ICT where access and communicating information have become increasingly easy, it was recognized that learning had to shift from receiving information to finding, managing, and applying information. The emphasis was thus for the curriculum to have a better balance between learning factual knowledge and learning skills to find information, apply information to solve problems, and communicate ideas effectively.

ICT was seen as essential in bringing about shifts in learning from mainly knowledge dissemination to more active engagement of the learners. Thus, ICT was integrated into 30 percent of the curriculum at all levels and as far as possible into all subjects. The use of ICT could broaden a teacher's pedagogical possibilities and open up a wider range of learning resources for students. In addition, ICT would allow a greater degree of independent learning; more able students could play an active role in their learning and expand their learning beyond the standard curriculum.

Through the integration of ICT into the curriculum, students were expected to acquire specific ICT skills at the various stages of schooling, starting in primary school. By the time they left secondary school, students would have acquired the minimum competencies in the use of the Internet and productivity applications such as word processors and spreadsheets.

Physical and Technological Infrastructure. Adequate physical and technological infrastructure was necessary for effective ICT integration. In mp1, a significant portion of the budget was used to create an ICT-rich environment that was conducive for learning. Under mp1, schools were provided with the necessary physical and technological infrastructure to allow students to spend up to 30 percent of the curriculum time using ICT by 2002. To achieve this target, mp1 set out national standards for the hardware and networking provisions as guidelines for schools from 1997 to 2002. All primary schools were provided with an initial student-computer ratio of 6.6:1, while secondary schools and JCs had an initial student-computer ratio of 5:1. Schools were given computer laboratories: three in each primary school, four in each secondary school, and five in each junior college.

In addition to the computer laboratories, students were also provided with access to ICT facilities in all learning areas in the school, including classrooms, libraries, and special rooms, to allow more convenient and effective ICT integration into the curriculum. Schools were allowed to opt for a mix of desktops and notebook computers to provide more flexibility in arranging students for group learning and overcoming space constraints. Schools were also encouraged to explore various configurations of placing the computers in the classrooms to better serve the learning needs of their students.

The MOE provided schoolwide networking in every school and allowed the Internet and digitized media resources to be accessed in all classrooms and learning areas. Networking allowed sharing of teaching and learning resources within and between schools by teachers and students. All schools were linked through a wide area network, which was eventually connected to the high-speed backbone of Singapore ONE.[6] Teachers and students from primary four and above were given e-mail accounts to facilitate communication and collaboration.

In parallel, in 1999, as part of the Program for Rebuilding and Improving Existing Schools (PRIME), the MOE provided a budget of S$4.5 billion to redevelop and reequip schools that were built over the past 20–30 years to the latest building standards and to support the educational programs such as mp1 (Teo 2001). In particular, to support mp1 implementation, PRIME provided these older schools with additional ICT facilities—computer laboratories, media resource libraries, and ICT learning resource rooms—larger classrooms, and an upgrade in power capacity where necessary. Beyond mp1 implementation, PRIME provided construction of extension blocks, alteration of existing school buildings, and construction of new buildings where appropriate. Construction was carried out in phases, determined by the age of the school, the state of existing facilities in the school, and availability and suitability of the school site.

As immediate access to technical support was important to build teachers' confidence, especially at the initial stages, the MOE outsourced technical support for the schools to a system integrator. The appointed system integrator provided a technology assistant in each school who gave first-level, onsite support in resolving hardware and software problems and in maintenance work.

Content and Learning Resources. Under mp1, one of the main approaches taken was integrating the use of educational software, largely CD-ROM-based software, into all subjects whenever the content and pedagogy found in the available commercial educational software were consistent with curricular objectives. In mp1, the MOE acquired a starter set of suitable commercially available educational software for schools and collaborated with local industry to encourage the development of a wide range of educational software that met the specific needs of the local curriculum.

To increase access to digital content for use in the curriculum, the MOE set up a central clearinghouse to source, evaluate, and recommend to schools suitable ICT-based learning resources, such as CD-based software titles and Internet sites. Recommendations on ICT-based learning resources made by the MOE clearinghouse were compiled and posted on the MOE intranet, which was accessible to all teachers from their school computers.

The Educational Software Procurement Scheme (ESPS) was also implemented at the start of mp1 to facilitate the procurement of software by schools directly from software publishers. Schools could purchase any number of software titles at special educational prices, which were, on average, 30–40 percent off the retail price. The ESPS also allowed teachers to purchase one personal copy of each software title at the special educational price.

The MOE actively promoted the collaboration with industry to ensure the continuous development of ICT-based content for use by the schools. To provide industry with incentives to collaborate, the MOE tapped into the various financial and resource support schemes for industry partners offered by statutory boards such as the National Computer Board (NCB), now known as the Infocomm Development Authority of Singapore (or iDA) and the Economic Development Board. For example, it used the MOE–Local Industry Upgrading Program launched in 1996 by the NCB to build the capacity of local companies for developing high-quality ICT-based resources, especially in areas where suitable titles were lacking. Many locally developed educational software packages are now recognized internationally, including the Active Primary Mathematics CD-ROM series, which features sound pedagogy, innovation, and content-rich activities. The MOE and a local publishing company, Times Media Pte Ltd, collaborated in the production of the Primary Mathematics CD-ROM series.

The MOE relied on Singapore ONE when it was launched for the delivery of interactive, multimedia applications and services through the networks. In 1999, under the IT2000 plan, iDA initiated the FastTrack@School program to help teachers and students use Singapore ONE for teaching and learning activities. This program encouraged industry partners to work with schools to develop useful and relevant broadband education content for the curriculum. More than 300 interactive, multimedia applications and services were successfully developed under this program.

Human Resources Development. Teachers played an important role in the successful implementation of mp1, that is, integrating ICT into the school curriculum and assessment. The shift in pedagogy required teachers to have a new set of skills, attitudes, and knowledge.

In mp1, every teacher went through 30 hours of school-based professional development on the integration of ICT into the curriculum. The workshops were conducted by senior ICT instructors from the ETD in the MOE. At these workshops, teachers were given examples of integrating the word processor, Internet, and other ICT tools into teaching and learning. Teachers were also given instruction on the design and conduct of ICT-based lessons. In addition to these training workshops, schools were encouraged to put in place structures to support teachers in the use of ICT, for example, to identify ICT champions at all levels, to adopt a buddy system for teachers, and to get ICT-savvy students to assist the teachers in class.

The MOE also introduced schemes to recognize teachers' creative use of ICT and motivate them to move on to higher levels of ICT use. One such award was the Hewlett Packard Innovation in Information Technology (HP INIT) Award, sponsored by Hewlett-Packard (Singapore) in 1999. In 2001, a new dimension was added to the HP INIT Award—collaboration and networking among teachers and specialists. The new dimension provided teachers with a platform to reflect on their own learning experiences through the innovative use of ICT, backed by strong pedagogical considerations.

A Computer Purchase Scheme for Teachers (CPST) was introduced to help teachers purchase their own computers. CPST was seen as essential in the initial stages to create an ICT culture among teachers. The MOE paid 20 percent of the purchase price for desktop computers and 40 percent for notebook computers.

At the National Institute of Education (NIE), the teacher-training programs were aligned with mp1 to ensure that all the graduating students had the essential skills for integrating ICT into the curriculum (Koh 1999). ICT was integrated into the NIE curricula for initial teacher training. In the early stages, teacher-trainees who did not have the necessary ICT skills, such as word processing, had to attend ICT skills training conducted by private training agencies. NIE focused on providing the teacher-trainees with the essential knowledge and basic skills for integrating ICT into their subject areas. Teacher-trainees were expected to participate in intra- and intergroup online discussions to apply what they had learned and to share with one another their experiences of integrating ICT into their practicum teaching. They were encouraged to design and conduct ICT-based lessons during their practical sessions. NIE also offered more advanced ICT-based pedagogical principles and skills as elective courses on constructivist learning using ICT and instructional multimedia design. For inservice teachers, NIE introduced the advanced diploma and advanced postgraduate diploma in education programs where teachers could upgrade their knowledge and skills in the use of ICT for teaching and learning.

RESEARCH AND DEVELOPMENT

In mp1, the MOE collaborated with industries, research institutes, and the NCB to undertake R&D in the use of ICT in learning. In 1997, the School Industry Partnership Scheme (SCHIPS) was initiated to explore the use of emerging technologies and pedagogies for teaching and learning. Two major projects included the development of the EduPAD and the Digital Media Repository (DMR). The EduPAD piloted under SCHIPS was a prototype equivalent of the current tablet personal computers (PCs) available in the market. The DMR was a centralized repository of digital resources for teaching and learning that was accessible via the networks by teachers anytime, anywhere.

ACHIEVEMENTS OF mp1

At the end of mp1, Singapore succeeded in laying a firm foundation that enabled all the schools to integrate ICT into the curriculum. Following are the significant achievements:

- All schools were provided with the necessary physical and ICT infrastructure for ICT-based teaching and learning. This infrastructure included networking within every school and access to the MOE's intranet and the Internet. Primary schools had a pupil-to-computer ratio of 6.6:1, while secondary schools and JCs had a ratio of 5:1.
- Teachers had acquired basic competencies in integrating ICT into the curriculum. More important, teachers had accepted ICT as a pedagogical tool in the classroom.
- There were pockets of excellence in the use of ICT in learning among some teachers and schools, providing models and directions for further innovations in the use of ICT in teaching and learning.

SECOND MASTER PLAN FOR ICT IN EDUCATION (2003–08)

Mp2 was launched in July 2002 by then–Senior Minister of State for Education Tharman Shanmugaratnam (the current minister for education) (Shanmugaratnam 2002). The second master plan consolidates and builds on the achievements of mp1. The focus of mp2 is on sustaining the momentum achieved from the successful implementation of mp1 to bring about a more pervasive and effective integration of ICT into the curriculum and engaged learning in students.

The underlying philosophy of mp1 remains relevant for mp2: to ensure that students acquire the necessary skills and knowledge that will meet the changing needs of society and work. The integration of ICT into the curriculum continues to be Singapore's key strategy in equipping students with the necessary ICT skills.

Table 8.2 A Comparison of the Focus of mp2 and mp1

mp1 Approach (From)	mp2 Approach (To)
Using ICT to enhance the delivery of the curriculum.	Adopting a seamless integration of ICT into the curriculum that starts right from the curriculum planning and design stage.
Using largely static printed learning resources and CD-ROM–based learning resources.	Using repositories of dynamic Web-based learning resources in the form of learning objects.
Providing teachers with a basic set of competencies for the integration of ICT into the curriculum.	Providing teachers with a wider repertoire of competencies for the integration of ICT into the curriculum.
Implementing largely teacher-centered pedagogies.	Implementing learner-centered pedagogies.
Providing all schools with standard ICT provisions.	Giving all schools greater autonomy to decide on the ICT provisions required, based on the learning needs of their students.
Adopting a centralized, phased approach to the integration of ICT into the curriculum.	Adopting an approach where schools have a greater sense of ownership of and accountability for the integration of ICT into the curriculum.
Implementing a one-size-fits-all plan for all schools to bring them up to a basic level of integration of ICT into the curriculum.	Adopting a mass-customization and an ability-driven plan that caters to specific groups of schools and students in terms of the integration of ICT into the curriculum, based on actual student needs.

In conceptualizing mp2, a systemic and holistic approach was adopted to address all key areas relating to the pervasive and effective use of ICT for teaching and learning. These key areas included (a) alignment of curriculum, instruction, and assessment; (b) provision of ICT-enabled infrastructure and support; (c) availability of ICT-based learning resources; (d) ongoing professional development; (e) R&D on the effective use of ICT-based learning resources, tools, and pedagogies and the possible use of emerging technologies in teaching and learning; and (f) building school capacity and capability to integrate ICT into the curriculum.

The current mp2 implementation focuses on changing pedagogical practices of classroom teachers to more fully harness ICT to bring about engaged learning in students. Specifically, the shifts in implementation focus from mp1 to mp2 are as shown in table 8.2.

MOVE TOWARD WEB-BASED LEARNING OBJECTS

The use of ICT-based learning resources in the curriculum is shifting from the use of the largely CD-ROM–based learning resources in mp1 to interactive Web-based learning resources in mp2. In mp1, the focus was on the acquisition of commercially available CD-ROM learning packages and the development of additional CD-ROM learning packages in collaboration with local industry. In mp2, in addition to using Internet-based and commercially available learning resources, selected teachers with the interest and talent are encouraged to develop and share their learning objects with other teachers. Examples of Web-based learning resources developed by the MOE and teachers can be found on the edu.MALL Web site (http://www.moe.gov.sg/edumall/index.htm).

By moving toward Web-based learning resources, teachers and students will be able to access learning resources anytime, anywhere using a range of devices (desktop computers, notebook/tablet computers, or handheld devices such as personal digital assistants [PDAs] and mobile phones) and platforms (e.g., Windows, Apple, or LINUX operating systems). By adopting the learning object framework for developing digital learning resources, teachers will have access to small units of learning that are highly customizable and reusable—allowing teachers to theoretically customize the learning paths of their students based on their students' individual learning styles, provided in a just-in-time and just-enough manner.

IMPROVED ICT PROVISIONS

The ICT norms in schools have been improved to provide greater access to computers by students for learning. The student–computer ratio is now 6.5:1 for primary schools and 4:1 for secondary schools, JCs, and centralized institutes. In mp1, almost all schools were connected to the Internet by a wired network through the MOE's network. The MOE is now segregating the schools' network from that of the ministry to give schools a more flexible network environment. Schools can experiment with new technologies such as a wireless network as well as higher bandwidth of direct access to the Internet. Under the iN2015 plan, schools will eventually connect to the Internet at a speed of 1 gigabit per second or more.

Under mp2, more and more teachers are developing their own ICT-based learning resources to meet their curricular needs. They are using various learning management systems (LMSs) available in the market or on the Internet to manage both the commercially available and school-created ICT-based learning resources. Hence, there is a need for interoperability among the LMSs to allow sharing of school-created ICT-based learning resources across all schools. The MOE has initiated a project for "intercluster sharing of resources" (or iSHARE) to develop a generic content management framework that will enable such sharing. The iSHARE framework is currently being implemented in one out of four zones of schools. By 2008, all schools should be able to share their school-created learning resources with one another.

At present, all secondary schools and JCs have an LMS, and about 90 percent of primary schools have an LMS. All primary schools are expected to have an LMS eventually.

MOVE TOWARD JUST-IN-TIME AND JUST-ENOUGH PROFESSIONAL DEVELOPMENT

As a result of the phased implementation approach to mp1, teachers and heads of departments (HODs) are at different levels of competencies in their ability to integrate ICT into the curriculum. Hence, in mp2, schools have the autonomy to decide on the type of professional development (PD) programs required, when they should be conducted, and who should be involved in the programs. To support schools in providing PD programs that are just-in-time and adequate for building the capacity of their teachers, the MOE offers on a school or cluster basis customized PD programs that are mostly subject-based to meet their specific needs. PD programs are in the form of face-to-face workshops, field work, and attachment programs focusing either on the baseline use of ICT for teaching and learning (e.g., use of the Internet), or higher levels of ICT use (e.g., discussion forums). Regardless of the learning modes, the PD programs emphasize the value-added use of ICT in the teaching and learning process and create the conditions for teachers to learn actively and collaboratively in a variety of learning environments. The MOE also organizes sessions to encourage regular exchange of ideas and professional reflections and thus build a sharing culture among teachers and HODs.

MOVE TOWARD GREATER SCHOOL AUTONOMY AND ACCOUNTABILITY IN IMPLEMENTATION

Under mp2, in line with the MOE's policy direction of giving top-down support for ground-up initiatives, schools are given greater autonomy to implement ICT programs according to their students' needs. To allow schools to exercise the autonomy given to them, ICT funds are now devolved to schools, with increased accountability from schools through the submission of their annual ICT plans to show how the funds supported their ICT programs for teaching and learning. The purpose of increased autonomy and accountability is better utilization of funds and deployment of limited resources, as well as greater ownership in mp2 implementation by the schools.

With schools at different levels of ICT implementation, the MOE consultancy teams are working with schools to build their capacity in ICT planning and in effective uses of ICT for teaching and learning. The consultancy teams also support schools' initiatives such as experimenting with the use of emerging technologies (e.g., tablet PCs, mobile devices, and 3-D virtual learning environments such as Quest Atlantis and Second Life) to encourage greater diversity and higher levels of ICT use.

Based on a review[7] conducted in 2004 to set implementation priorities, the MOE has developed baseline ICT standards for students' learning experiences to ensure that all schools achieve a minimum level of ICT use. These standards will be rolled out in all primary schools in 2007 and in all secondary schools in 2008.

Since mp1, the MOE has continued to introduce recognition schemes to acknowledge teachers' efforts in harnessing the use of ICT in education. Examples of the recognition include the Microsoft-MOE Professional Development Award sponsored by Microsoft in 2004 and the Lenovo Innovation Award sponsored by Lenovo launched in 2007.

BUILDING R&D CAPABILITY

In mp2, the MOE encourages R&D to support innovations in ICT-based pedagogical practices. In 2003, the MOE established an R&D Section within the ETD to undertake applied R&D work with the schools and to encourage experimentation with innovative ICT-based pedagogical practices. In 2005, the MOE established the Learning Sciences Lab (LSL) at the NIE to undertake fundamental research on learning that is enabled by ICT in the schools (Looi et al. 2005). LSL's charter is to expose school leaders, teachers, and students to workable ideas and prototypes of using ICT in education that can potentially transform teaching and learning through engaging in a continuous process of experimentation.

To encourage experimentation at schools, the MOE introduced more schemes to recognize and support schools that are ready to achieve higher levels of ICT use in education. In 2005, the MOE launched the LEAD ICT@Schools Scheme (Leading Experimentation and Development in ICT), which will support not only schools that conduct research on emerging ICT-based pedagogies, but also schools that want to experiment with existing ICT-based pedagogies on a significant scale. Schools recognized under this scheme will have additional funds for ICT implementation. There are currently about 66 schools (or about 15 percent) on the scheme.

In line with the iN2015 vision, the MOE launched the FutureSchools@Singapore (FS@SG) project in 2007, in which it will support and develop 15 schools (about 5 percent of schools) by 2015 over a few phases into peaks of excellence in the use of ICT for teaching and learning. While these FS@SG schools would be provided with state-of-the-art, ICT-enabled teaching and learning environments, including learning in a 1-to-1 computing environment for all students, the aim of the project is really to foster and sustain innovations in curriculum, instruction, and assessment that would fully leverage on ICT to bring about engaged learning in students. The successful models and ICT-based learning resources and tools will be adapted for use by the LEAD ICT schools and, in turn, will then be adapted by the rest of the schools after these models, resources, and tools have been proven to be effective for learning in the LEAD ICT Schools.

The MOE, in partnership with the iDA, will continue to collaborate with LSL and other academic groups at NIE and schools to conduct further research on developing and prototyping pedagogical models and expand the scope and nature of formative assessments.

ACHIEVEMENTS IN mp2

In mp2, the MOE has worked with school leaders, on a just-in-time and just-enough basis, to provide the necessary conditions for classroom teachers to innovate with the use of ICT in the curriculum. There is a sustainable mechanism and framework for sharing innovative pedagogical practices and models and teacher-created digital educational resources among schools and teachers. There is also an alignment of key stakeholders to ensure that research findings are translated into actual practices by teachers in the classrooms.

An example of a significant experiment with innovative use of ICT in teaching and learning is the BackPack.Net project. The MOE partnered with iDA and Microsoft in 2003 to promote student-centered learning through the use of tablet PCs, digital inking applications, and other innovative ICT technologies. Two of the four pioneer schools, Crescent Girls' School and Catholic High School, are Microsoft's first in Asia—and in the world—in terms of the scale of use of tablet PCs and inking technology (Bienskowski et al. 2005). This collaboration also led to the establishment of the Classroom of the Future at NIE in 2003 to showcase the future possibilities in using ICT in teaching and learning.

BUDGET FOR mp1 AND mp2

For mp1, the MOE announced a budget of S$2 billion for the six-year plan. However, with declining ICT costs and better understanding of mp1 implementation as it progressed, the actual amount spent was much less than the announced budget. The focus of mp2 is on changing pedagogical practices of teachers rather than investing in ICT infrastructure, so the ICT expenditure has been modest relative to the mp1 budget—an average of S$1.3 million per school for 2003–2005. This translated to a total expenditure of about S$470 million over a three-year period. The cost for mp1 was higher than for mp2 because of the capital investment required to equip all schools with the necessary ICT infrastructure for teaching and learning.

DIGITAL OPPORTUNITIES FOR ALL

As we move forward in the digital age, it is critical that all Singaporeans are able to avail themselves of the digital opportunities and possibilities. An ICT culture would bring the benefits of an ICT-enabled lifestyle to people of all ages and from all walks of life. Hence, the government saw the need to invest in ICT facilities to increase access to computers and the Internet, particularly for students from poor socioeconomic backgrounds. In 1999, under the IT2000 master plan, Internet@library was launched to give everyone easy access to the Internet at 10 public libraries.

Under mp2, to narrow the digital divide, the MOE increased the appropriate integration of ICT into the curriculum, lowered the student–computer ratio, enhanced student access to computers by providing more open access areas, and provided cheaper access to the Internet through school–industry partnerships. Singapore's target is for all students, regardless of socioeconomic backgrounds, to have equal access to ICT facilities in the schools and for all households with school-going children to have at least an Internet-ready personal computing device for learning purposes.

To help households gain access to an Internet-ready device, iDA collaborated with industry and introduced the NEU PC Scheme in 1999. It offered needy families Internet-ready computers at highly subsidized prices, and more than 19,000 families benefited from this scheme over six years. However, as of 2006, 14 percent of households with school-going children still did not have access to an Internet-ready personal computing device. So the government enhanced the scheme to benefit even more needy families under the 2006 NEU PC Plus Scheme, and students from low-income families can obtain a brand new desktop computer, bundled with three years of unlimited broadband access, for less than S$300.

SOME LESSONS FROM mp1 AND mp2 IMPLEMENTATION

There is already an abundance of literature on the lessons learned and the challenges faced in master planning for ICT in education. For example, the World Bank's ICT and Education,[8] UNESCO's ICT in Education,[9] and the United Kingdom's BECTA[10] Web sites provide useful inputs on master planning for ICT in education. Some specific examples of publications that would be useful for policy makers include chapters by Mitchel Resnick (2002) and Robert Hawkins (2002) in the *Global Information Technology Report 2001–2002,* the handbook on monitoring and evaluating ICT in an education project by Daniel Wagner and his colleagues (2005), and a framework for analyzing national policies and programs on ICT-based education reform by Robert Kozma (2005).

Following are some of the lessons learned that are specific to the context of Singapore's master planning for ICT in education.

ADDRESSING FUNDAMENTAL ISSUES IN EDUCATION

To ensure success in master planning for ICT in education, fundamental issues in education must first be resolved before an attempt is made to introduce a systemwide use of ICT into education. These issues include relevant curricula, good basic school infrastructure, and adequate number of qualified, trained teachers.

When Singapore launched its mp1 in 1997, Singapore education was shifting from an efficiency-driven education system to an ability-driven education system, that is, from one that was highly structured and standardized to one that would be able to cater to a wider range of learners, taking into consideration their talents and interests (Chiang 1998). Singapore had brought down the school dropout rate from 11 percent in 1980 to 0.4 percent in 1997 for primary schools, and from 19 percent in 1980 to 4.4 percent in 1997 for secondary schools. A centralized, standardized curriculum was implemented in all schools. Singapore had about 21,500 qualified, trained teachers in schools in 1997, up from 18,000 in 1980. Today, Singapore has about 27,000 teachers and this number will be increasing to at least 30,000 by 2010 (Ministry of Education 2006). A strong school leadership runs all schools effectively, and there is a sufficient number of schools with good basic infrastructure to deliver a good, quality education. Supported by steady economic growth over the years and a sound and robust education system in 1997, Singapore was able to mobilize additional resources back then to launch mp1 successfully—to provide all schools with the necessary ICT-enabled teaching and learning environments and almost all teachers with the necessary training to acquire the basic competencies to integrate ICT into the curriculum.

SYSTEMATIC AND SYSTEMIC IMPLEMENTATION APPROACH

In conceptualizing the master plan for ICT in education, a systematic and systemic approach for implementing the plan must be taken.

It is important to systematically identify all the key dimensions of the master plan that are critical to the success of its implementation. In the case of Singapore, the critical dimensions, as outlined in the earlier section, included the following:

- An adequate ICT-enabled teaching and learning infrastructure conducive to the integration of ICT into the curriculum, which included technical support for teachers.
- An alignment of curriculum, instruction, and assessment to direct and provide incentives for the integration of ICT into teaching and learning.
- Easy access to ICT-based learning resources and tools for the integration of ICT into the curriculum.
- Just-in-time and just-enough professional development programs for teachers and school leaders to integrate ICT into the curriculum.
- An R&D program to develop capabilities in harnessing emerging technologies to transform teaching and learning.

Both mp1 and mp2 were implemented systematically: The integration of ICT into the curriculum and assessment was supported and complemented by other MOE initiatives. These other major initiatives were directed at reviewing and revising teaching and assessment methods, including nurturing thinking skills and creativity and encouraging knowledge generation and application. The initiatives that were implemented over the years included, for example, Thinking Schools, Learning Nation (Goh 1997; Ministry of Education 1998), Project Work (2000),[11] and the more recent Innovation and Enterprise (2004)[12] and Teach Less, Learn More (2005).[13] The curriculum was appropriately reduced, without sacrificing rigor and standards, to create space and time for teachers to carry out pedagogical innovations that include the use of ICT in their teaching.

PAYING ATTENTION TO TEACHERS' READINESS FOR ICT INTEGRATION INTO THE CURRICULUM

One of the key challenges in the successful implementation of the ICT master plan for education is ensuring teachers' readiness in changing their classroom practices to integrate ICT into the curriculum in a meaningful manner. To succeed in the implementation, attention must be paid to the cultural or people dimension.

Before most teachers will be willing to change their classroom practices, they need to be persuaded by realistic models of ICT-based pedagogies that demonstrate some transformation of the educational experiences of their students. As there may be a steep learning curve in the integration of ICT into the curriculum, most teachers will not be convinced to change their classroom practices if the application of ICT were to merely allow them to go about their teaching faster or to do more of the same. It is important to change teachers' beliefs through the use of success stories that clearly demonstrate the value-adding impact of the use of ICT in teaching and learning.

Once teachers become convinced of the value of the integration of ICT into the curriculum, policy makers must consistently and constantly communicate positive messages and offer incentives to teachers and school leaders that encourage a culture of experimentation and exploration in ICT integration—with the explicit acknowledgment that some of their efforts in experimentation and exploration might not be successful. It is important to build a sharing culture to encourage sustainable collaboration and professional development among the teachers and school leaders. This allows the learning experiences gained at professional development programs to be expanded to a wider community, thereby creating a multiplier effect. It also provides mutual support and generation of innovative ICT practices in education through regular exchange of ideas, professional reflections, and mentoring.

ALIGNMENT OF INTENT AND INTERESTS OF KEY STAKEHOLDERS

The Singapore experience showed that, to implement the ICT master plan for education in an expedient manner, there is a need for alignment of intent and interests among the key stakeholders, which may include, for example, school leaders, teachers, students, parents, teacher trainers, researchers, and industry. With this alignment, there will be synergy among the various parties to implement the ICT master plan for education, which will lead to a minimization of unnecessary cancellation of efforts carried out at the school level. Successful practices and models of the integration of the ICT into the curriculum by innovative teachers and schools can be adapted and adopted by other teachers and schools without every teacher and school incurring the same overhead costs for experimentation and exploration. Learning sciences researchers working in partnership with the MOE, schools, and industry will be able to scale up their successful research findings beyond the schools participating in the research to all schools. The wider community will be able to provide a supportive environment outside the schools to reinforce the learning within schools.

To ensure alignment of key stakeholders in the implementation of the ICT master plan for education, it is important to communicate the interest and approach in a timely fashion to all key stakeholders. Time and effort must be invested to implement, monitor, and refine the communication plan as the implementation progresses.

COLLABORATIVE AND MULTIDISCIPLINARY APPROACH TO IMPLEMENTATION

The implementation of the ICT master plan for education is a complex process that requires a wide range of expertise and resources for successful implementation. While learning should always drive how ICT should be integrated into the curriculum, the successful incorporation of ICT into teaching and learning requires expertise and resources that may go beyond what might be available in the education community.

The MOE had to work with industry partners and learning sciences researchers to explore emerging technologies that could be potentially useful for teaching and learning. The establishment of the appropriate ICT-enabled teaching and learning environments within each school requires considerable technical expertise—more than what the average school teacher has. To develop highly interactive Web-based learning resources, the MOE collaborated with industry partners and with the institutes of higher learning. Some of the development work, for example, was carried out in collaboration with students in the local polytechnics as part of their industrial attachment to the MOE. Hence, it was important to collaborate with economic agencies such as the iDA of Singapore, institutes of higher learning, and industry to extend the capability of the MOE to fully implement the ICT master plan.

To generate new ideas and possibilities for the integration of ICT into the curriculum, the MOE found it beneficial to have a multidisciplinary team to work on the various projects. A multidisciplinary team of, for example, educational technologists, curriculum specialists, subject-matter experts, classroom teachers, and ICT experts, working together, generated ideas that were far superior than if each of them worked individually on the project.

For example, the multidisciplinary project team of the MOE, LSL from NIE, and 16 schools worked together to foster teachers' interest in using interactive whiteboards (IWBs) to enhance learning and teaching and to make their instructional practices more learner centered. Through professional development activities and sharing successful practices of using IWBs, teachers were able to develop innovative approaches of IWB use that brought about motivation, engagement, and learning gains for pupils. Besides NIE, which provided the research expertise, there was collaboration with the British Council (BC) and Tanglin Trust School (TTS). BC was instrumental in providing good examples of IWB use for English learning. Singapore teachers, in designing their own lessons, adapted ideas that they had learned from the BC. TTS teachers seeded more lesson ideas, and other teachers were able to observe TTS teachers in action using IWB in their classes. Besides linking schools with BC and TTS, NIE also brought in expertise on IWB from the United Kingdom to further exchange IWB ideas with the teachers.

CENTRALIZED APPROACH VS. GROUND-UP INITIATIVES FROM SCHOOLS

Under mp1, the MOE took an essentially centralized, one-size-fits-all approach to the implementation of the ICT master plan as schools did not have the necessary capabilities and expertise to implement the integration of ICT into the curriculum on their own. A centralized, top-down approach was also effective in ensuring that resources were optimally deployed to schools for the integration of ICT into the curriculum. Typically, the top-down implementation approach would involve a few schools that were willing and ready to either prototype or pilot test the pedagogical models or ICT-based resources and tools. When the pilots had been proven to be successful and the key operational implementation issues had been resolved, the models and resources would be rolled out in phases to all schools. This centralized, top-down approach is an effective implementation strategy at the initial phase of any implementation where expertise in schools or within the education community is limited.

Under mp2, schools are at different stages of ICT integration into the curriculum because of the phased approach taken in the implementation of mp1. In mp2, a completely centralized, one-size-fits-all, top-down approach is not appropriate; it would lead to faster and capable schools being held back in their implementation, while the resources provided to the slower schools with less capability would be wasted as they would not be ready for the implementation. In mp2, the

MOE provides top-down support for ground-up initiatives from schools for routine ICT integration into the curriculum, but continues to adopt some form of centralized, top-down approach for novel integration of ICT into the curriculum that pushes the frontiers of teaching and learning.

CONCLUSION

The use of ICT in education can be only as effective as the good teachers and school leaders who are able to leverage on ICT to motivate students to learn and to create the necessary conditions for that learning to occur. Hence, the key to successful implementation of mp2 is to focus on improving the capabilities of teachers to effectively integrate ICT into the curriculum through constant innovations in their classroom practices (Zhao and Cziko 2001; Zhao et al. 2002). To build the teachers' capability to innovate in their classroom practices, the MOE will continue to do the following:

- Build communities of practice for teachers that will enable them to engage and support one another in professional sharing and to exchange success stories of innovative ICT-based practices for adoption in their classrooms.
- Build school leaders' capability and expertise in technology planning to enable them to implement effective schoolwide integration of ICT into the curriculum.
- Build selected teachers' capability, through collaboration with industry and institutes of higher learning, of developing interactive Web-based learning objects to support the effective integration of ICT into the curriculum.
- Work toward a seamless ICT-enabled teaching and learning environment that allows teachers to get access and share both commercially available and school-created ICT-based learning resources.
- Exploit the potential integration of emerging technologies into the curriculum to enhance learning.
- Scale up the research findings on proven ICT-enabled pedagogical models and successful practices to influence classroom practices of all teachers.

NOTES

1. *The Global Competitiveness Report 2006–2007: Country Highlights.* Retrieved December 26, 2006, from http://www.weforum.org/en/fp/gcr_2006-07_highlights/index.htm.
2. For details on specific program carried out under the second master plan, visit the edu.MALL Web site at http://www.moe.gov.sg/edumall/index.htm.
3. For more details, visit Infocomm Development Authority of Singapore's Web site at http://www.ida.gov.sg.
4. The full iN2015 reports are found at http://www.in2015.sg/reports.html.

5. Secondary education (years 7–10 or 11) has four streams: Special, Express, Normal (academic), and Normal (technical). The Normal (technical) stream caters to students who are most likely to take up technical-vocational training for their postsecondary education.

6. The Singapore ONE backbone used fiber-optic technology and ATM switching, giving transmission speeds up to 622 Mbps.

7. A summary of the findings can be found at http://www.moe.gov.sg/edumall/mp2/mp2.htm.

8. http://www.worldbank.org/education/edtech/.

9. http://www.unescobkk.org/index.php?id=494.

10. http://www.becta.org.uk/.

11. See the MOE Web site on Project Work at http://www.moe.gov.sg/projectwork/.

12. See the MOE Bluesky Web site at http://www.moe.gov.sg/bluesky/index.htm.

13. "Teach Less, Learn More" was launched by the Ministry of Education to shift the focus in classroom teaching and learning from "quantity" to "quality." "More quality" in terms of classroom interaction, opportunities for expression, the learning of lifelong skills, and the building of character through innovative and effective teaching approaches and strategies. "Less quantity" in terms of rote learning, repetitive tests, and following prescribed answers and set formulae.

REFERENCES

Bienskowski, M. A., G. Haertal, R. Yamaguchi, A. Molina, F. Adamson, and L. Peck-Theis. 2005. *Singapore Tablet PC Program Study: Executive Summary.* Report No. P16685. Menlo Park, CA: SRI International. http://ctl.sri.com/publications/downloads/TabletPC_ExecSummary.pdf (accessed December 26, 2006).

Chang, J. H. 2003. "Culture, State and Economics Development in Singapore." *Journal of Contemporary Asia* 33 (1): 85–105.

Cheah, H. M., and T. S. Koh. 2001. "Singapore: Integration of ICT into Education." *Journal of Southeast Asian Education* 2 (1): 147–164.

Chia, S. Y., and J. J. Lim. 2003. "Singapore: A Regional Hub in ICT." In *Towards a Knowledge-Based Economy: East Asia's Changing Industrial Geography,* ed. S. Masuyama and D. Vandenbrink, 259–298. Singapore: Institute of Southeast Asian Studies.

Chiang, C. F. (1998). "Education: New Directions." In *Singapore: The Year in Review 1998,* ed. G. L. Ooi and R. S. Rajan, 65–76. Singapore: The Institute of Policy Studies and Times Academic Press.

Committee on National Computerisation. 1981. *Report of the Committee on National Computerisation.* Singapore: Telecommunication Authority of Singapore.

Cordeiro, C. M., and S. Al-Hawamdeh. 2001. "National Information Infrastructure and the Realization of Singapore IT2000 Initiative." *Information Research* 6 (2). http://InformationR.net/ir/6-2/paper96.htm (accessed December 26, 2006).

Economic Review Committee. 2002. *Report by Sub-Committee on Enhancing Human Capital.* Singapore: Ministry of Trade and Industry.

Goh, C. T. 1997. "Shaping Our Future: Thinking Schools, Learning Nation." Opening address, 7th International Conference on Thinking, Suntec City, Singapore, June 2. http://www.moe.gov.sg/speeches/1997/020697.htm (accessed December 26, 2006).

Hawkins, R. J. 2002. "Ten Lessons for ICT and Education in the Developing World." In *The Global Information Technology Report 2001–2002,* ed. G. Kirkman, P. K. Cornelius,

J. D. Sachs, and K. Schwab, 38–43. New York: Oxford University Press. http://www.cid.harvard.edu/cr/pdf/gitrr2002_ch04.pdf (accessed December 26, 2006).

Infocomm Development Authority. 2000. *Infocomm 21: Singapore Where the Digital Future Is*. Singapore: Infocomm Development Authority.

———. 2003. *Connected Singapore: A New Blueprint for Infocomm Development*. Singapore: Infocomm Development Authority.

Koh, T. S. (1999). "IT Masterplan Implementation at the National Institute of Education: An Overview." In *Enhancing Learning: Challenge of Integrating Thinking and Information Technology into the Curriculum*, ed. M. Waas, 76–82. Singapore: Educational Research Association.

Kozma, R. 2005. "National Policies That Connect ICT-Based Education Reform to Economic and Social Development. *Human Technology* 1 (2): 117–156. http://www.humantechnology.jyu.fi/articles/volume1/2005/kozma.pdf (accessed December 26, 2006).

Looi, C. K., D. Hung, J. Bopry, and T. S. Koh. 2004. "Singapore's Learning Science Lab: Seeking Transformations in ICT-Enabled Pedagogy." *Educational Technology Research and Development* (U.S.) 52 (4): 91–115.

Ministry of Education. 1998. *Learning to Think, Thinking to Learn: Towards Thinking Schools, Learning Nation*. Singapore: Ministry of Education.

———. 2006. *Education Statistics Digest*. Singapore: Ministry of Education.

National Computer Board. 1992. *A Vision of an Intelligent Island: The IT2000 Report*. Singapore: SNP Publishers.

National IT Plan Working Committee. 1985. *National IT Plan: A Strategic Framework*. Singapore: National Computer Board.

Resnick, M. 2002. "Rethinking Learning in the Digital Age." In *The Global Information Technology Report 2001–2002*, ed. G. Kirkman, P. K. Cornelius, J. D. Sachs, and K. Schwab, 32–37. New York: Oxford University Press. http://llk.media.mit.edu/papers/mres-wef.pdf (accessed December 26, 2006).

Shanmugaratnam, T. 2002. "IT in Learning: Preparing for a Different Future." Opening address, ITOPIA 2002, Suntec City, Singapore, July 24. http://www.moe.gov.sg/speeches/2002/sp24072002.htm (accessed December 26, 2006).

Teo, C. H. 1997. "Opening New Frontiers in Education with Information Technology (IT)." Opening address, Launch of the Masterplan for IT in Education, Suntec City, Singapore, April 28. http://www.moe.gov.sg/speeches/1997/280497.htm (accessed December 26, 2006).

———. 2001. Speech delivered at the launch of the book *Architecture of Learning: New Singapore Schools*, Rosyth School, Singapore, March 31. http://www.moe.gov.sg/speeches/2001/sp31032001a.htm (accessed December 26, 2006).

Wagner, D. A., R. Day, T. James, R. B. Kozma, J. Miller, and T. Unwin. 2005. *Monitoring and Evaluation of ICT in Education Projects: A Handbook for Developing Countries*. Washington, DC: The International Bank for Reconstruction and Development/World Bank. http://www.infodev.org/en/Document.9.aspx (accessed December 26, 2006).

Wong, P. K. 2001. "The Contribution of IT to the Rapid Economic Development of Singapore." In *Information Technology, Productivity and Economic Growth: International Evidence and Implications for Economic Development*, ed. M. Pohjola, 221–241. New York: Oxford University Press.

Zhao, Y., and G. A. Cziko. 2001. "Teacher Adoption of Technology: A Perceptual Control Theory Perspective." *Journal of Technology and Teacher Education* 9 (1): 5–30.

Zhao, Y., K. Pugh, S. Sheldon, and J. L. Byers. 2002. "Conditions for Classroom Technology Innovations." *Teachers College Record* 104 (3): 482–515.

Conclusion: The Engine Drivers

This book documents the various facets and stages of education change in Singapore since 1965 and how they contributed to enhancing the nation's competitiveness in the global economy. The key goal of this volume is to enable readers to understand the close relationship of educational development and manpower planning in the development of human resources and technological capability in Singapore. What will continue to drive the system in the future is the recognition of Singapore's vulnerability in economic, social, and political spheres. Because the country is devoid of natural resources, human resources are seen as the most fundamental element in Singapore's nation-building process and, consequently, education and training are at the heart of the nation's wider economic plans. This explains why Singapore links education so intimately to its economic priorities, the continued high investment in education, and a pragmatic vision that allows for continual fine-tuning and reform. The book is written primarily with the objective of sharing Singapore's experience in synergizing the demands of two key sectors—education and the economy—with developing countries. The central thesis is that Singapore's successful economic restructuring since 1965 owes much to its leaders' ability to establish a close link between policies for skills formation and the demand for skills at each phase of the country's economic growth. This skills formation is achieved through the government's educational policies to develop each child to his or her maximum potential and to fine-tune the educational system to meet the manpower needs of the economy.

The voluminous literature and reports on education in developing countries, such as those on the African continent, have consistently highlighted the improvements in literacy rates but, at the same time, pointed to the continual key education problems and issues that have plagued them for decades—accessibility to basic education for females, high dropout rates, severe shortage of teachers, insufficient schools, lack of funds for educational purposes and textbooks, and lack of transparency. In Sub-Saharan Africa, for example, primary school enrollments and literacy rates are still among the lowest in the world. In many rural societies, children are required by parents to work in the fields, and they attend school only when they are not needed in the fields. When they do attend, it is not uncommon for them to bring along their younger siblings to the classroom because no one will be at home to look after the young ones. This arrangement often adversely affects the education of the children. While primary school enrollment has improved, consistency and quality of education remain low in many places. Existing constraints that affect efficiency include limited availability and distribution of teaching materials, rote learning, outdated curricula, inadequate physical facilities and equipment, class size or teacher-pupil ratio, and teacher supply and performance in classroom. These are substantial and largely unsolved challenges facing developing countries.[1]

Singapore, too, had these problems during the 1950s to the early 1970s. Singapore's education since 1965 exemplifies the general rule that the development of widespread basic education is necessary, though not sufficient, for sustaining economic growth. During the early phases of growth (in the 1960s and early 1970s), the government's priority was to create jobs, so that the people and the country could survive. It attempted to expand quickly the accessibility to primary education for all Singaporeans. This would at least create a young labor force with basic education to support the labor-intensive factories provided for by largely foreign companies. Besides, rapid construction of schools and recruitment of teachers would also provide employment opportunities. However, up to the 1970s, the rapid drive toward universal primary education and high enrollment in secondary education was not matched by improvement in education quality, including the professional status of teachers. There was high education wastage. On the economic front, labor shortage was severe; productivity of the Singapore worker was low; and, largely as a consequence of being heavily dependent on multinational corporations for technology, the indigenous technology base was poorly developed. Urgent measures were taken by the education planners to upgrade the quality of the education system and to reduce educational wastage in the 1980s.

What then are the engine drivers? Singapore's quality education and manpower training are where they are today as a result of the effective role played by three key participants. First and foremost is the Singapore government.

Throughout this book we have emphasized the way in which education and training practices were shaped by the overarching nation-building agenda of the Singapore government. It fostered rapid economic growth by putting stress on meritocracy, high academic achievement, and the relevance of education to manpower planning. Education promotes income growth, which in turn promotes further investment in education. This had been the guiding principle for Lee Kuan Yew and his first generation of leaders when Singapore gained independence in 1965. Without natural resources, the strategy for long-term survival was to create a nation capable of fully utilizing its only assets—namely, human resources—as the basis of its main competitive advantage in the world economy.[2] Singapore's education and training strategies were consistently in line with the nation's economic trajectory to sustainable growth. Education policy is well integrated with economic policy and manpower planning. The Singapore government takes a very proactive role in ensuring that all citizens are literate. It invests heavily in education, especially at the secondary level, and in the lifelong training of the labor force. Besides defense, the education sector receives the largest share (about 4 percent) of the gross domestic product each year. Planning and implementation for large-scale expansion of primary and secondary education were centralized at the Ministry of Education and carefully supervised by experienced educators. Since 1965, the government has undergone its own learning process in discovering how to link education and training to the needs of its changing economy. As a latecomer to sustained growth through industrialization, the government was able to learn from the older industrial economies the types of skills required for the various stages of economic growth and the appropriate principles and policies on which its own programs should be built.

The second key participants are the postsecondary education institutions. Aside from gaining admission to the local universities, postsecondary education is the final education process that prepares students to be integrated into society and work for a living, contributing back to the society. Although the education level of Singapore's workforce has shifted positively in the past 10 years, education levels are still lagging behind those in the developed countries. On average, more than 75 percent of the workforce in developed countries possesses postsecondary education or beyond. But in Singapore, only 35 percent of the current workforce has postsecondary education and beyond. To sustain Singapore's long-term competitiveness, 65 percent of its population must have postsecondary education and beyond by 2015. Notwithstanding the significant role played by the schools in nurturing the academic quality and character development of young Singaporeans, the postsecondary education institutions—the Institute of Technical Education, the junior colleges, and the polytechnics—provide a vital "ladder" in manpower planning and training to meet the anticipated needs of the new economy. Upon completion of secondary education, students have many options. They can study at a pre-university institution, such as a junior college (for a two-year course) or at a centralized institute (for a three-year course). Students also have the option of pursuing a wide range of specialized diploma courses at one of the five polytechnics or at a specialized institution such as Nanyang Academy of Fine Arts. For the less academically inclined, the Institute of Technical Education prepares students with the technical knowledge and skills required for various industry sectors. The courses offered at the polytechnics tend to be market driven and career oriented, offering students practical and valuable experience. Upon graduation, polytechnic students can choose either to enter the workforce or to further their education at universities.

The third key participants are Singapore's universities. Singaporeans place a high premium on university education. The universities provide Singaporeans with dynamic and enriching learning opportunities, as well as mold the young adults into responsible and respectable citizens. The universities receive substantial government funding, yet they remain autonomous. They can chart their own destiny; differentiate themselves; and pursue new heights of excellence in education, research, and service. The Singapore government will increase the number of publicly subsidized university places from 25 percent (in 2007) to 30 percent of each cohort by 2015. This would provide an additional 2,400 publicly subsidized places that are broadly aligned to Singapore's long-term manpower needs and allow for a diversity of university-level paths to meet the needs of the market and aspirations of parents and students. However, expanding the university sector is a complex issue; it took nearly 30 years before the country established its three full-fledged and publicly funded universities (the National University of Singapore in 1980, the Nanyang Technological University in 1991, and the Singapore Management University in 2000). Singapore's experience here reminds policy makers in developing countries of three crucial points: (a) expansion of the university sector is guided primarily by economic considerations, (b) the courses that the universities provide are aligned to the needs and development of the national economy, and (c) the country's universities need to be of high quality and produce graduates who are able to find jobs.

In summary, many developing countries have learned and some have attempted to transfer aspects of Singapore's state-led education and economic development model into their own respective systems. While many developing countries have also adopted the so-called "state development model," we would like to reiterate that in the case of Singapore, behind the mechanisms and processes of economic and education change is the force that drives them all—the political leadership of Singapore. The leaders who were entrusted by the populace to lead the small island city-state had both the capacity to make sound social and macroeconomic policies and the political will to make changes. This collective responsibility and accountability depicts a high level of multiagency coordination and integration of policy making in Singapore, and demonstrates clearly the crucial link between economic development and school, technical, and university education and training. Education was (and is) seen as the key to a good life and, since the early years after independence, the political leadership worked hard to provide education for all. The state makes heavy investments in education, from preschool to tertiary education, as this is the key to sustainable development. While it is true that educational policies and developments in Singapore before the 1990s were not all smooth sailing, the major goal of education in Singapore was never compromised. All young

Singaporeans, regardless of race, language, gender, or religion, will be educated to the very best of their ability. For developing countries, this is perhaps one of the most significant challenges in the new millennium.

NOTES

1. In Arab countries and North Africa, heavy investment in education in recent years has resulted in these countries now approaching universal primary enrollment; the major exceptions are Morocco, Saudi Arabia, and Yemen, where access to primary schools remains problematic, especially for girls. The spending on education in this region now averages 4.4 percent of GDP and 14.9 percent of total spending. These levels are comparable to those in the high-performing Asian economies. While the people are beginning to enjoy the social benefits of education (such as literacy and life expectancy), in terms of overall economic growth and increases in per-capita income, the payoffs from education in the region have been low. Unemployment rates are hovering around 20 percent of the workforce, real wages have declined, and, on the whole, education has become a less attractive investment option for parents and young people.

2. It must be noted that the city-state's situation is evidently very different from many developing countries. In coordinating the supply of trained personnel to meet the needs of the expanding economy, Singapore has one distinct advantage when compared with other countries. Its small geographical size and compactness (supported by an excellent communication infrastructure) allow for efficient planning, cohesive decision making, channeling of information, and deployment of personnel within and between the government and private sectors.

Index

ECO-AUDIT

Environmental Benefits Statement

The World Bank is committed to preserving endangered forests and natural resources. The Office of the Publisher has chosen to print ***Toward a Better Future*** on 60# Roland Opaque with 30% post-consumer waste, in accordance with the recommended standards for paper usage set by the Green Press Initiative, a nonprofit program supporting publishers in using fiber that is not sourced from endangered forests. For more information, visit www.greenpressinitiative.org.

Savings:
- 9 trees
- 6 million BTUs energy
- 759 pounds CO_2 equivalent
- 3,150 gallons water
- 405 pounds solid waste

green press INITIATIVE